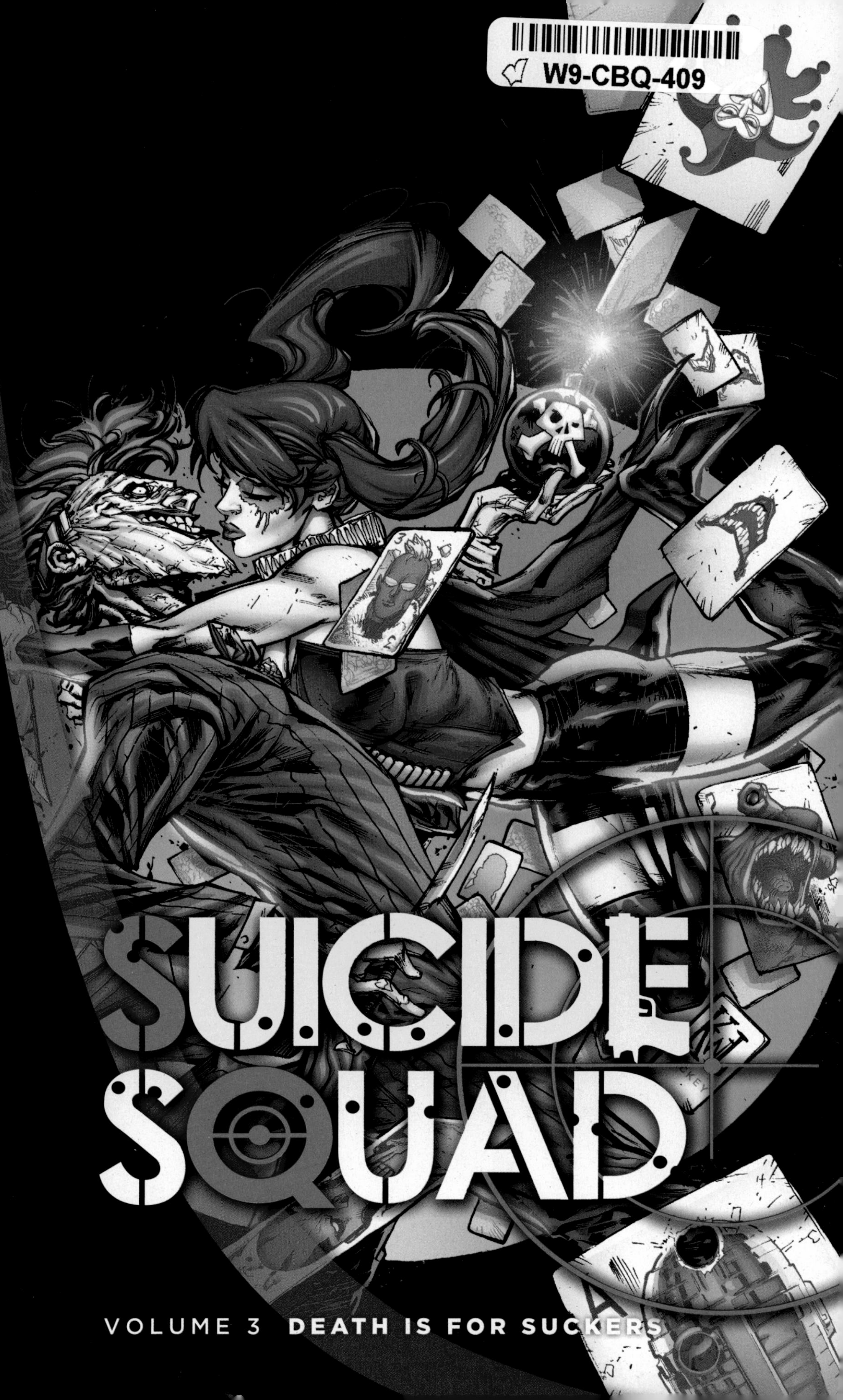

SUICIDE SQUAD

VOLUME 3 **DEATH IS FOR SUCKERS**

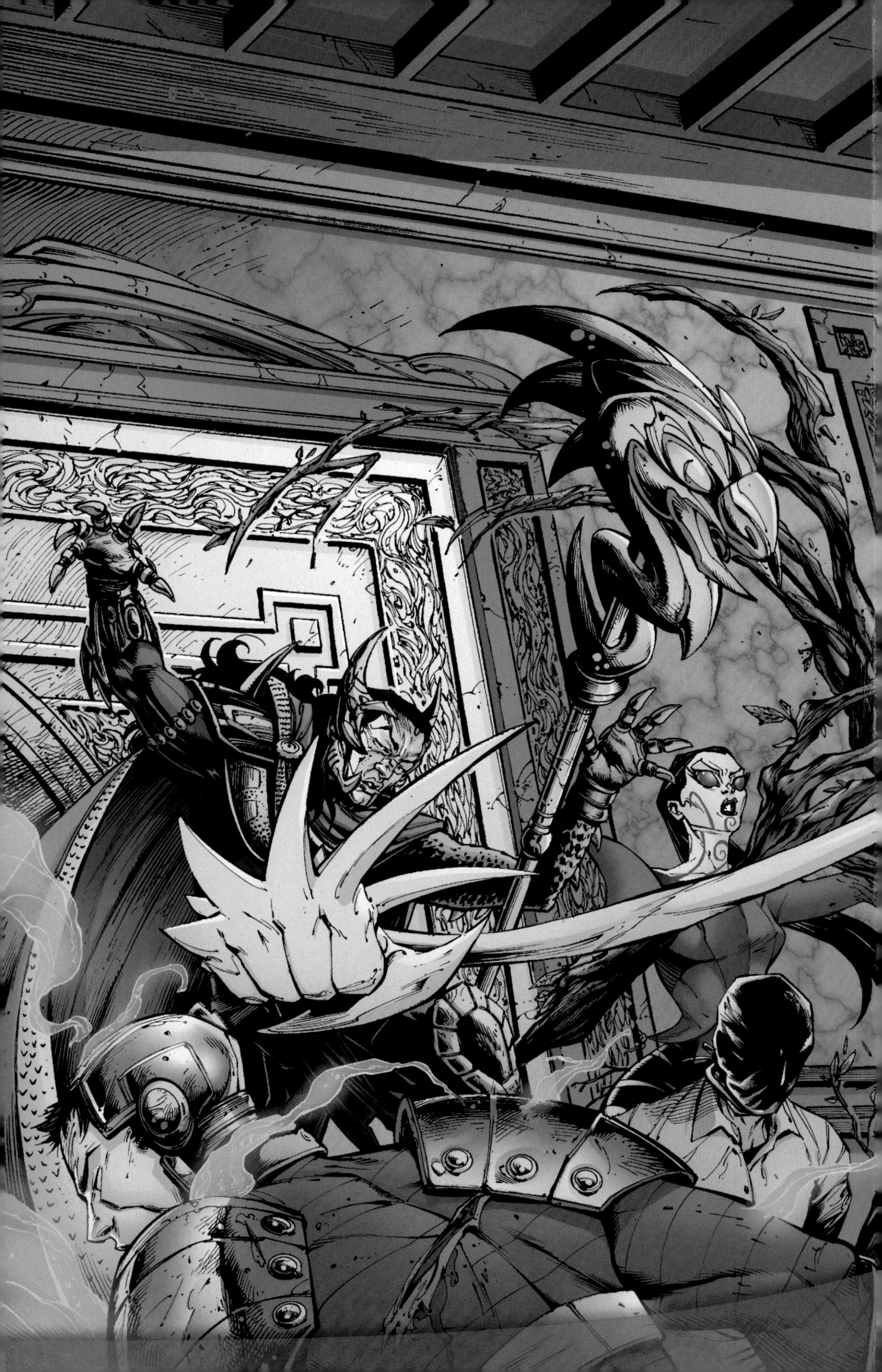

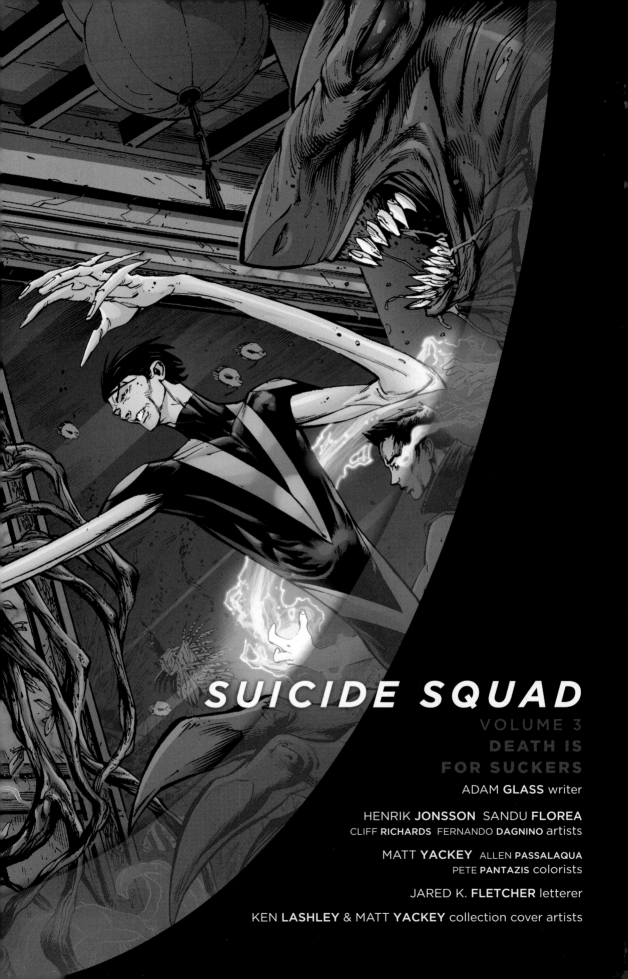

SUICIDE SQUAD

VOLUME 3
DEATH IS
FOR SUCKERS

ADAM **GLASS** writer

HENRIK **JONSSON** SANDU **FLOREA**
CLIFF **RICHARDS** FERNANDO **DAGNINO** artists

MATT **YACKEY** ALLEN **PASSALAQUA**
PETE **PANTAZIS** colorists

JARED K. **FLETCHER** letterer

KEN **LASHLEY** & MATT **YACKEY** collection cover artists

MIKE MARTS Group Editor – Original Series RACHEL GLUCKSTERN Editor – Original Series
RICKEY PURDIN DARREN SHAN Assistant Editors – Original Series JEB WOODARD Group Editor – Collected Editions
ROWENA YOW Editor – Collected Edition STEVE COOK Design Director – Books ROBBIE BIEDERMAN Publication Design

BOB HARRAS Senior VP – Editor-in-Chief, DC Comics

DIANE NELSON President DAN DIDIO and JIM LEE Co-Publishers
GEOFF JOHNS Chief Creative Officer AMIT DESAI Senior VP – Marketing & Global Franchise Management
NAIRI GARDINER Senior VP – Finance SAM ADES VP – Digital Marketing BOBBIE CHASE VP – Talent Development
MARK CHIARELLO Senior VP – Art, Design & Collected Editions JOHN CUNNINGHAM VP – Content Strategy
ANNE DEPIES VP – Strategy Planning & Reporting DON FALLETTI VP – Manufacturing Operations
LAWRENCE GANEM VP – Editorial Administration & Talent Relations ALISON GILL Senior VP – Manufacturing & Operations
HANK KANALZ Senior VP – Editorial Strategy & Administration JAY KOGAN VP – Legal Affairs
DEREK MADDALENA Senior VP – Sales & Business Development JACK MAHAN VP – Business Affairs
DAN MIRON VP – Sales Planning & Trade Development NICK NAPOLITANO VP – Manufacturing Administration
CAROL ROEDER VP – Marketing EDDIE SCANNELL VP – Mass Account & Digital Sales
COURTNEY SIMMONS Senior VP – Publicity & Communications JIM (SKI) SOKOLOWSKI VP – Comic Book Specialty & Newsstand Sales
SANDY YI Senior VP – Global Franchise Management

SUICIDE SQUAD VOLUME 3: DEATH IS FOR SUCKERS

Published by DC Comics. Copyright © 2013 DC Comics. All Rights Reserved.

Originally published in single magazine form in SUICIDE SQUAD 14-19 © 2013 DC Comics. All Rights Reserved.
All characters, their distinctive likenesses and related elements featured in this publication are trademarks of DC Comics.
The stories, characters and incidents featured in this publication are entirely fictional.
DC Comics does not read or accept unsolicited ideas, stories or artwork.

DC Comics, 2900 W. Alameda Avenue, Burbank, CA 91505
Printed by Transcontinental Interglobe Beauceville, Canada. 3/18/16. Fifth Printing.
ISBN: 978-1-4012-4316-6

Library of Congress Cataloging-in-Publication Data

Glass, Adam, 1968-
Suicide Squad. Volume 3, Death is for suckers / Adam Glass, Henrik Jonsson, Fernando Dagnino, Cliff Richards.
pages cm
"Originally published in single magazine form as Suicide Squad 14-19."
ISBN 978-1-4012-4316-6
1. Graphic novels. I. Jonsson, Henrik. II. Dagnino, Fernando, 1973- III. Richards, Cliff. IV. Title. V. Title: Death is for suckers.
PN6728.S825G59 2013
741.5'973—dc23
                                    2013020545

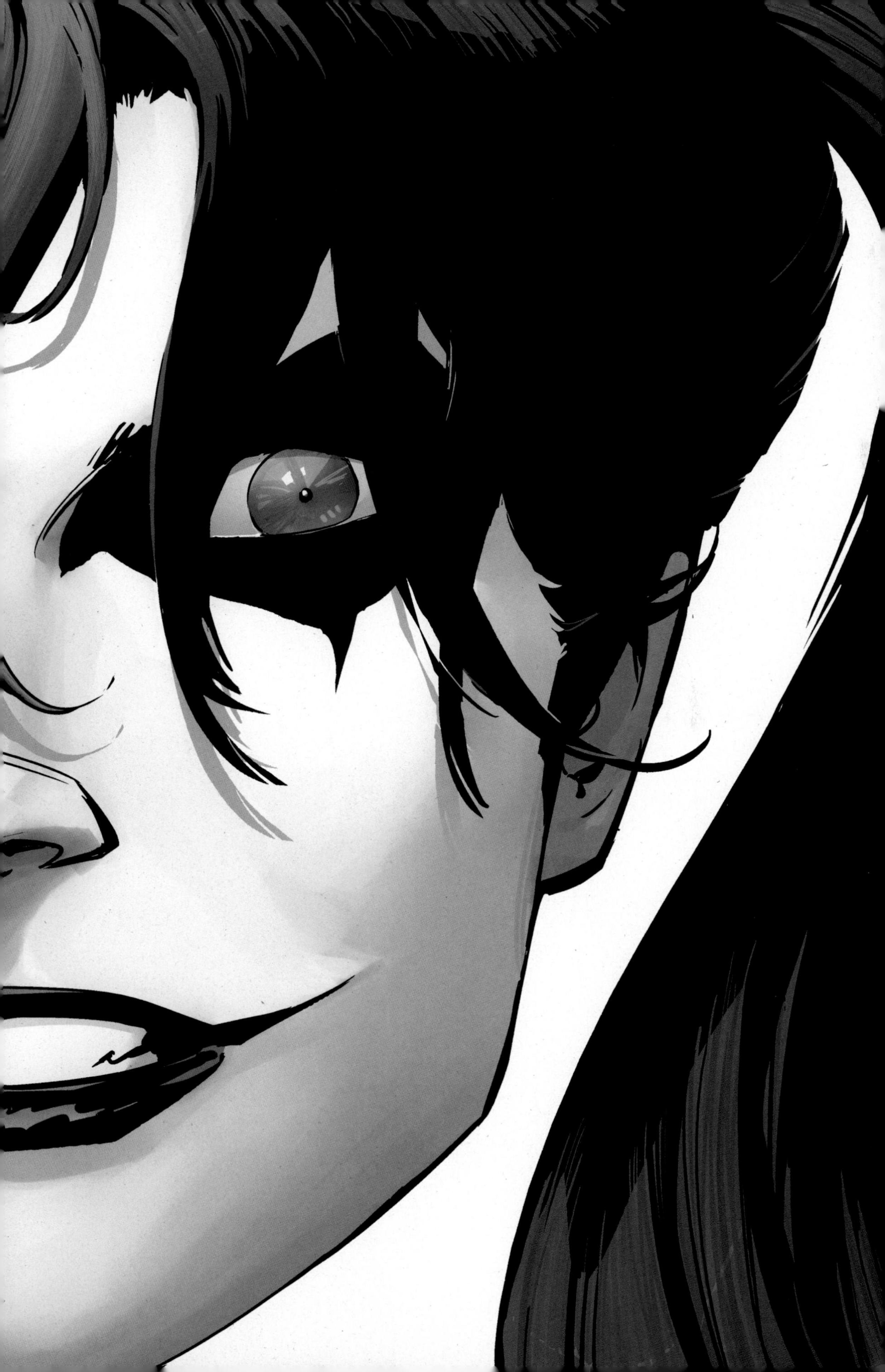

RUNNING WITH THE DEVIL: PART ONE

ADAM GLASS writer **FERNANDO DAGNINO** artist cover art by **GREG CAPULLO & FCO PLASCENCIA**

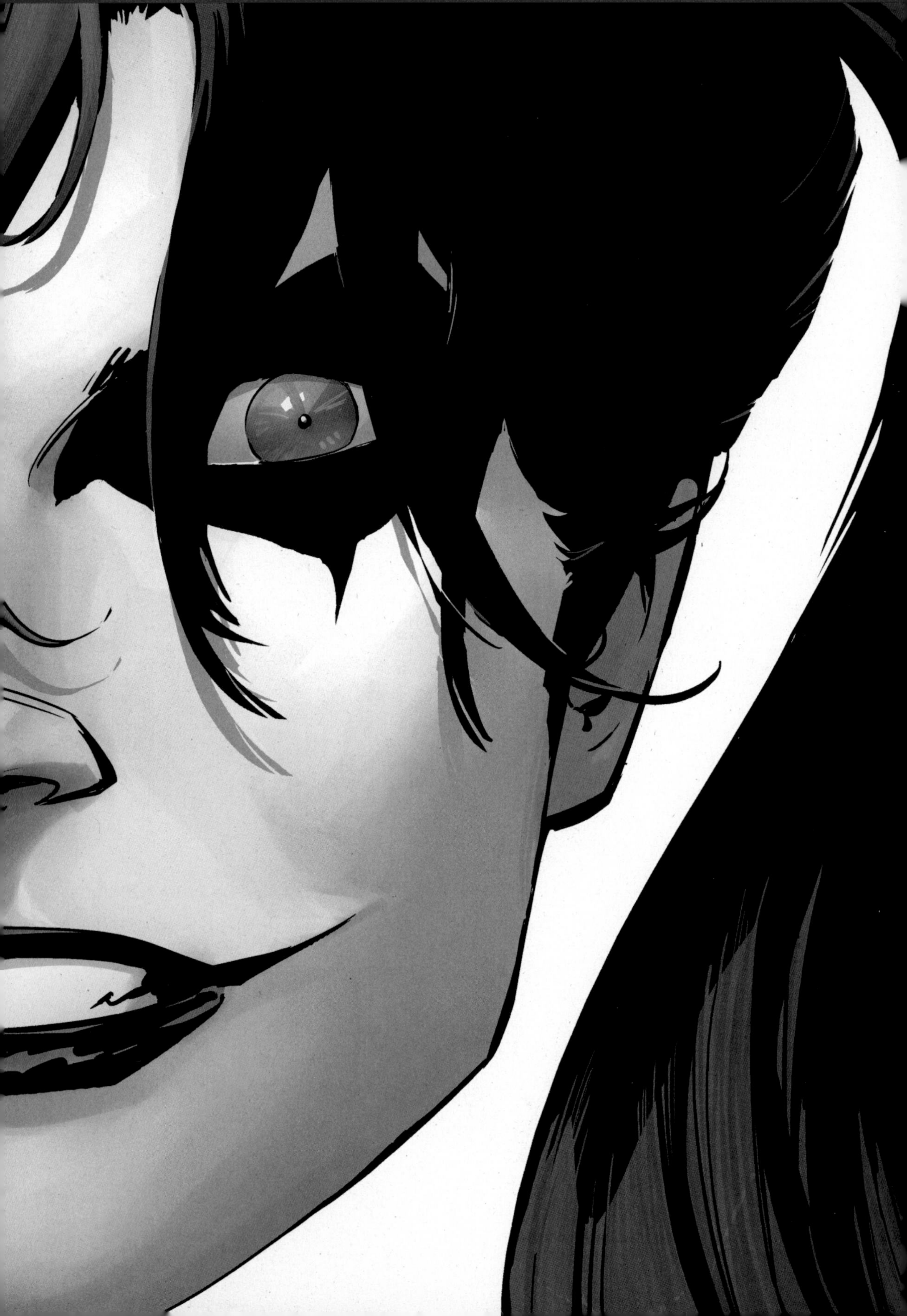

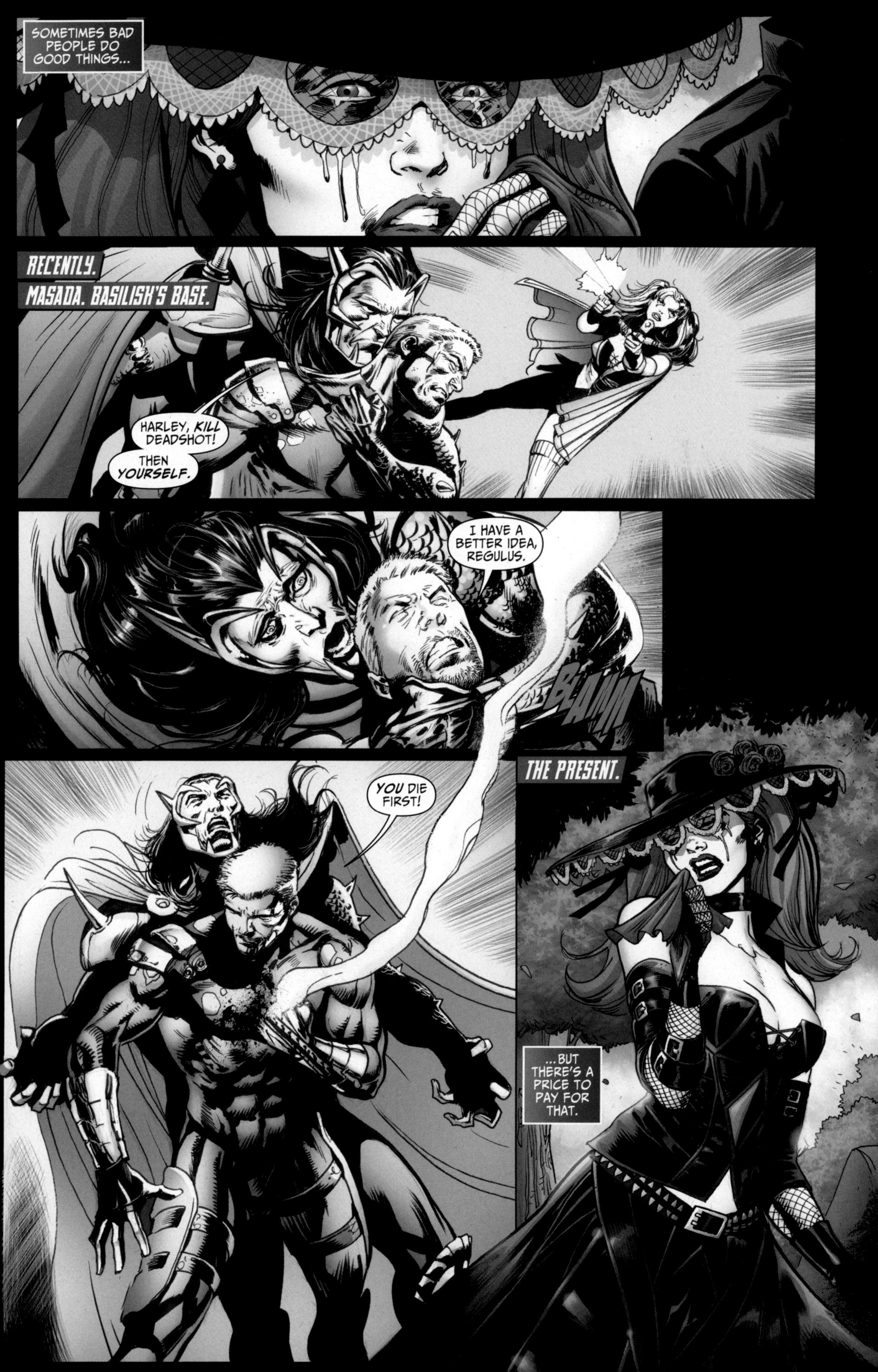
SOMETIMES BAD PEOPLE DO GOOD THINGS...
RECENTLY.
MASADA. BASILISK'S BASE.
HARLEY, KILL DEADSHOT!
THEN YOURSELF.
I HAVE A BETTER IDEA, REGULUS.
BLAM
YOU DIE FIRST!
THE PRESENT.
...BUT THERE'S A PRICE TO PAY FOR THAT.

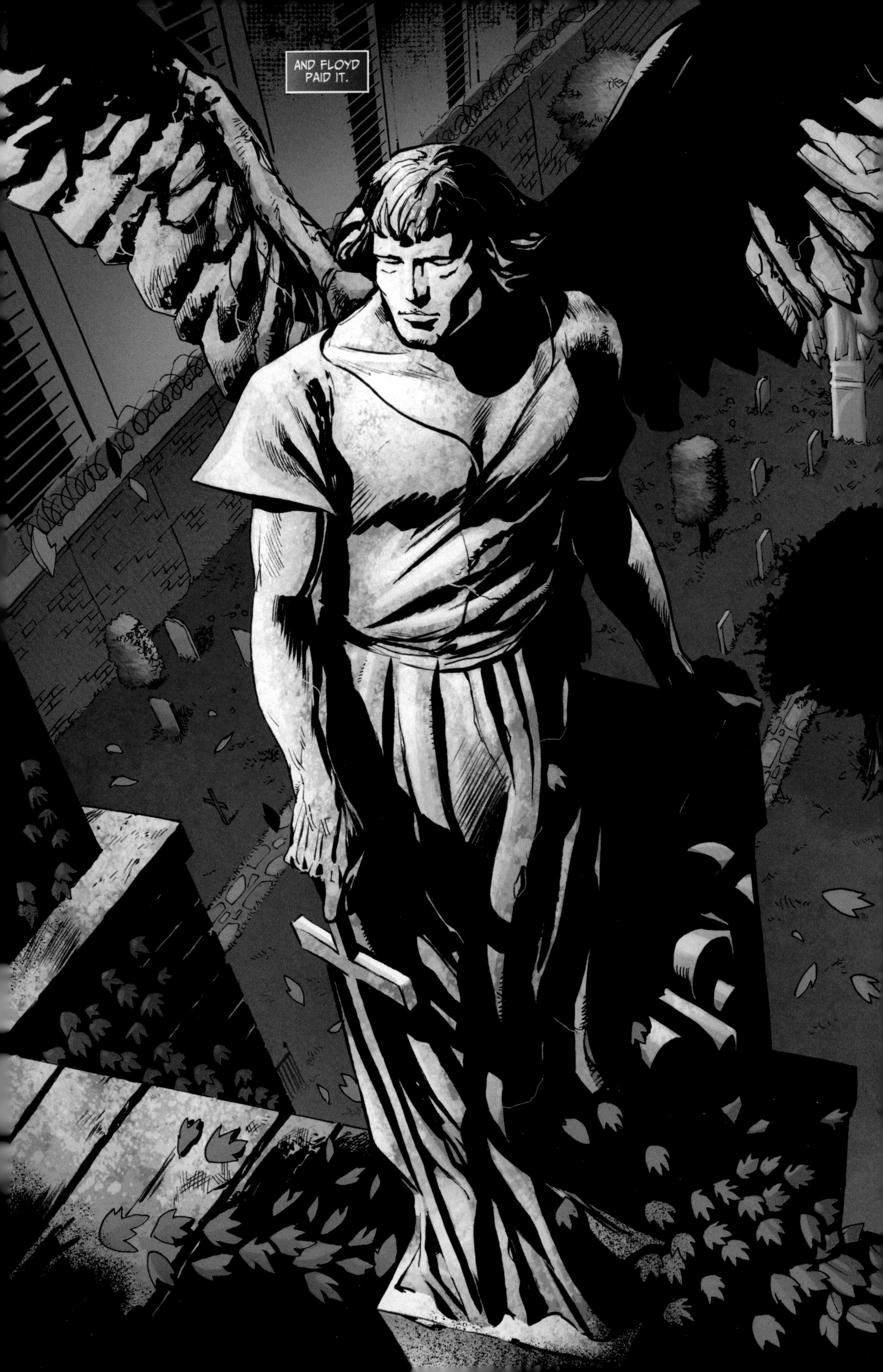
AND FLOYD PAID IT.

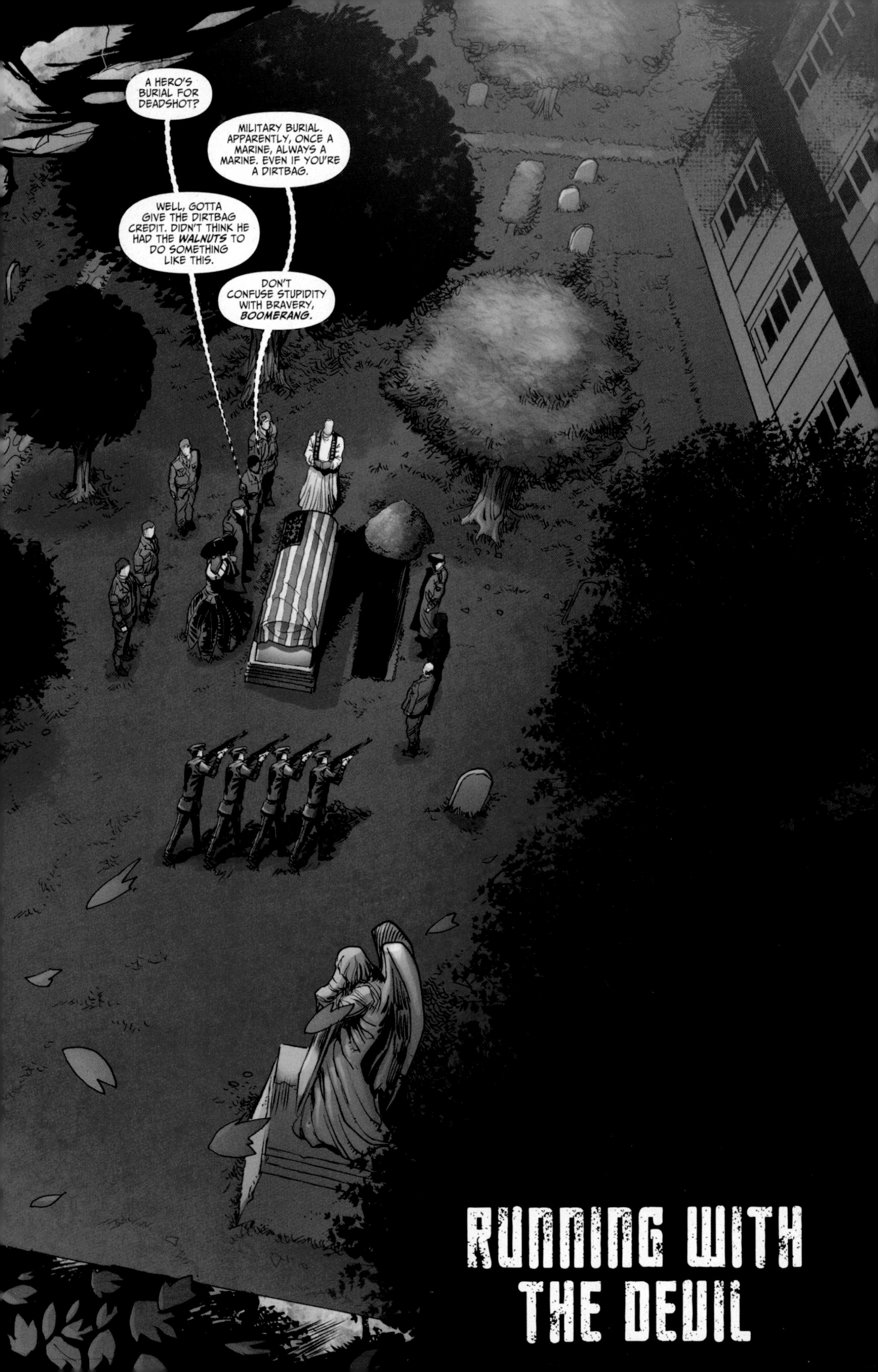
A HERO'S BURIAL FOR DEADSHOT?
MILITARY BURIAL. APPARENTLY, ONCE A MARINE, ALWAYS A MARINE. EVEN IF YOU'RE A DIRTBAG.
WELL, GOTTA GIVE THE DIRTBAG CREDIT. DIDN'T THINK HE HAD THE WALNUTS TO DO SOMETHING LIKE THIS.
DON'T CONFUSE STUPIDITY WITH BRAVERY, BOOMERANG.
RUNNING WITH THE DEVIL

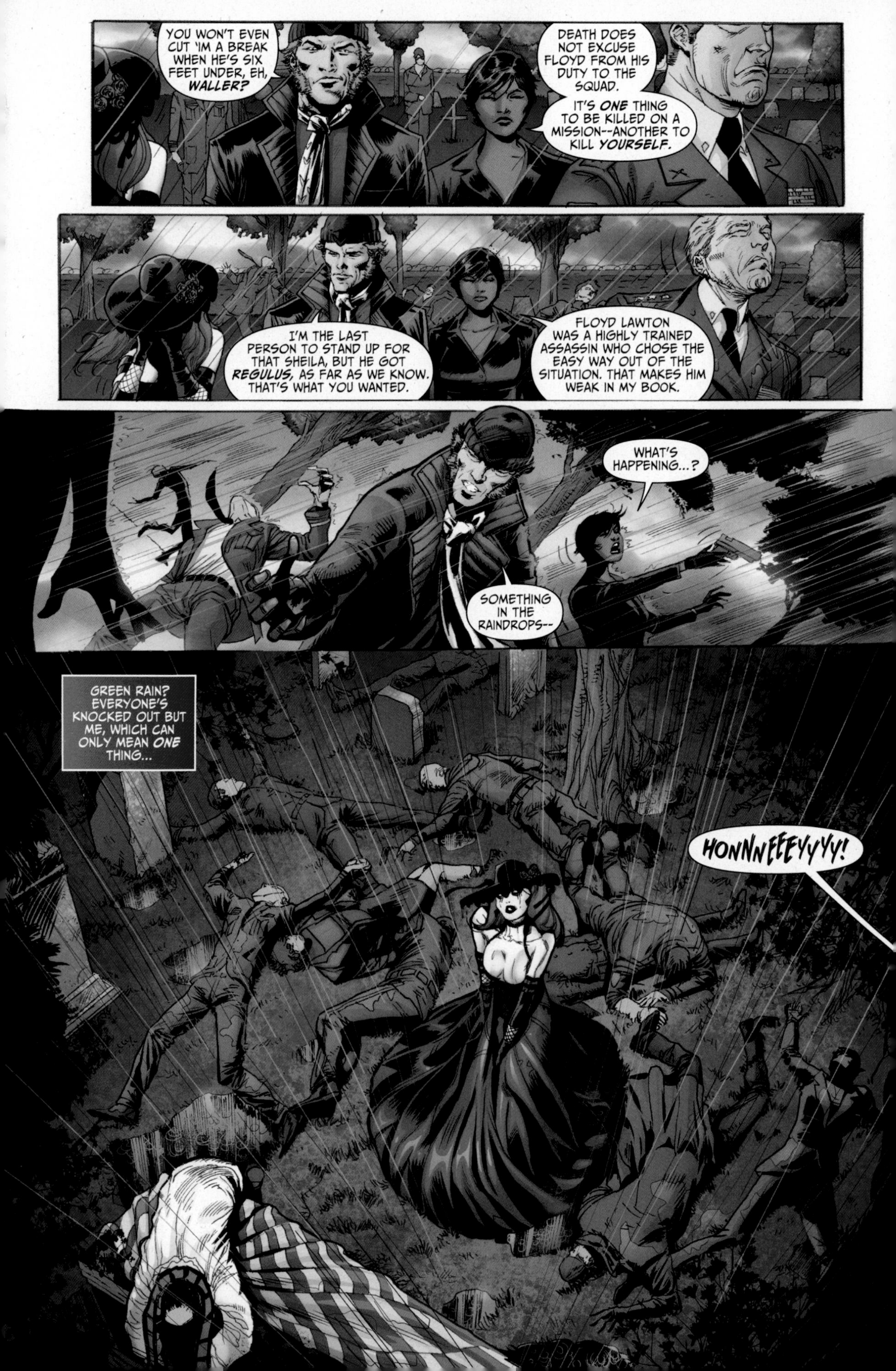
YOU WON'T EVEN CUT 'IM A BREAK WHEN HE'S SIX FEET UNDER, EH, WALLER?
DEATH DOES NOT EXCUSE FLOYD FROM HIS DUTY TO THE SQUAD.
IT'S ONE THING TO BE KILLED ON A MISSION--ANOTHER TO KILL YOURSELF.
I'M THE LAST PERSON TO STAND UP FOR THAT SHEILA, BUT HE GOT REGULUS, AS FAR AS WE KNOW. THAT'S WHAT YOU WANTED.
FLOYD LAWTON WAS A HIGHLY TRAINED ASSASSIN WHO CHOSE THE EASY WAY OUT OF THE SITUATION. THAT MAKES HIM WEAK IN MY BOOK.
WHAT'S HAPPENING...?
SOMETHING IN THE RAINDROPS--
GREEN RAIN? EVERYONE'S KNOCKED OUT BUT ME, WHICH CAN ONLY MEAN ONE THING...
HONNNEEEYYYY!

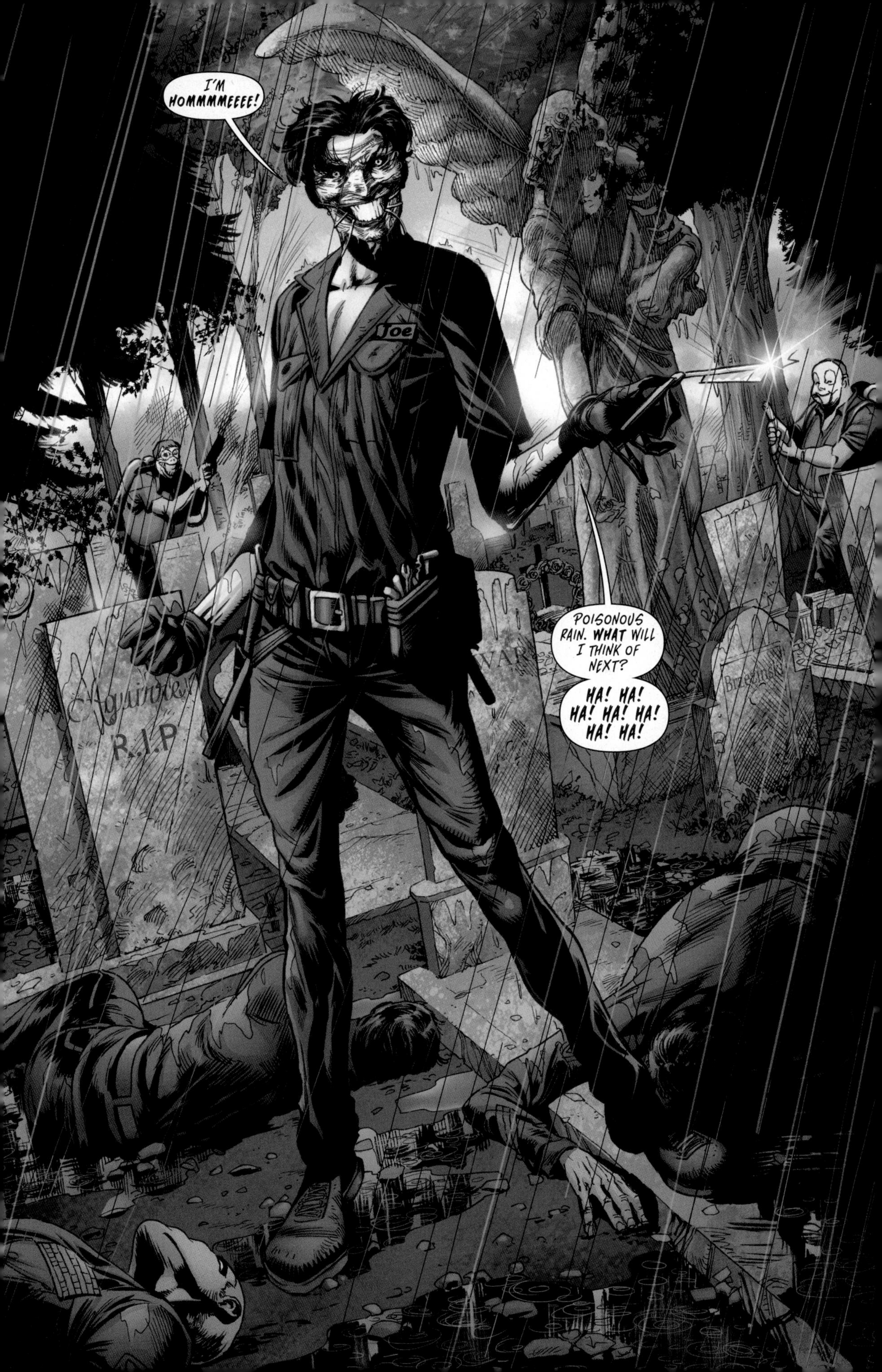
I'M HOMMMMEEEE!
Joe
Aguirre R.I.P
WAR
Brzezinski
POISONOUS RAIN. WHAT WILL I THINK OF NEXT?
HA! HA! HA! HA! HA! HA! HA!

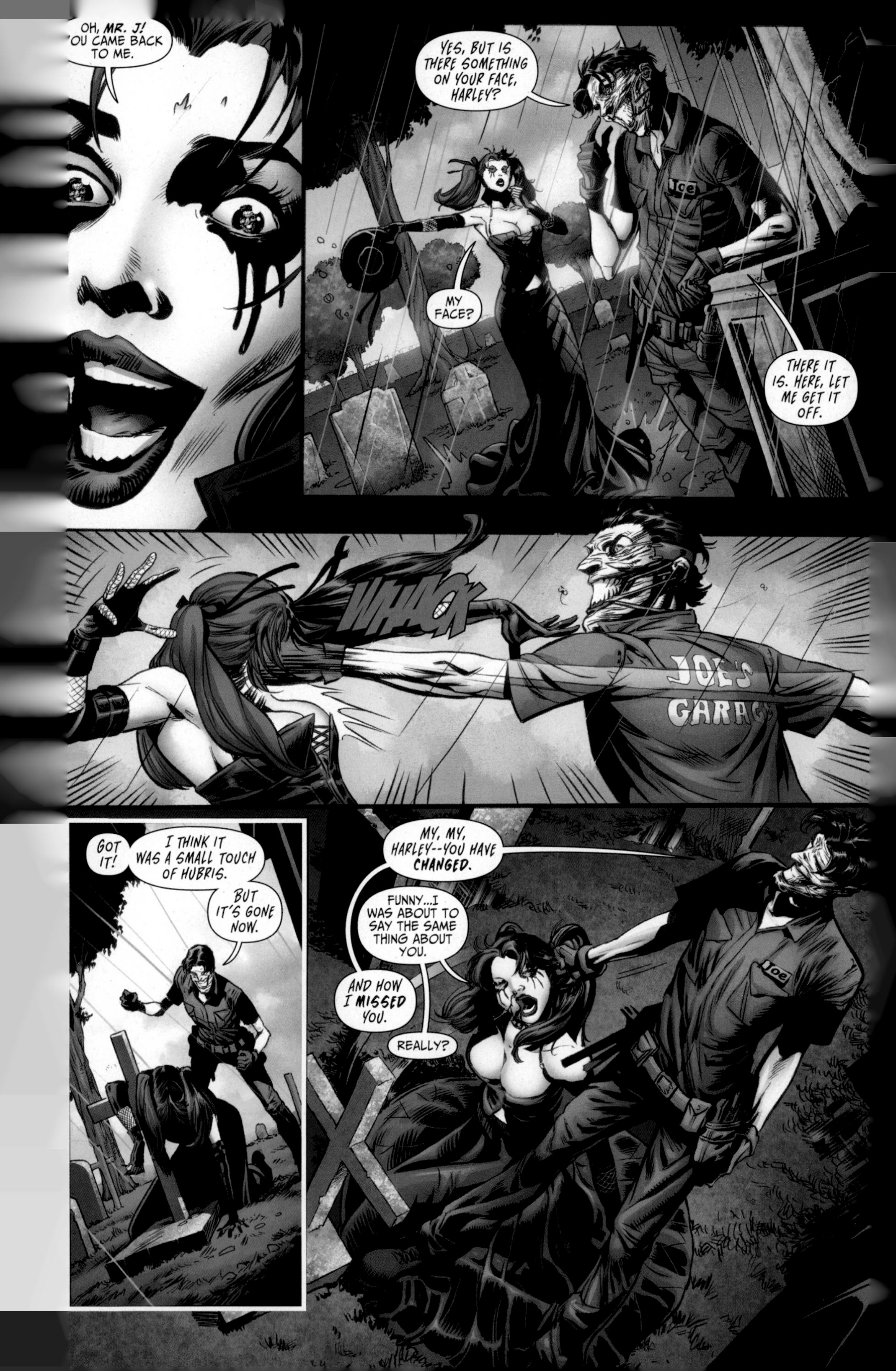

OH, MR. J! YOU CAME BACK TO ME.
YES, BUT IS THERE SOMETHING ON YOUR FACE, HARLEY?
MY FACE?
THERE IT IS. HERE, LET ME GET IT OFF.
WHACK
JOE'S GARAG
GOT IT!
I THINK IT WAS A SMALL TOUCH OF HUBRIS.
BUT IT'S GONE NOW.
MY, MY, HARLEY--YOU HAVE CHANGED.
FUNNY...I WAS ABOUT TO SAY THE SAME THING ABOUT YOU.
AND HOW I MISSED YOU.
REALLY?

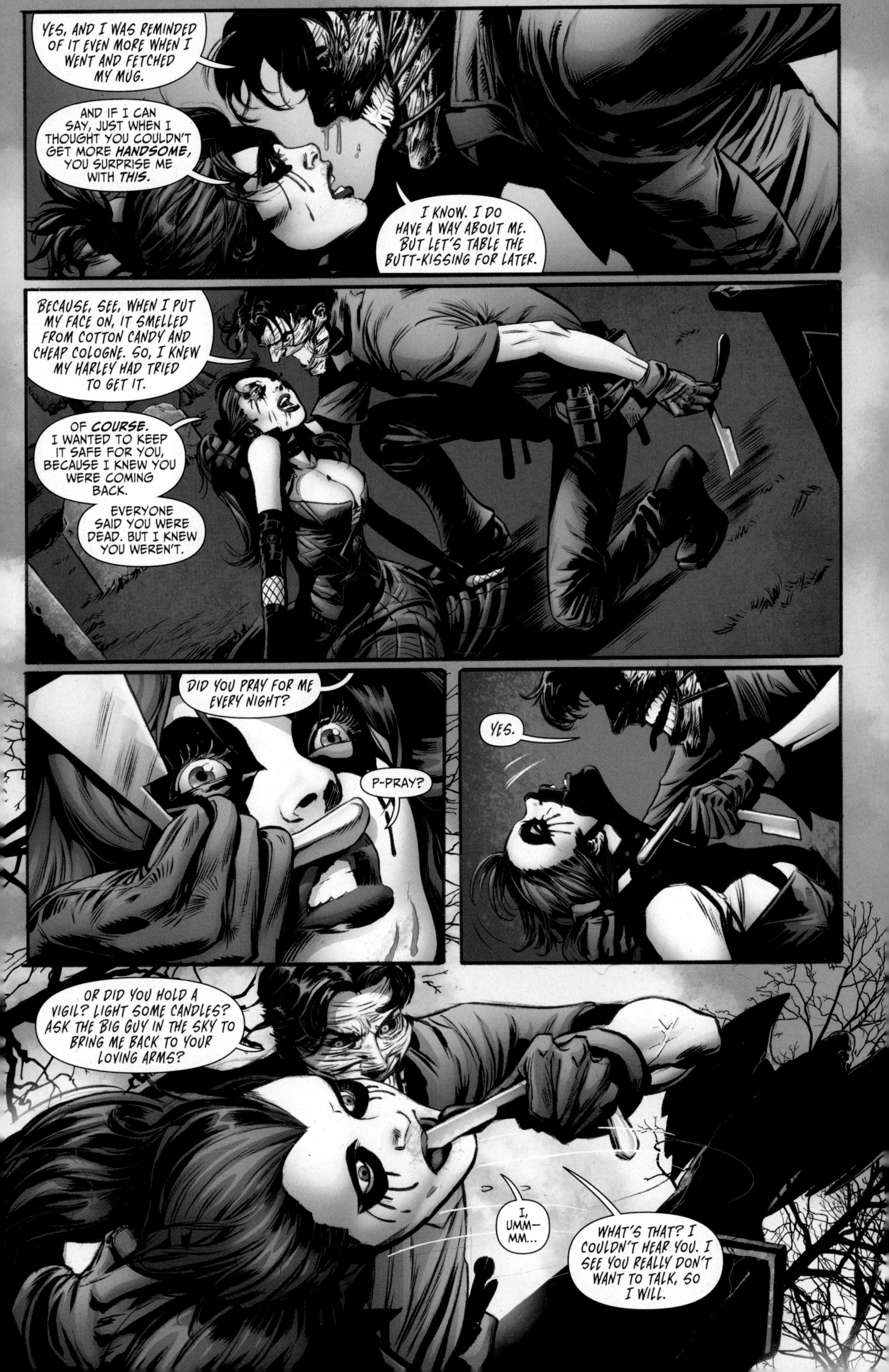
YES, AND I WAS REMINDED OF IT EVEN MORE WHEN I WENT AND FETCHED MY MUG.
AND IF I CAN SAY, JUST WHEN I THOUGHT YOU COULDN'T GET MORE HANDSOME, YOU SURPRISE ME WITH THIS.
I KNOW. I DO HAVE A WAY ABOUT ME. BUT LET'S TABLE THE BUTT-KISSING FOR LATER.
BECAUSE, SEE, WHEN I PUT MY FACE ON, IT SMELLED FROM COTTON CANDY AND CHEAP COLOGNE. SO, I KNEW MY HARLEY HAD TRIED TO GET IT.
OF COURSE. I WANTED TO KEEP IT SAFE FOR YOU, BECAUSE I KNEW YOU WERE COMING BACK.
EVERYONE SAID YOU WERE DEAD. BUT I KNEW YOU WEREN'T.
DID YOU PRAY FOR ME EVERY NIGHT?
P-PRAY?
YES.
OR DID YOU HOLD A VIGIL? LIGHT SOME CANDLES? ASK THE BIG GUY IN THE SKY TO BRING ME BACK TO YOUR LOVING ARMS?
I, UMM—MM...
WHAT'S THAT? I COULDN'T HEAR YOU. I SEE YOU REALLY DON'T WANT TO TALK, SO I WILL.

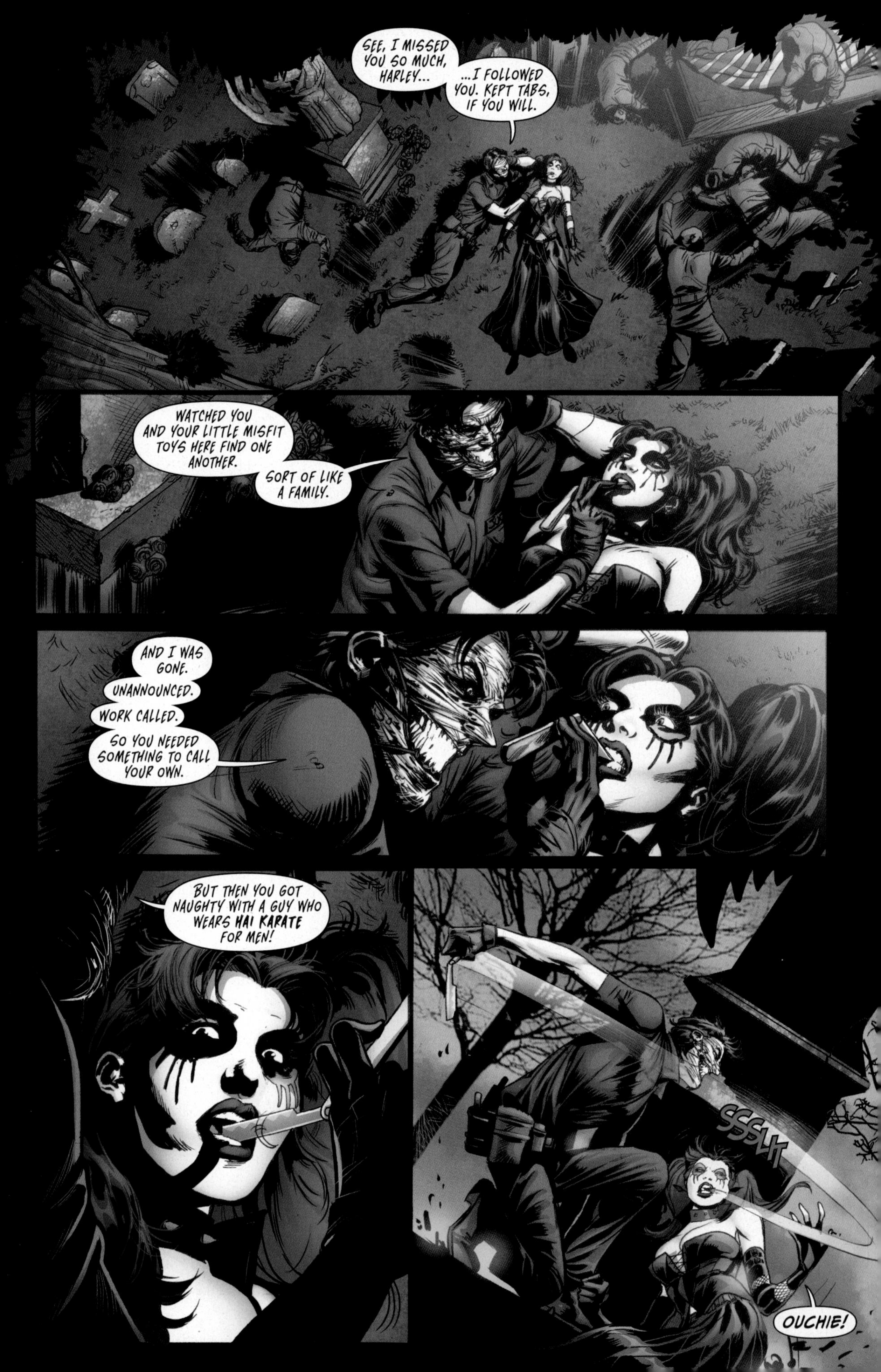
SEE, I MISSED YOU SO MUCH, HARLEY...
...I FOLLOWED YOU. KEPT TABS, IF YOU WILL.
WATCHED YOU AND YOUR LITTLE MISFIT TOYS HERE FIND ONE ANOTHER.
SORT OF LIKE A FAMILY.
AND I WAS GONE.
UNANNOUNCED.
WORK CALLED.
SO YOU NEEDED SOMETHING TO CALL YOUR OWN.
BUT THEN YOU GOT NAUGHTY WITH A GUY WHO WEARS HAI KARATE FOR MEN!
SSSLK
OUCHIE!

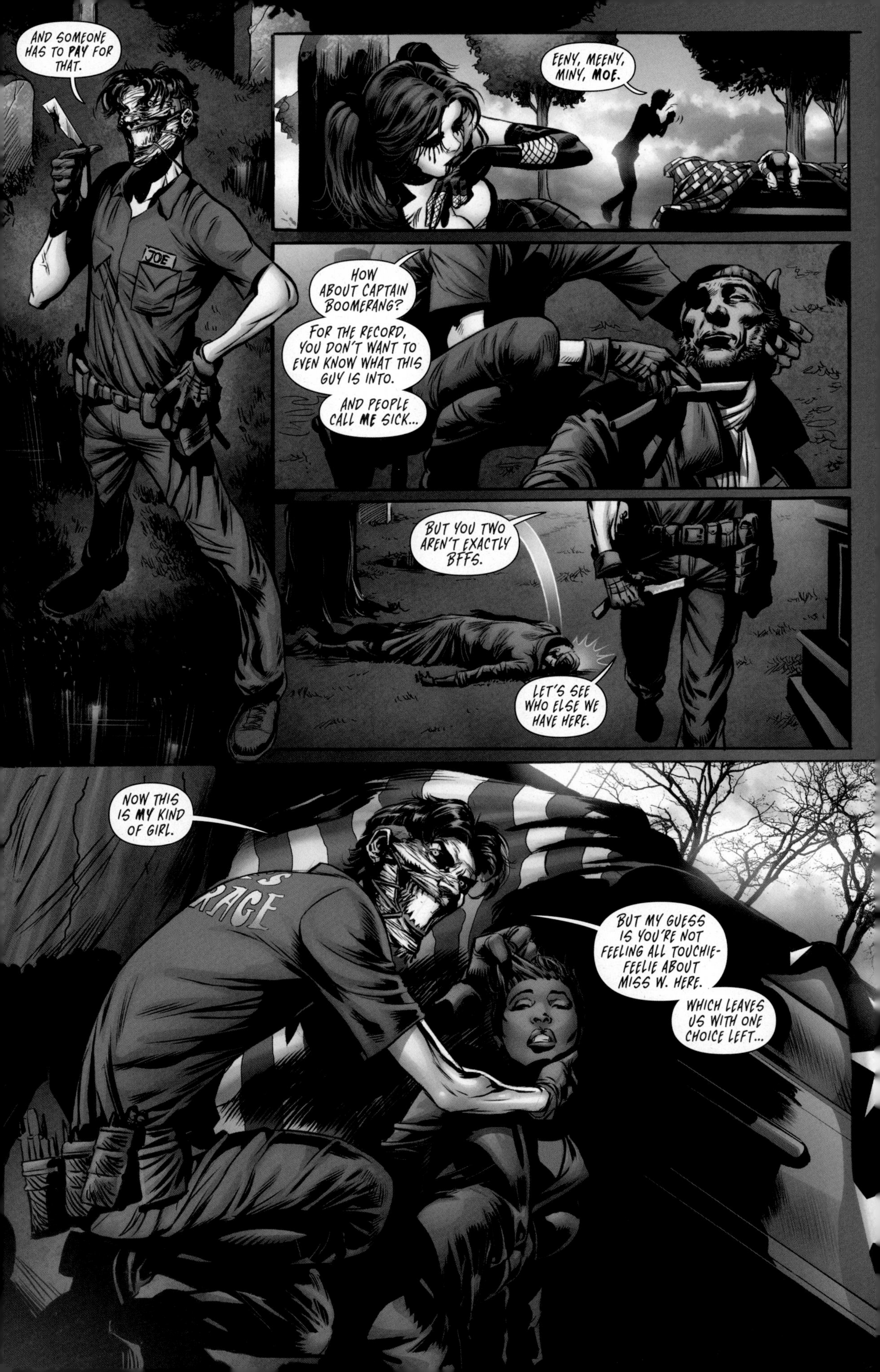

AND SOMEONE HAS TO PAY FOR THAT.
EENY, MEENY, MINY, MOE.
HOW ABOUT CAPTAIN BOOMERANG?
FOR THE RECORD, YOU DON'T WANT TO EVEN KNOW WHAT THIS GUY IS INTO.
AND PEOPLE CALL ME SICK...
BUT YOU TWO AREN'T EXACTLY BFFS.
LET'S SEE WHO ELSE WE HAVE HERE.
NOW THIS IS MY KIND OF GIRL.
BUT MY GUESS IS YOU'RE NOT FEELING ALL TOUCHIE-FEELIE ABOUT MISS W. HERE.
WHICH LEAVES US WITH ONE CHOICE LEFT...

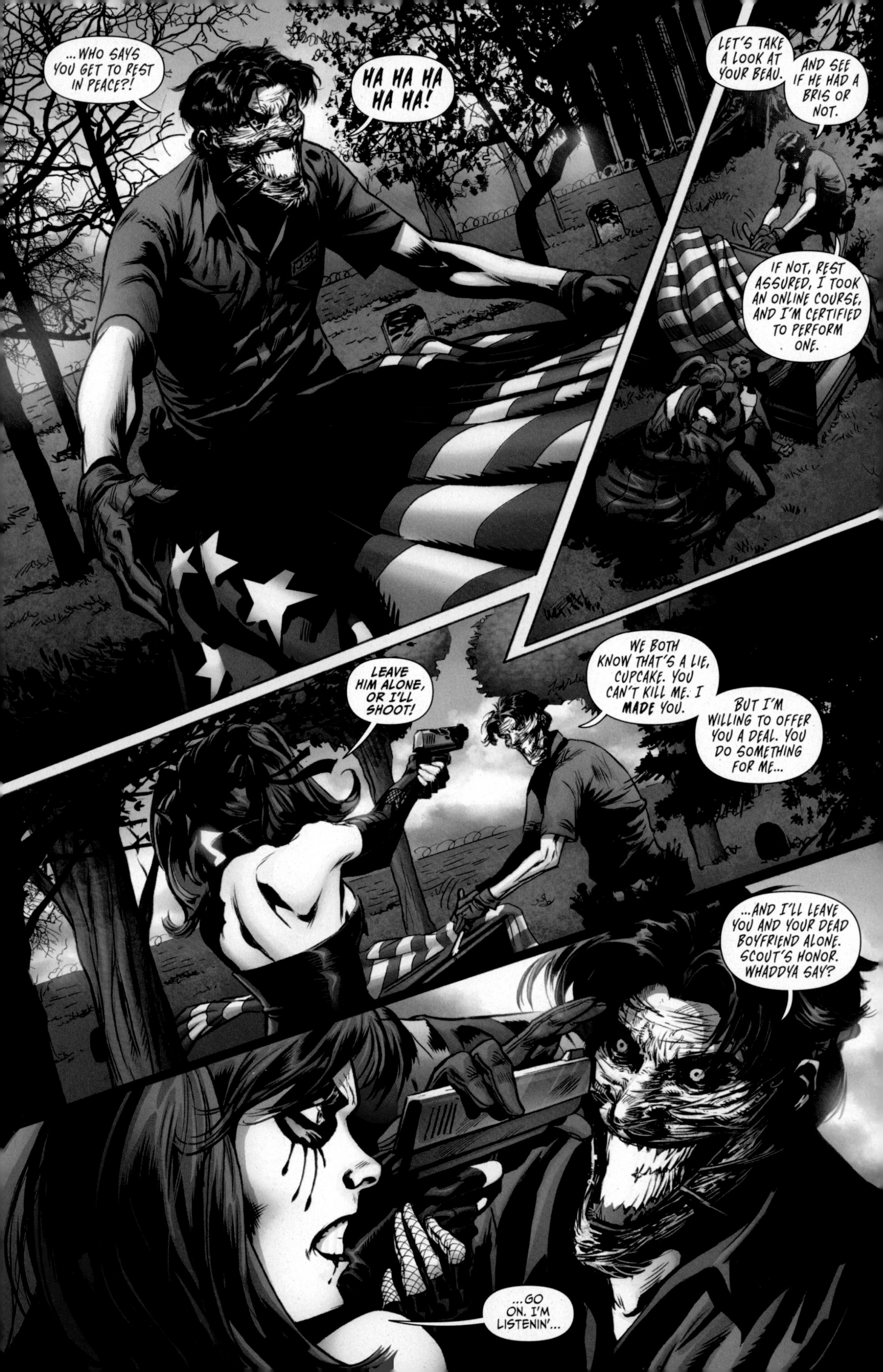
...WHO SAYS YOU GET TO REST IN PEACE?!
HA HA HA HA HA!
LET'S TAKE A LOOK AT YOUR BEAU.
AND SEE IF HE HAD A BRIS OR NOT.
IF NOT, REST ASSURED, I TOOK AN ONLINE COURSE, AND I'M CERTIFIED TO PERFORM ONE.
LEAVE HIM ALONE, OR I'LL SHOOT!
WE BOTH KNOW THAT'S A LIE, CUPCAKE. YOU CAN'T KILL ME. I MADE YOU.
BUT I'M WILLING TO OFFER YOU A DEAL. YOU DO SOMETHING FOR ME...
...AND I'LL LEAVE YOU AND YOUR DEAD BOYFRIEND ALONE. SCOUT'S HONOR. WHADDYA SAY?
...GO ON. I'M LISTENIN'...

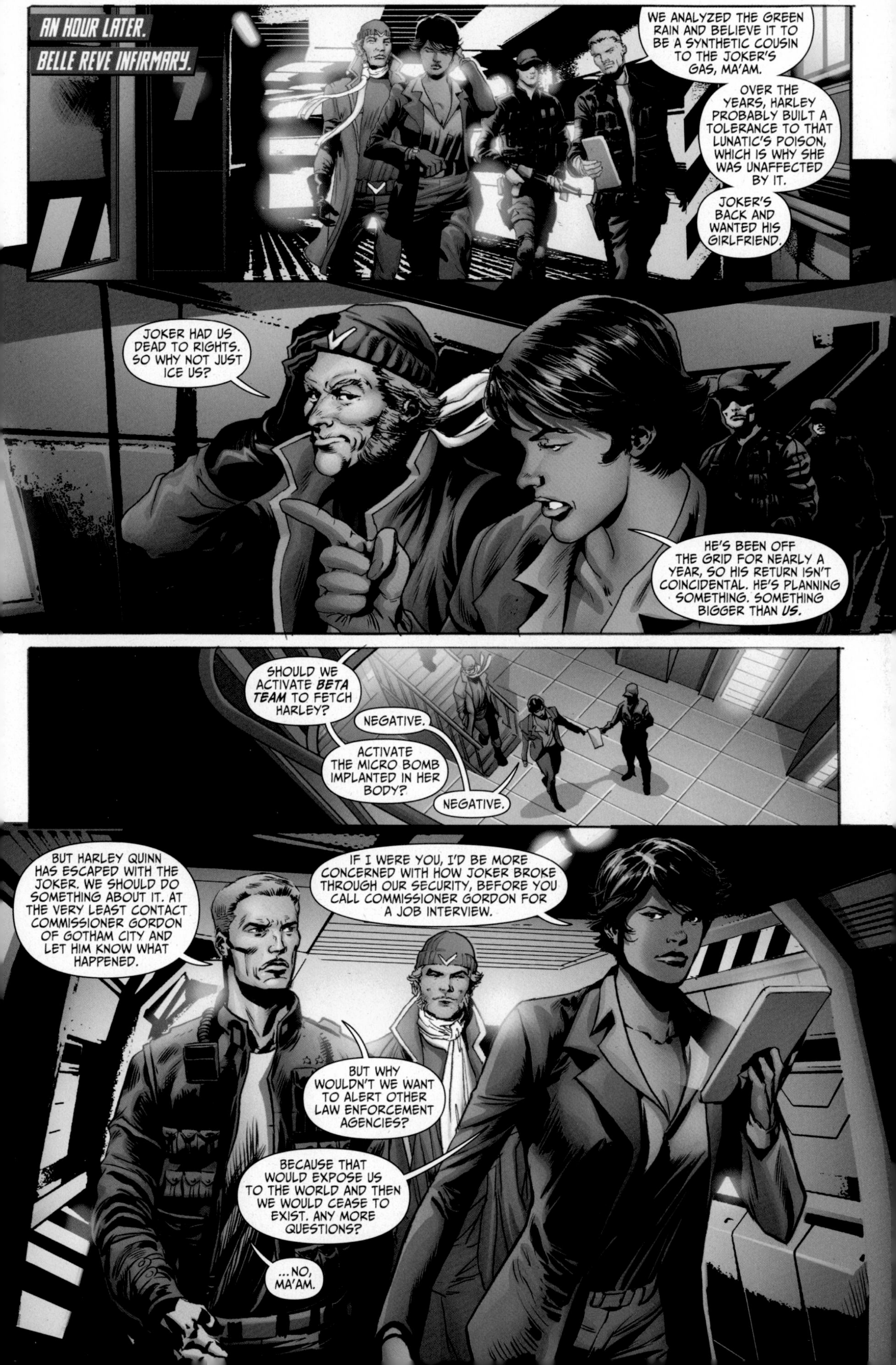
AN HOUR LATER.
BELLE REVE INFIRMARY.
WE ANALYZED THE GREEN RAIN AND BELIEVE IT TO BE A SYNTHETIC COUSIN TO THE JOKER'S GAS, MA'AM.
OVER THE YEARS, HARLEY PROBABLY BUILT A TOLERANCE TO THAT LUNATIC'S POISON, WHICH IS WHY SHE WAS UNAFFECTED BY IT.
JOKER'S BACK AND WANTED HIS GIRLFRIEND.
JOKER HAD US DEAD TO RIGHTS. SO WHY NOT JUST ICE US?
HE'S BEEN OFF THE GRID FOR NEARLY A YEAR, SO HIS RETURN ISN'T COINCIDENTAL. HE'S PLANNING SOMETHING. SOMETHING BIGGER THAN *US.*
SHOULD WE ACTIVATE *BETA TEAM* TO FETCH HARLEY?
NEGATIVE.
ACTIVATE THE MICRO BOMB IMPLANTED IN HER BODY?
NEGATIVE.
BUT HARLEY QUINN HAS ESCAPED WITH THE JOKER. WE SHOULD DO SOMETHING ABOUT IT. AT THE VERY LEAST CONTACT COMMISSIONER GORDON OF GOTHAM CITY AND LET HIM KNOW WHAT HAPPENED.
IF I WERE YOU, I'D BE MORE CONCERNED WITH HOW JOKER BROKE THROUGH OUR SECURITY, BEFORE YOU CALL COMMISSIONER GORDON FOR A JOB INTERVIEW.
BUT WHY WOULDN'T WE WANT TO ALERT OTHER LAW ENFORCEMENT AGENCIES?
BECAUSE THAT WOULD EXPOSE US TO THE WORLD AND THEN WE WOULD CEASE TO EXIST. ANY MORE QUESTIONS?
...NO, MA'AM.

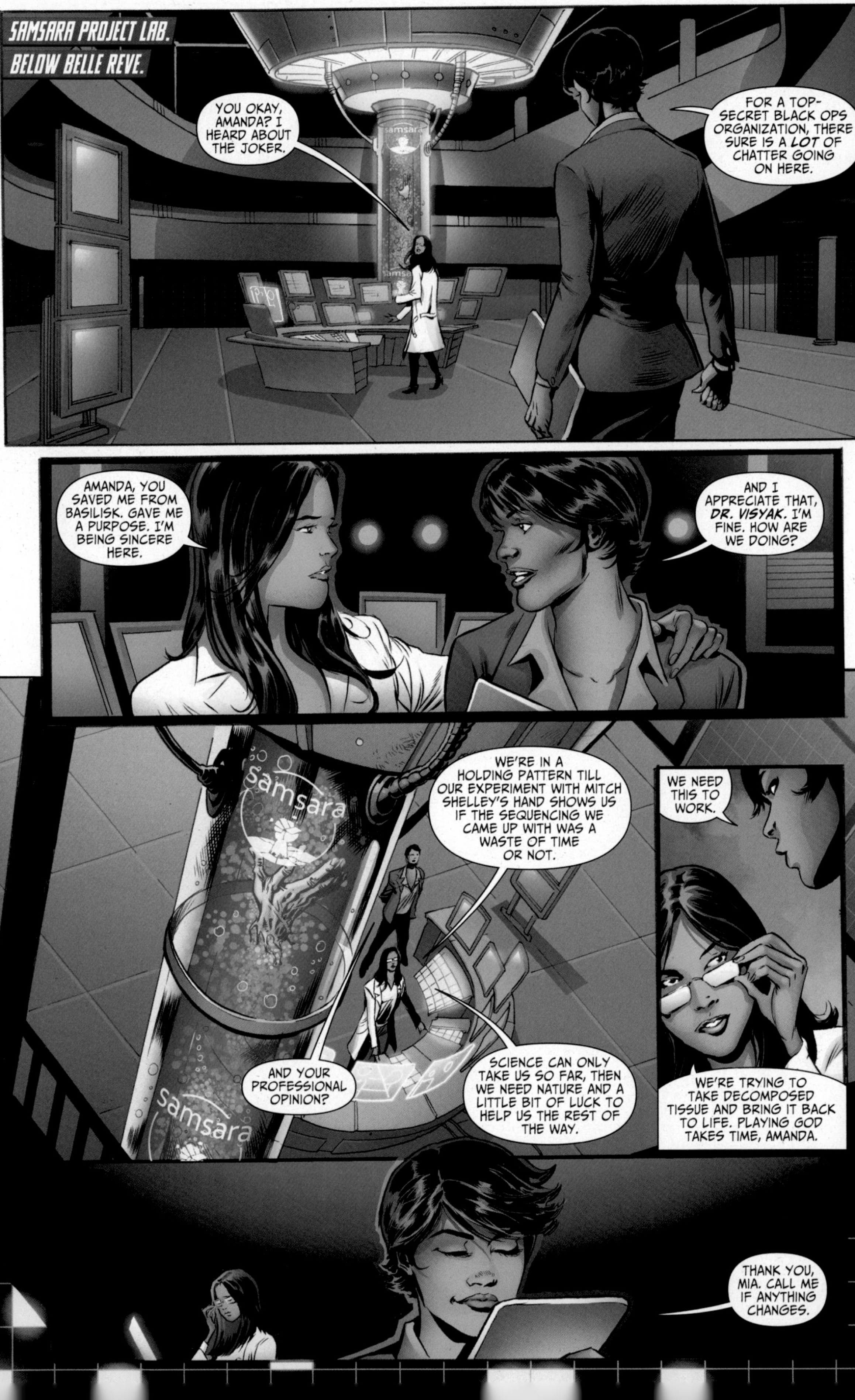
SAMSARA PROJECT LAB.
BELOW BELLE REVE.
YOU OKAY, AMANDA? I HEARD ABOUT THE JOKER.
FOR A TOP-SECRET BLACK OPS ORGANIZATION, THERE SURE IS A LOT OF CHATTER GOING ON HERE.
AMANDA, YOU SAVED ME FROM BASILISK. GAVE ME A PURPOSE. I'M BEING SINCERE HERE.
AND I APPRECIATE THAT, DR. VISYAK. I'M FINE. HOW ARE WE DOING?
WE'RE IN A HOLDING PATTERN TILL OUR EXPERIMENT WITH MITCH SHELLEY'S HAND SHOWS US IF THE SEQUENCING WE CAME UP WITH WAS A WASTE OF TIME OR NOT.
AND YOUR PROFESSIONAL OPINION?
SCIENCE CAN ONLY TAKE US SO FAR, THEN WE NEED NATURE AND A LITTLE BIT OF LUCK TO HELP US THE REST OF THE WAY.
WE NEED THIS TO WORK.
WE'RE TRYING TO TAKE DECOMPOSED TISSUE AND BRING IT BACK TO LIFE. PLAYING GOD TAKES TIME, AMANDA.
THANK YOU, MIA. CALL ME IF ANYTHING CHANGES.

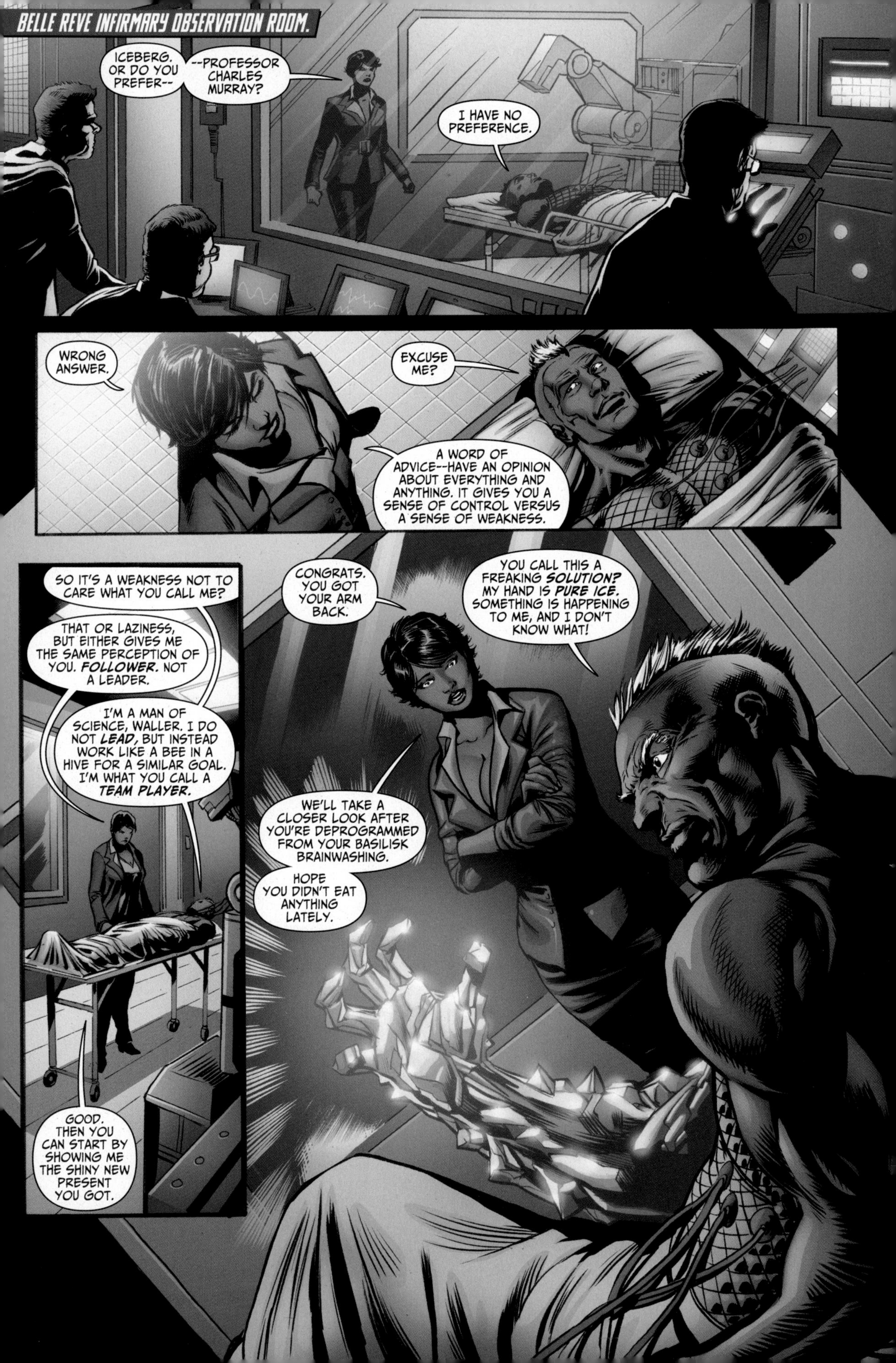
BELLE REVE INFIRMARY OBSERVATION ROOM.
ICEBERG. OR DO YOU PREFER--
--PROFESSOR CHARLES MURRAY?
I HAVE NO PREFERENCE.
WRONG ANSWER.
EXCUSE ME?
A WORD OF ADVICE--HAVE AN OPINION ABOUT EVERYTHING AND ANYTHING. IT GIVES YOU A SENSE OF CONTROL VERSUS A SENSE OF WEAKNESS.
SO IT'S A WEAKNESS NOT TO CARE WHAT YOU CALL ME?
THAT OR LAZINESS, BUT EITHER GIVES ME THE SAME PERCEPTION OF YOU. FOLLOWER. NOT A LEADER.
I'M A MAN OF SCIENCE, WALLER. I DO NOT LEAD, BUT INSTEAD WORK LIKE A BEE IN A HIVE FOR A SIMILAR GOAL. I'M WHAT YOU CALL A TEAM PLAYER.
GOOD. THEN YOU CAN START BY SHOWING ME THE SHINY NEW PRESENT YOU GOT.
CONGRATS. YOU GOT YOUR ARM BACK.
YOU CALL THIS A FREAKING SOLUTION? MY HAND IS PURE ICE. SOMETHING IS HAPPENING TO ME, AND I DON'T KNOW WHAT!
WE'LL TAKE A CLOSER LOOK AFTER YOU'RE DEPROGRAMMED FROM YOUR BASILISK BRAINWASHING.
HOPE YOU DIDN'T EAT ANYTHING LATELY.

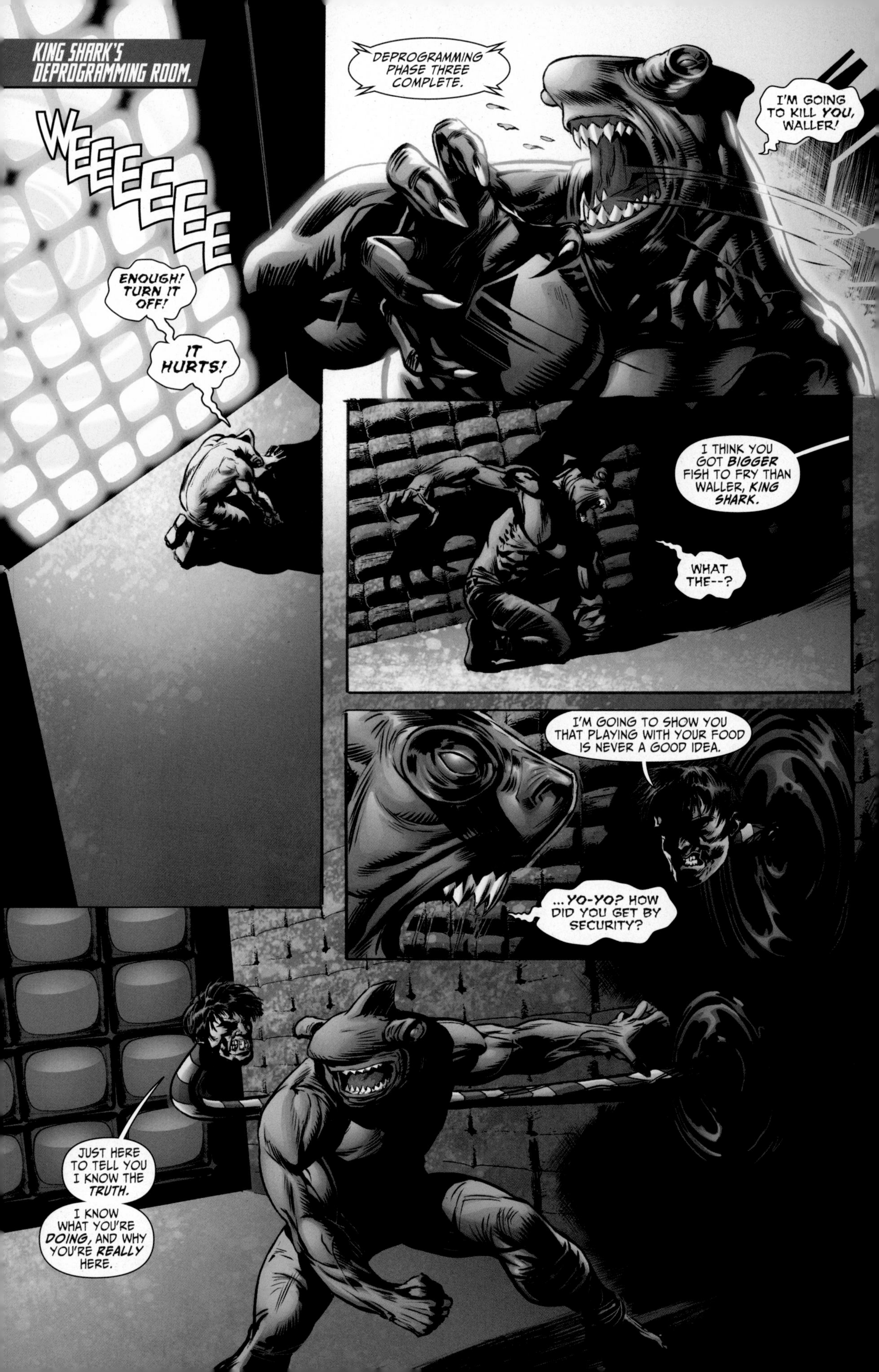
KING SHARK'S DEPROGRAMMING ROOM.
WEEEEEEE
DEPROGRAMMING PHASE THREE COMPLETE.
I'M GOING TO KILL YOU, WALLER!
ENOUGH! TURN IT OFF!
IT HURTS!
I THINK YOU GOT BIGGER FISH TO FRY THAN WALLER, KING SHARK.
WHAT THE--?
I'M GOING TO SHOW YOU THAT PLAYING WITH YOUR FOOD IS NEVER A GOOD IDEA.
...YO-YO? HOW DID YOU GET BY SECURITY?
JUST HERE TO TELL YOU I KNOW THE TRUTH.
I KNOW WHAT YOU'RE DOING, AND WHY YOU'RE REALLY HERE.

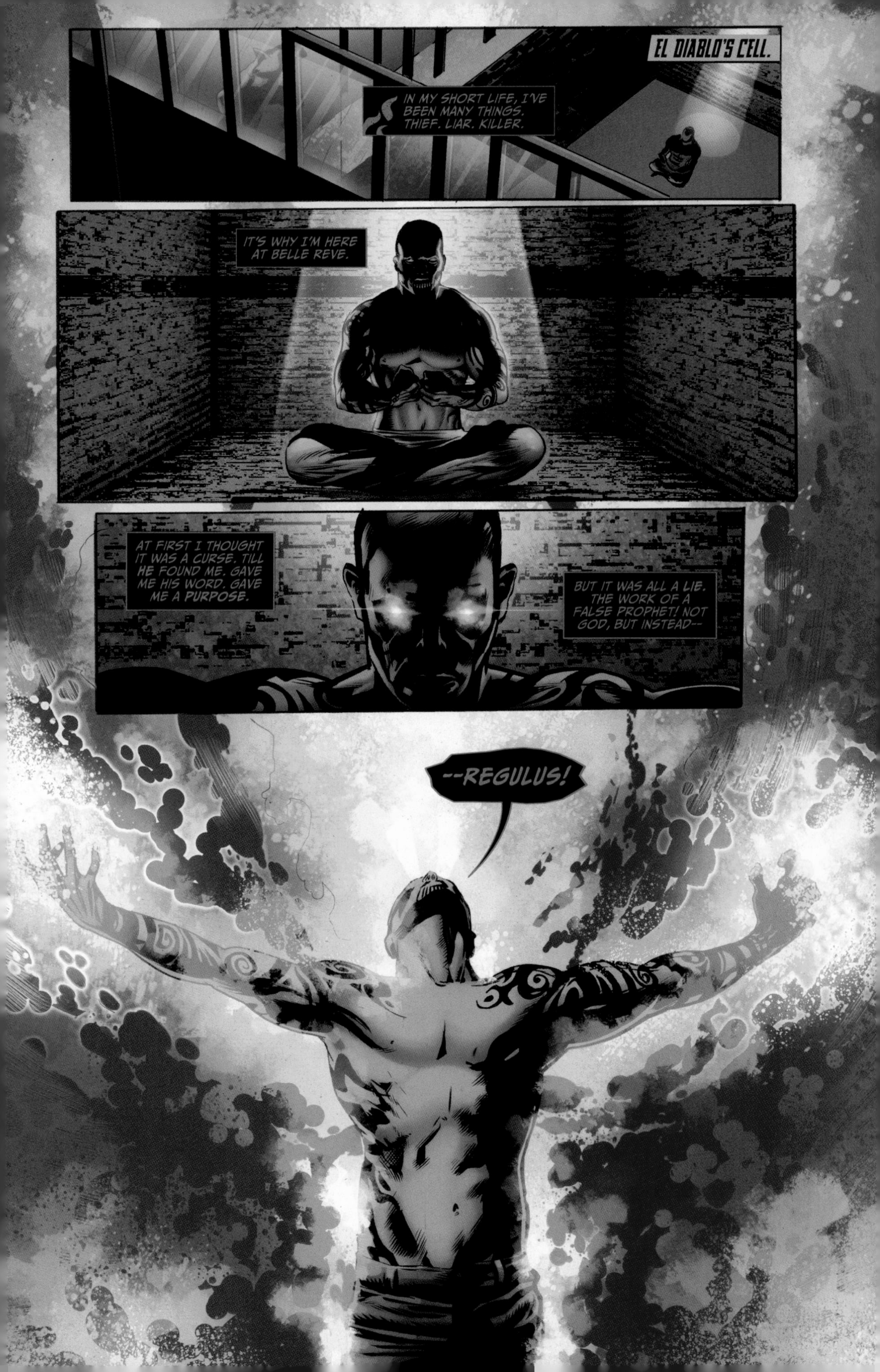
EL DIABLO'S CELL.
IN MY SHORT LIFE, I'VE BEEN MANY THINGS. THIEF. LIAR. KILLER.
IT'S WHY I'M HERE AT BELLE REVE.
AT FIRST I THOUGHT IT WAS A CURSE. TILL HE FOUND ME. GAVE ME HIS WORD. GAVE ME A PURPOSE.
BUT IT WAS ALL A LIE. THE WORK OF A FALSE PROPHET! NOT GOD, BUT INSTEAD--
--REGULUS!

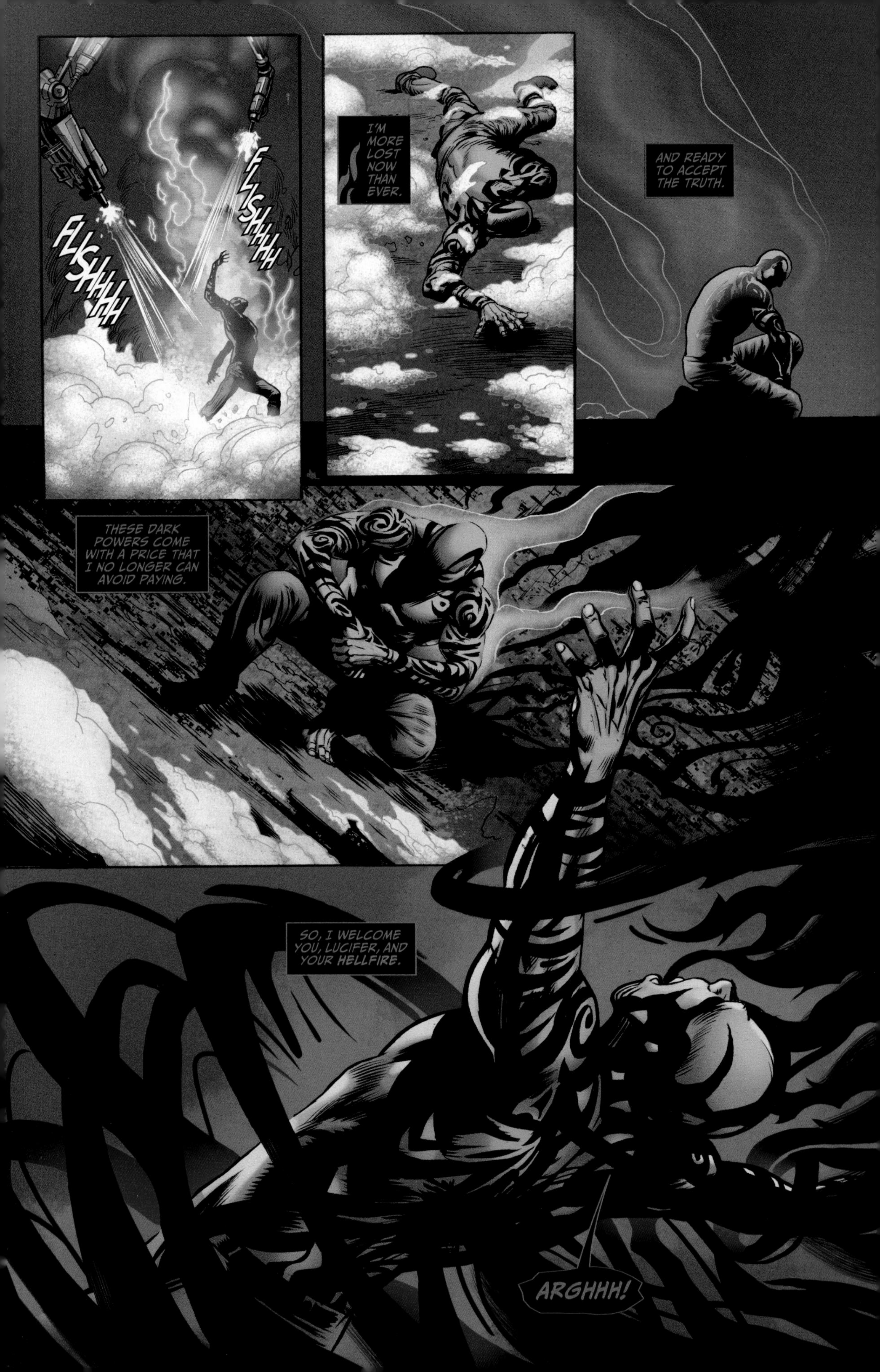
FLISHHHH
FLISHHHH
I'M MORE LOST NOW THAN EVER.
AND READY TO ACCEPT THE TRUTH.
THESE DARK POWERS COME WITH A PRICE THAT I NO LONGER CAN AVOID PAYING.
SO, I WELCOME YOU, LUCIFER, AND YOUR HELLFIRE.
ARGHHH!

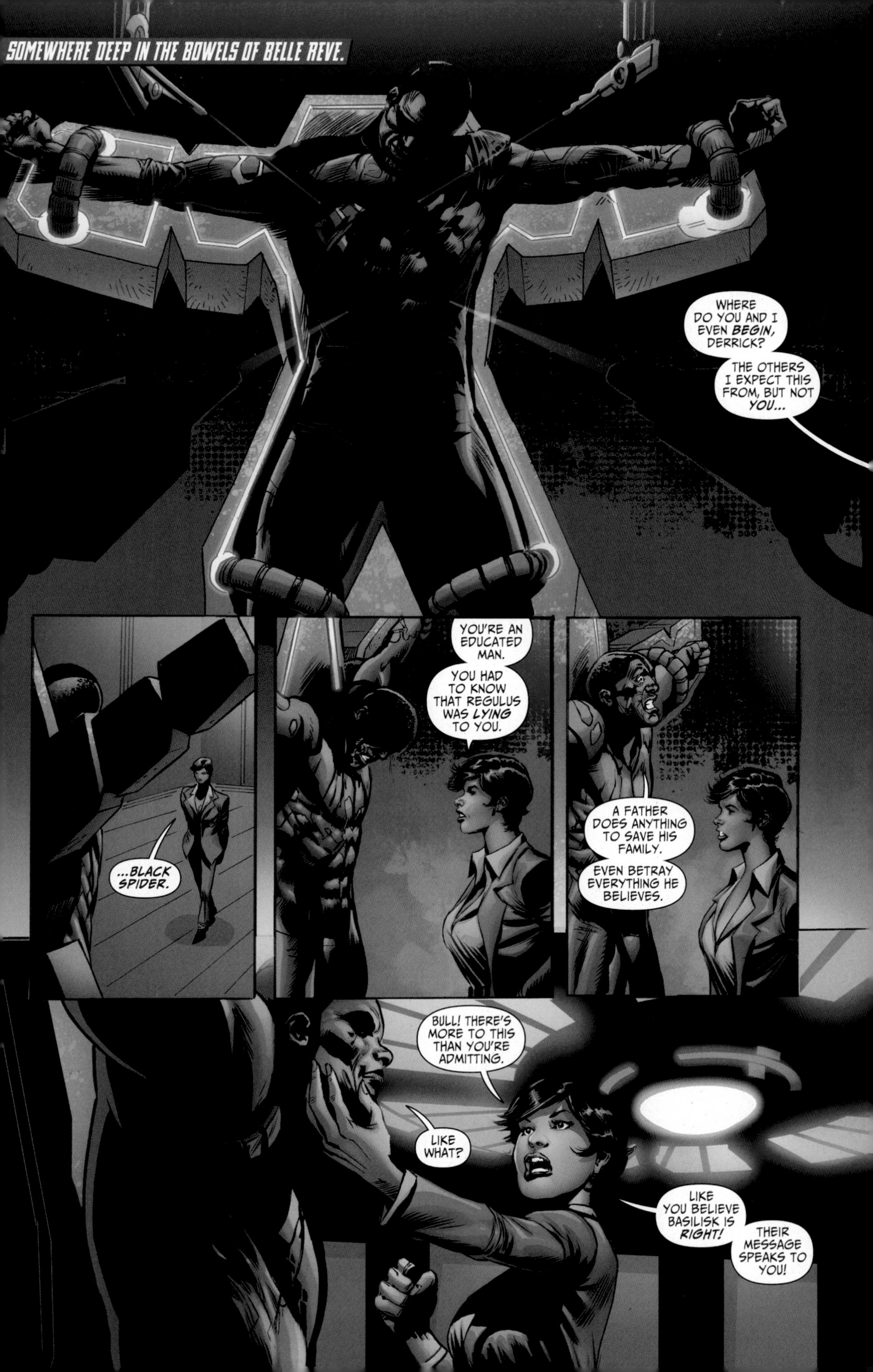
SOMEWHERE DEEP IN THE BOWELS OF BELLE REVE.
WHERE DO YOU AND I EVEN BEGIN, DERRICK?
THE OTHERS I EXPECT THIS FROM, BUT NOT YOU...
...BLACK SPIDER.
YOU'RE AN EDUCATED MAN.
YOU HAD TO KNOW THAT REGULUS WAS LYING TO YOU.
A FATHER DOES ANYTHING TO SAVE HIS FAMILY.
EVEN BETRAY EVERYTHING HE BELIEVES.
BULL! THERE'S MORE TO THIS THAN YOU'RE ADMITTING.
LIKE WHAT?
LIKE YOU BELIEVE BASILISK IS RIGHT!
THEIR MESSAGE SPEAKS TO YOU!

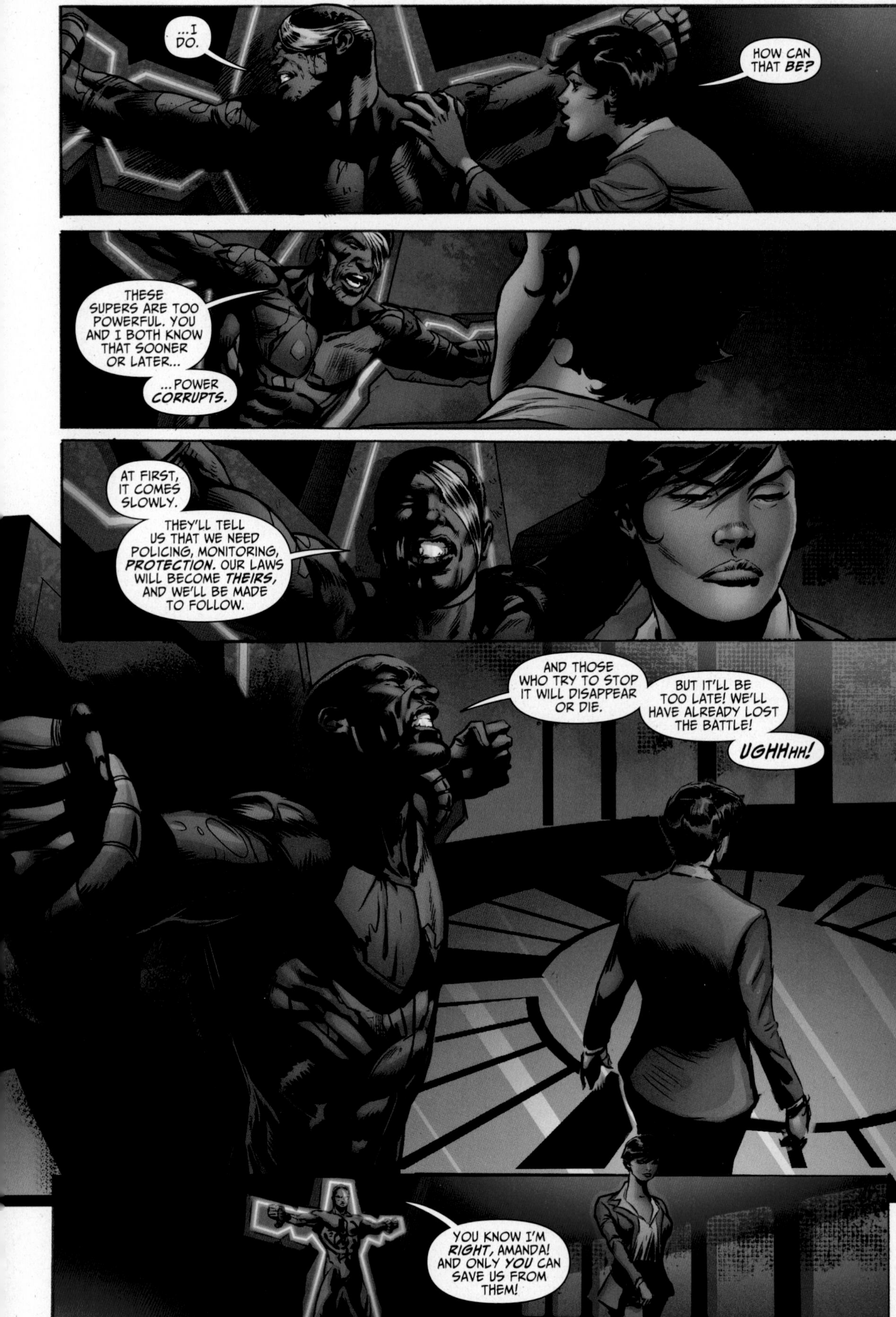
...I DO.
HOW CAN THAT *BE?*
THESE SUPERS ARE TOO POWERFUL. YOU AND I BOTH KNOW THAT SOONER OR LATER...
...POWER *CORRUPTS.*
AT FIRST, IT COMES SLOWLY.
THEY'LL TELL US THAT WE NEED POLICING, MONITORING, *PROTECTION.* OUR LAWS WILL BECOME *THEIRS,* AND WE'LL BE MADE TO FOLLOW.
AND THOSE WHO TRY TO STOP IT WILL DISAPPEAR OR DIE.
BUT IT'LL BE TOO LATE! WE'LL HAVE ALREADY LOST THE BATTLE!
UGHHhh!
YOU KNOW I'M *RIGHT,* AMANDA! AND ONLY *YOU* CAN SAVE US FROM THEM!

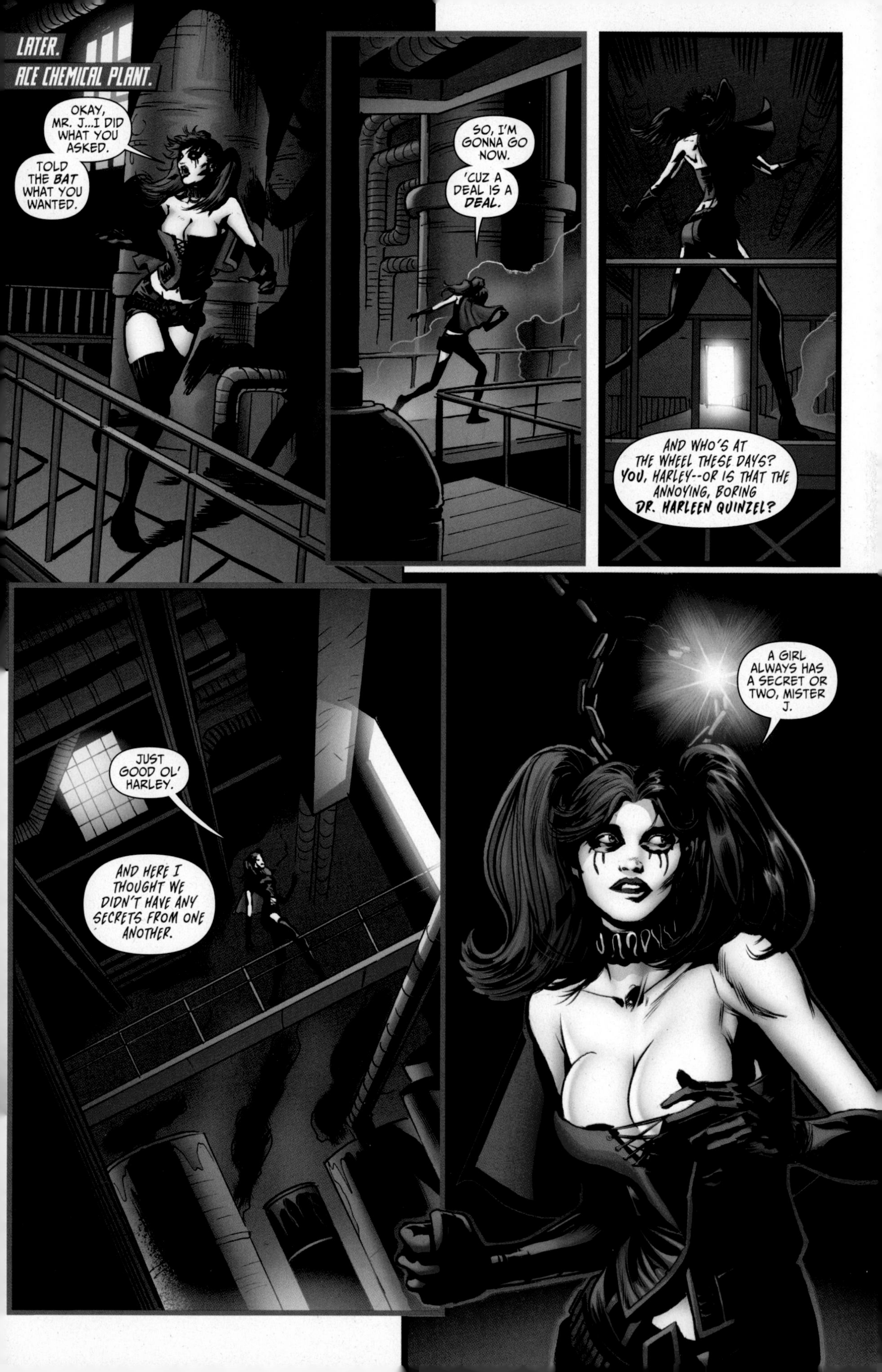
LATER.
ACE CHEMICAL PLANT.
OKAY, MR. J...I DID WHAT YOU ASKED.
TOLD THE BAT WHAT YOU WANTED.
SO, I'M GONNA GO NOW.
'CUZ A DEAL IS A DEAL.
AND WHO'S AT THE WHEEL THESE DAYS? YOU, HARLEY--OR IS THAT THE ANNOYING, BORING DR. HARLEEN QUINZEL?
JUST GOOD OL' HARLEY.
AND HERE I THOUGHT WE DIDN'T HAVE ANY SECRETS FROM ONE ANOTHER.
A GIRL ALWAYS HAS A SECRET OR TWO, MISTER J.

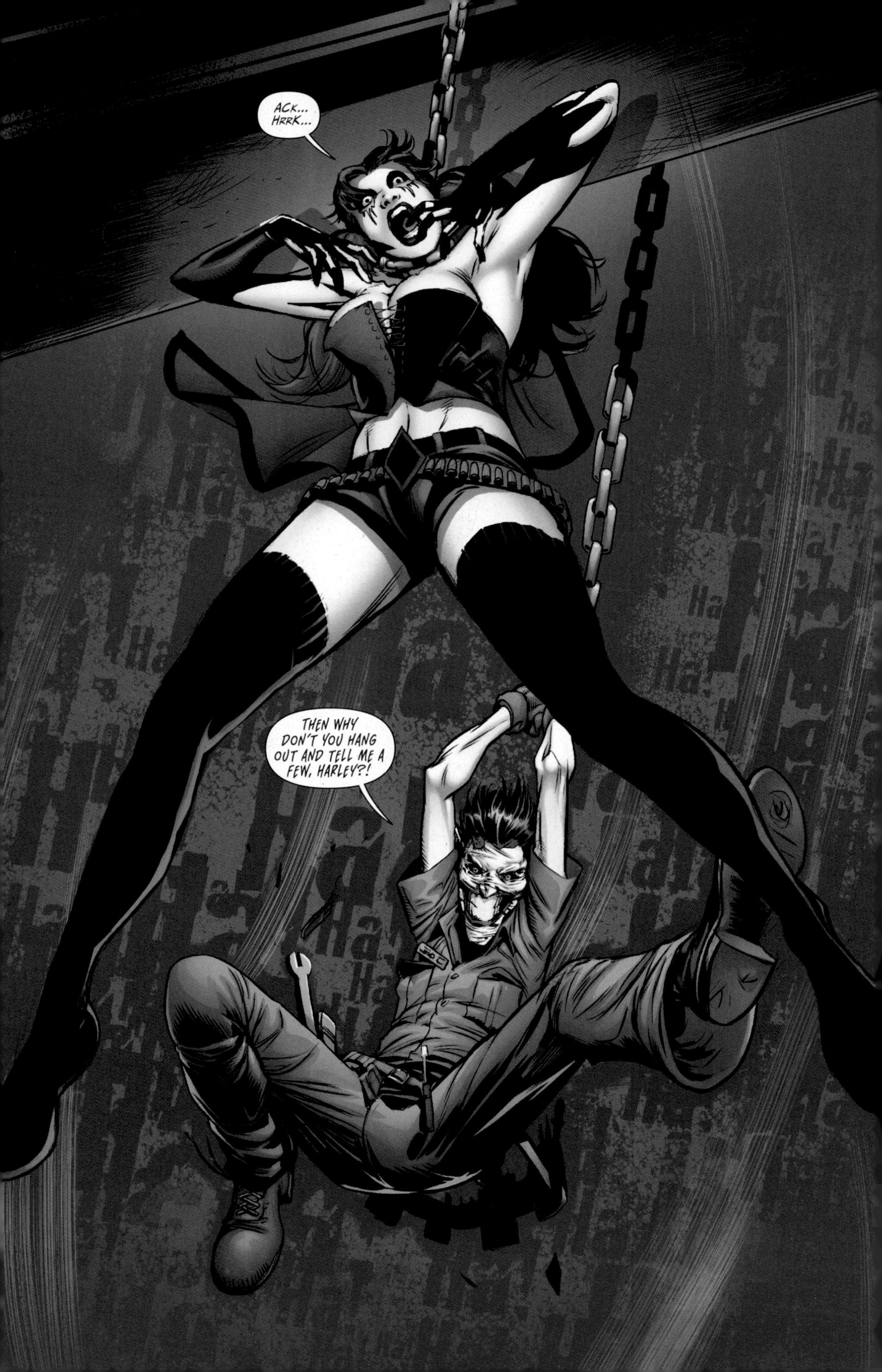
ACK... HRRK...
THEN WHY DON'T YOU HANG OUT AND TELL ME A FEW, HARLEY?!

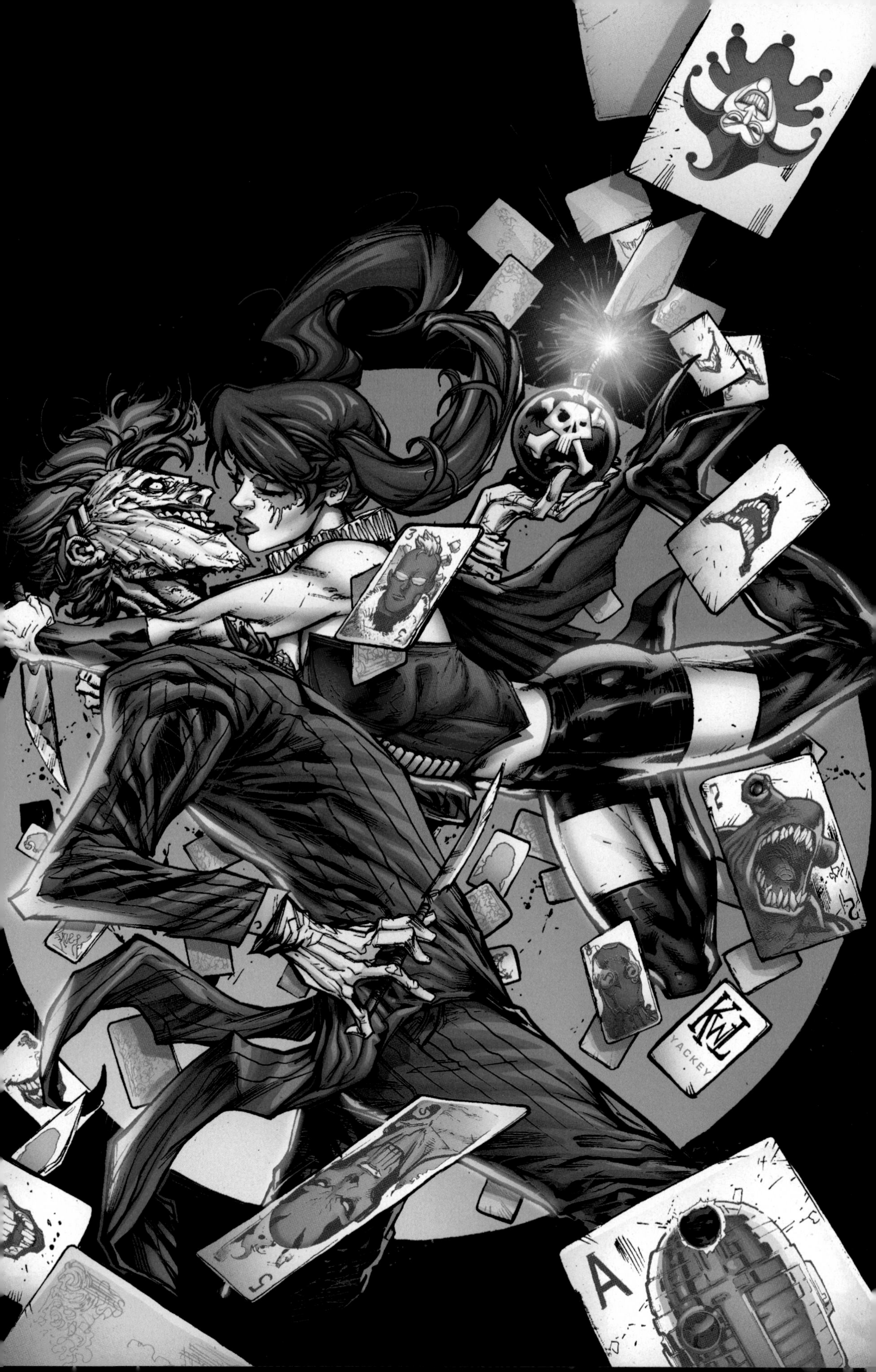
YACKEY

RUNNING WITH THE DEVIL: PART TWO

ADAM GLASS writer **FERNANDO DAGNINO** artist cover art by **KEN LASHLEY & MATT YACKEY**

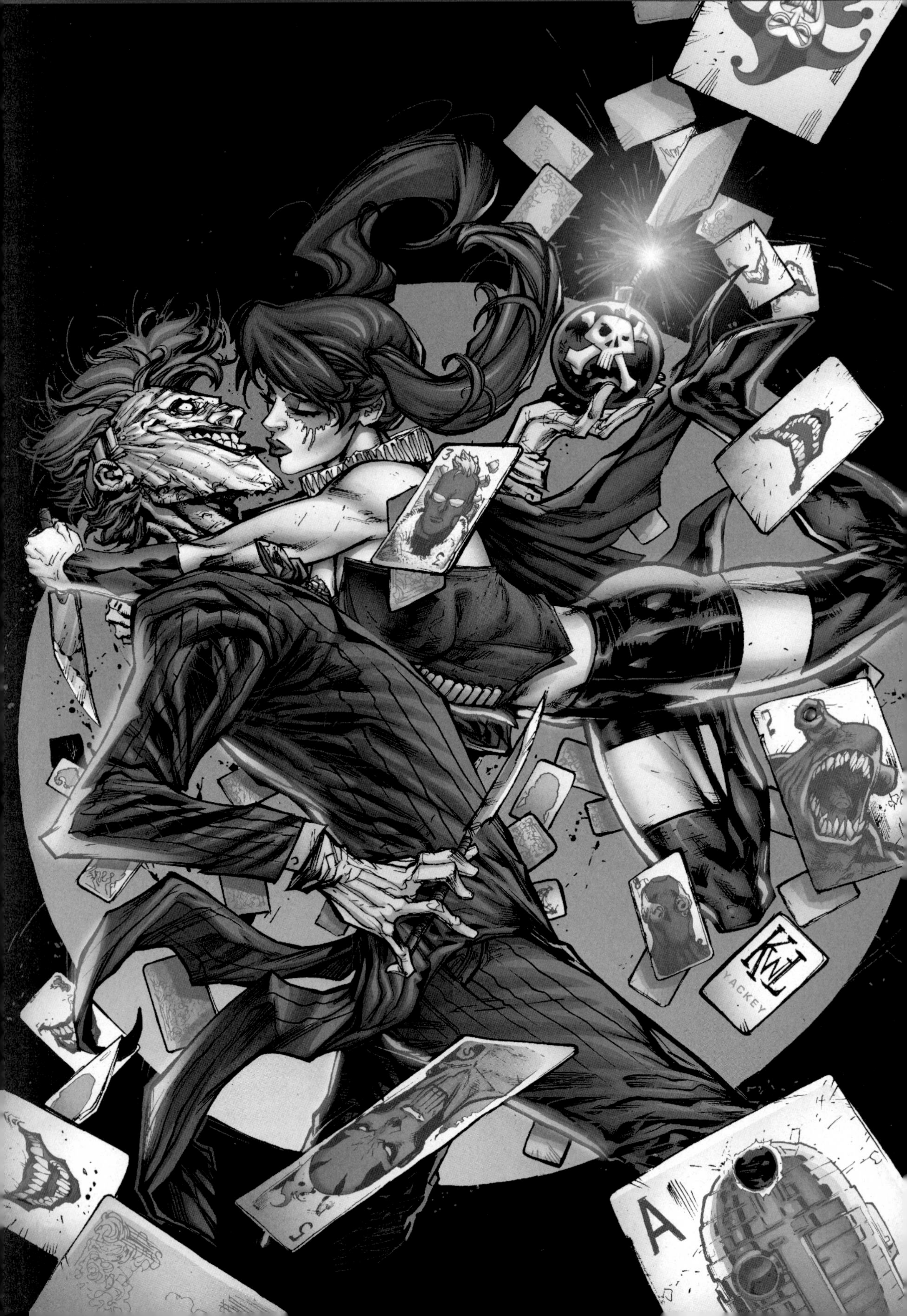

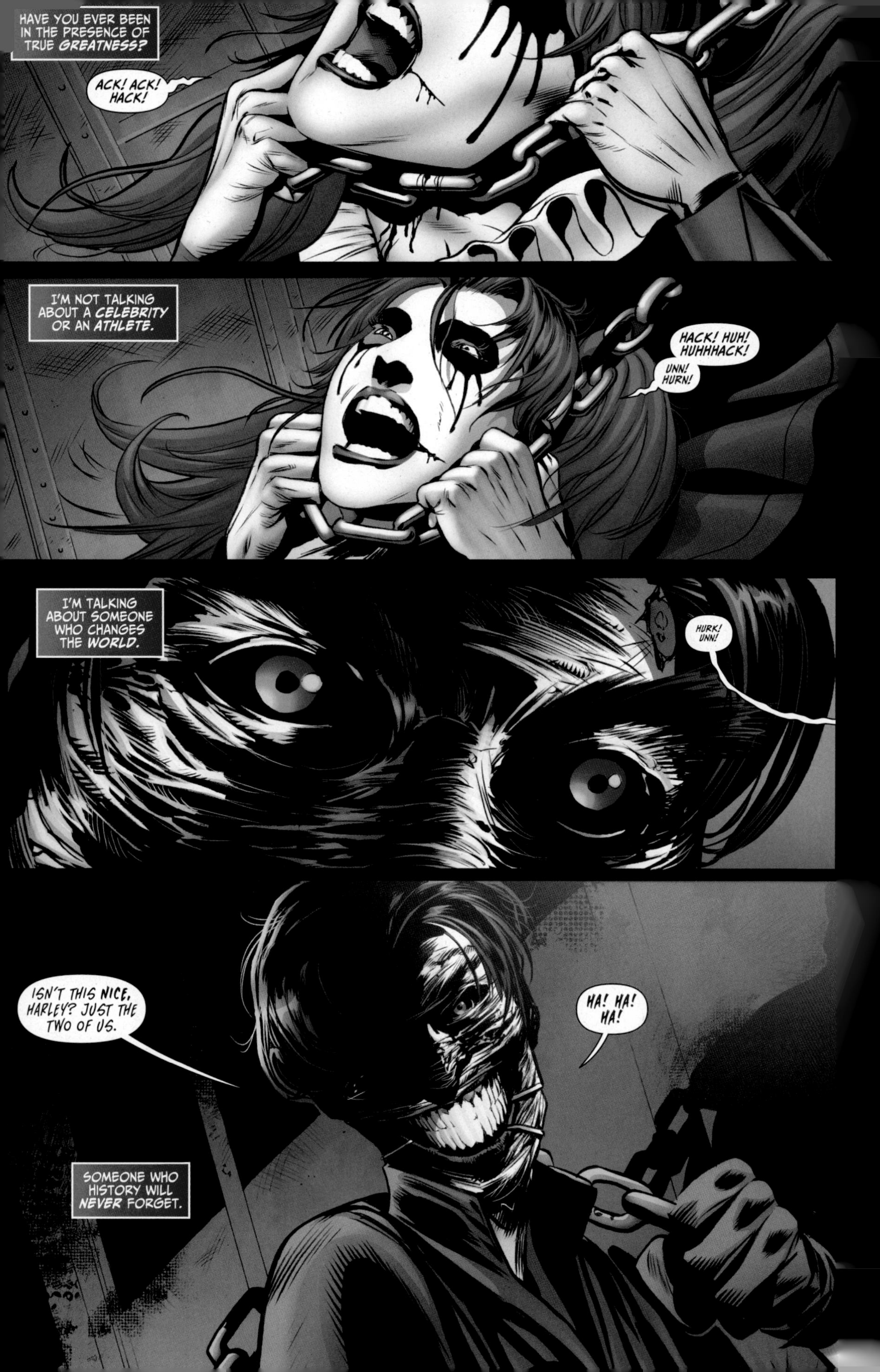
HAVE YOU EVER BEEN IN THE PRESENCE OF TRUE GREATNESS?
ACK! ACK! HACK!
I'M NOT TALKING ABOUT A CELEBRITY OR AN ATHLETE.
HACK! HUH! HUHHHACK!
UNN! HURN!
I'M TALKING ABOUT SOMEONE WHO CHANGES THE WORLD.
HURK! UNN!
ISN'T THIS NICE, HARLEY? JUST THE TWO OF US.
HA! HA! HA!
SOMEONE WHO HISTORY WILL NEVER FORGET.

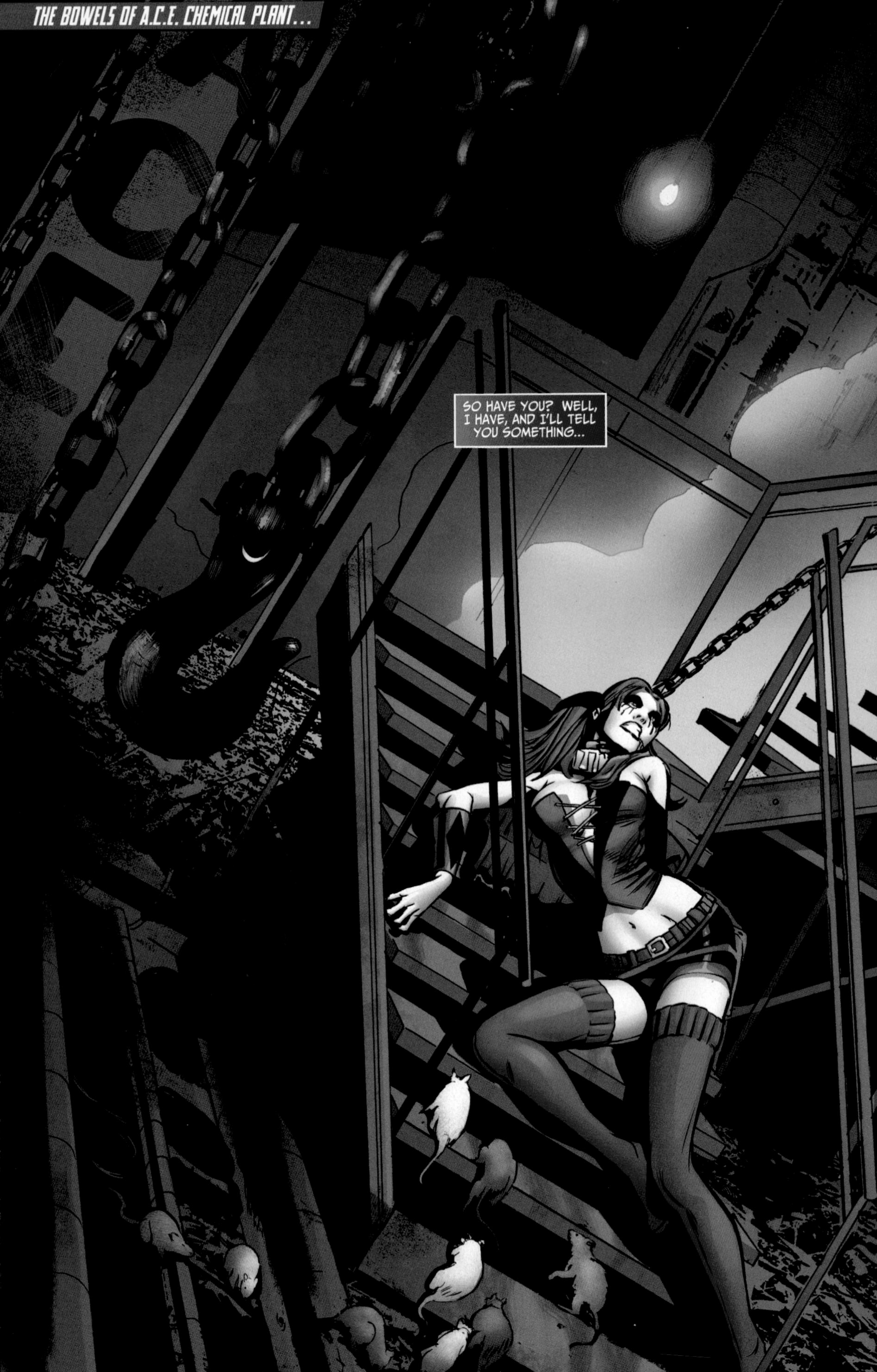
THE BOWELS OF A.C.E. CHEMICAL PLANT...
SO HAVE YOU? WELL, I HAVE, AND I'LL TELL YOU SOMETHING...

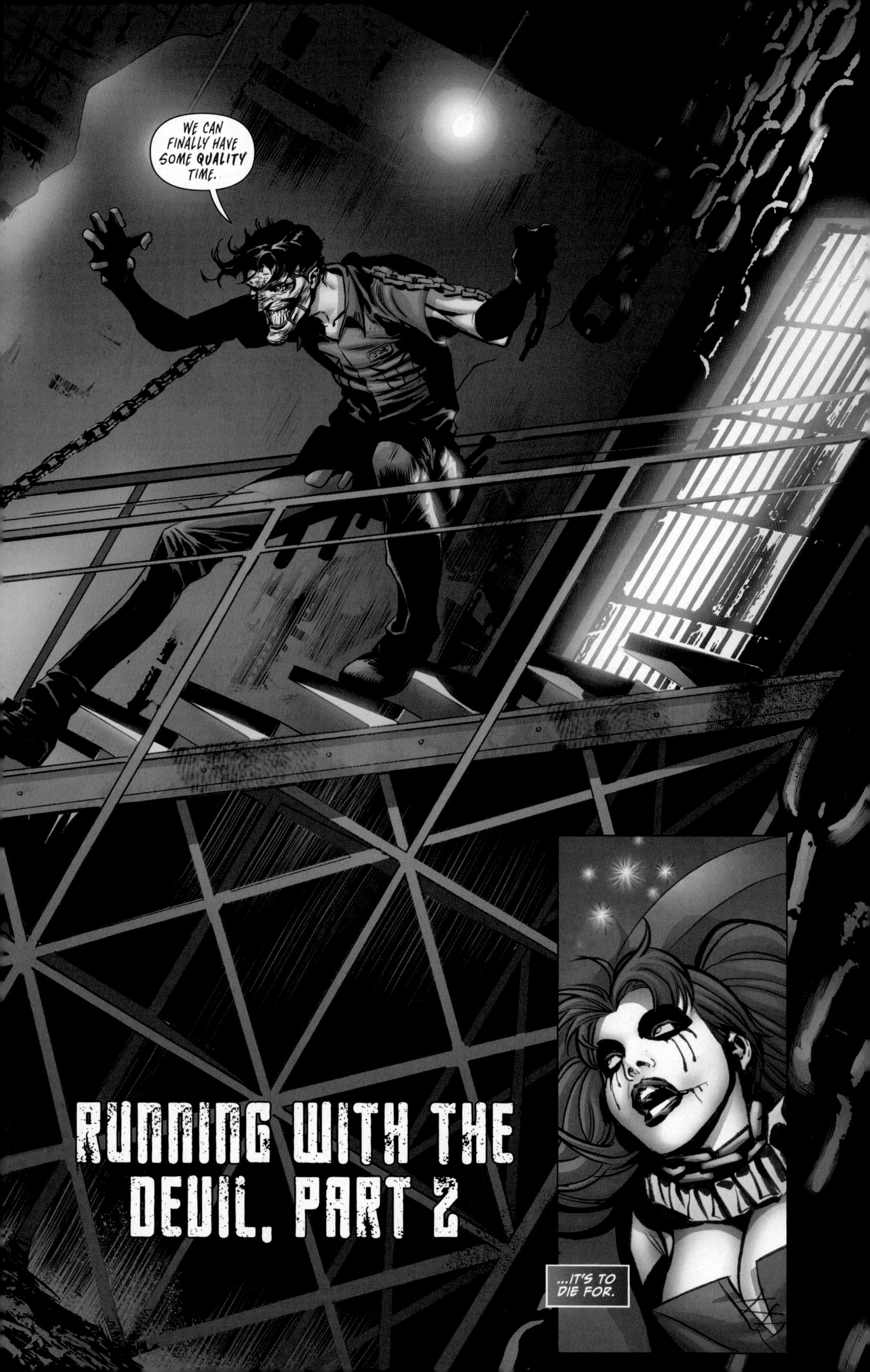
WE CAN FINALLY HAVE SOME QUALITY TIME.
RUNNING WITH THE DEVIL, PART 2
...IT'S TO DIE FOR.

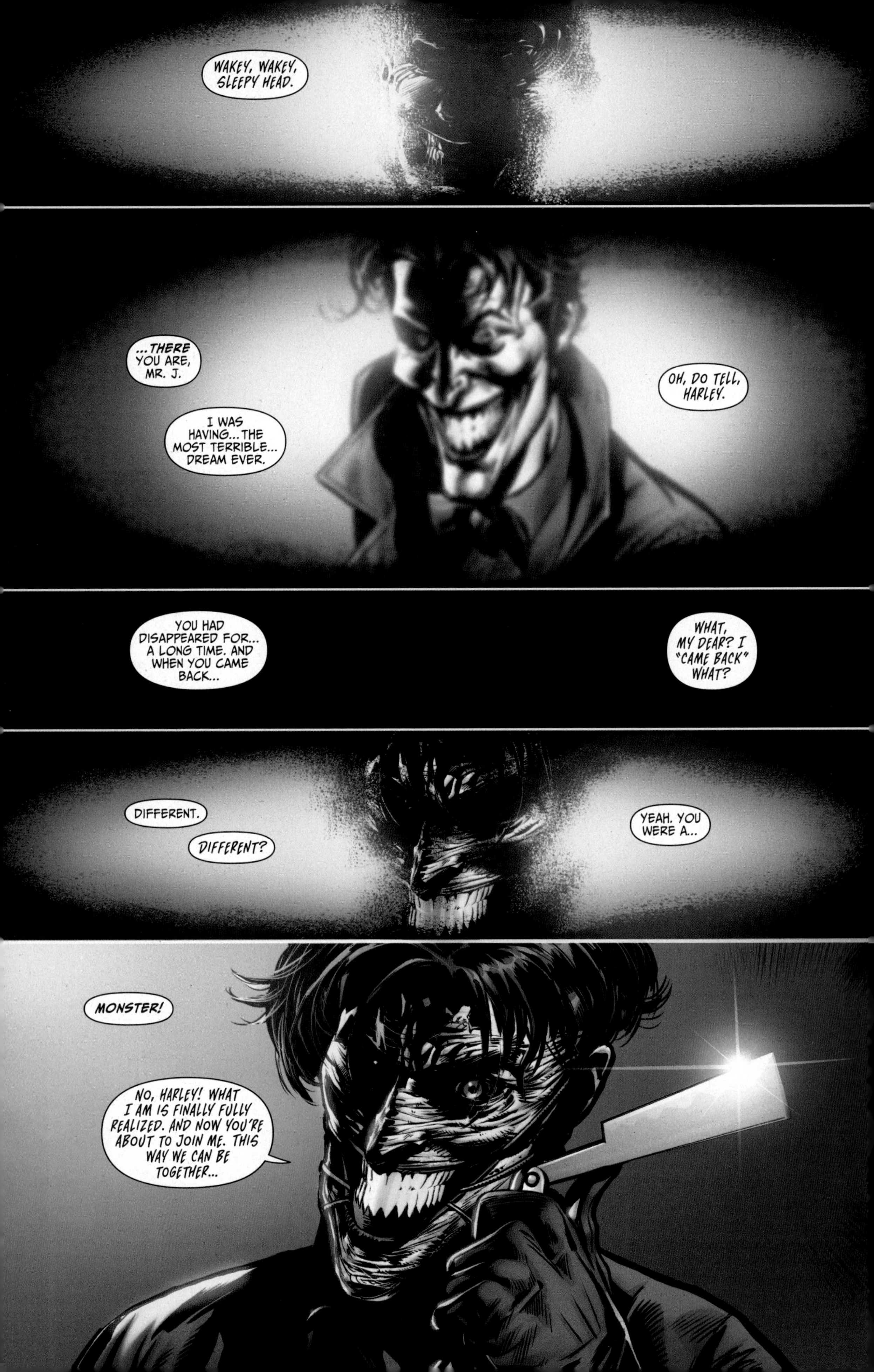
WAKEY, WAKEY, SLEEPY HEAD.
...THERE YOU ARE, MR. J.
I WAS HAVING... THE MOST TERRIBLE... DREAM EVER.
OH, DO TELL, HARLEY.
YOU HAD DISAPPEARED FOR... A LONG TIME. AND WHEN YOU CAME BACK...
WHAT, MY DEAR? I "CAME BACK" WHAT?
DIFFERENT.
DIFFERENT?
YEAH. YOU WERE A...
MONSTER!
NO, HARLEY! WHAT I AM IS FINALLY FULLY REALIZED. AND NOW YOU'RE ABOUT TO JOIN ME. THIS WAY WE CAN BE TOGETHER...

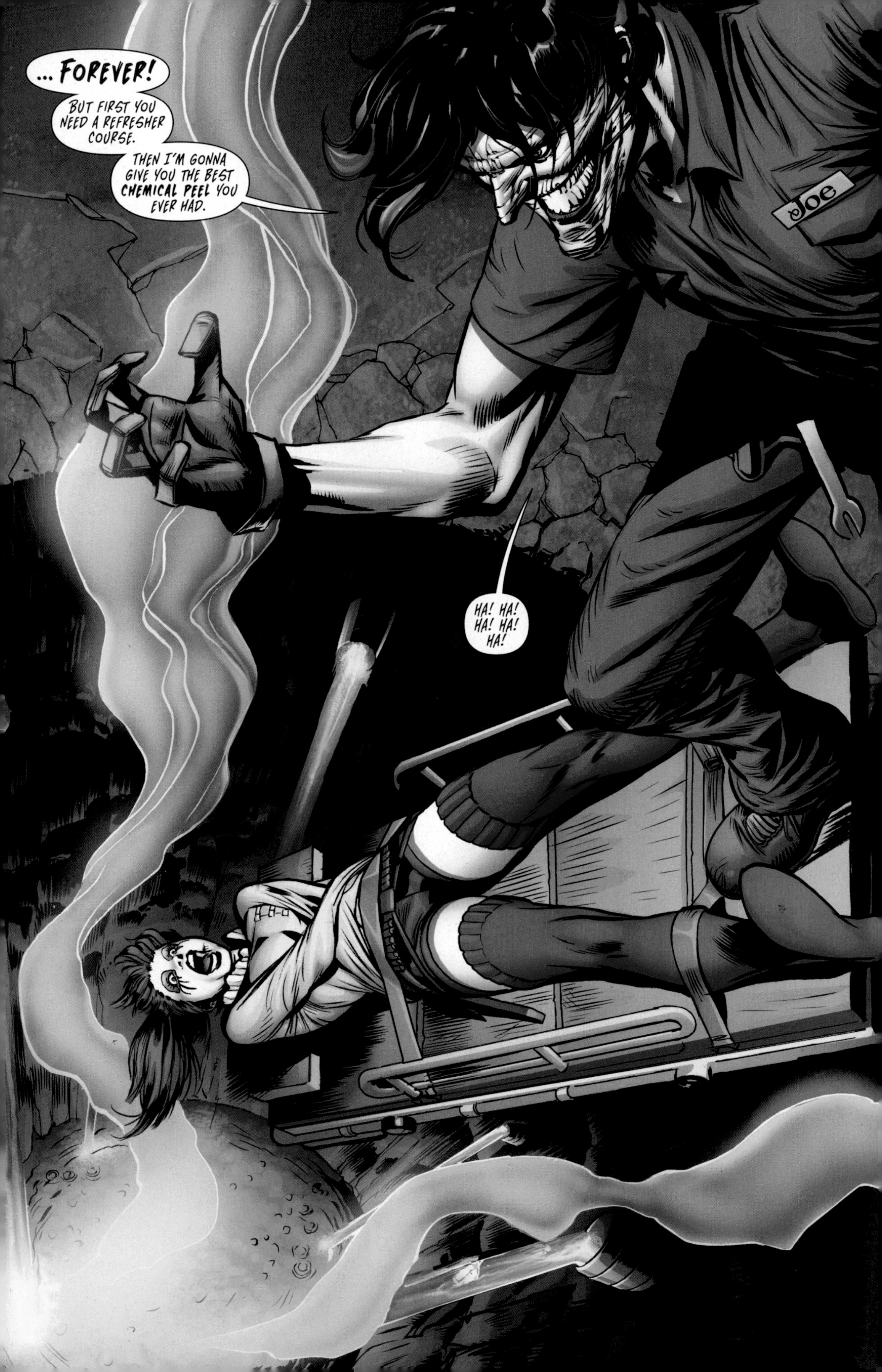

... FOREVER!
BUT FIRST YOU NEED A REFRESHER COURSE.
THEN I'M GONNA GIVE YOU THE BEST CHEMICAL PEEL YOU EVER HAD.
HA! HA! HA! HA! HA!
Joe

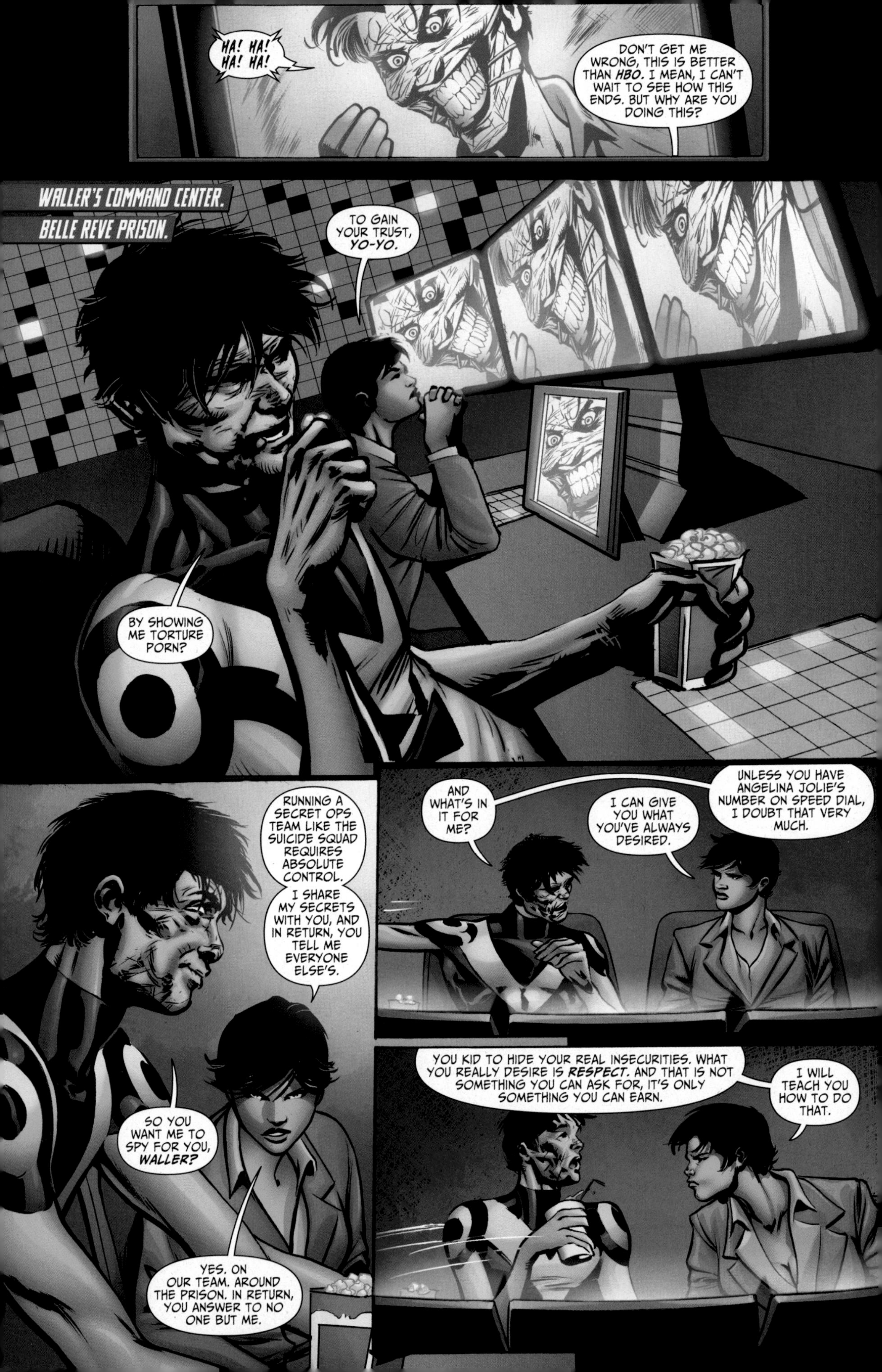
HA! HA! HA! HA!
DON'T GET ME WRONG, THIS IS BETTER THAN HBO. I MEAN, I CAN'T WAIT TO SEE HOW THIS ENDS. BUT WHY ARE YOU DOING THIS?
WALLER'S COMMAND CENTER.
BELLE REVE PRISON.
TO GAIN YOUR TRUST, YO-YO.
BY SHOWING ME TORTURE PORN?
RUNNING A SECRET OPS TEAM LIKE THE SUICIDE SQUAD REQUIRES ABSOLUTE CONTROL.
I SHARE MY SECRETS WITH YOU, AND IN RETURN, YOU TELL ME EVERYONE ELSE'S.
SO YOU WANT ME TO SPY FOR YOU, WALLER?
YES. ON OUR TEAM. AROUND THE PRISON. IN RETURN, YOU ANSWER TO NO ONE BUT ME.
AND WHAT'S IN IT FOR ME?
I CAN GIVE YOU WHAT YOU'VE ALWAYS DESIRED.
UNLESS YOU HAVE ANGELINA JOLIE'S NUMBER ON SPEED DIAL, I DOUBT THAT VERY MUCH.
YOU KID TO HIDE YOUR REAL INSECURITIES. WHAT YOU REALLY DESIRE IS RESPECT. AND THAT IS NOT SOMETHING YOU CAN ASK FOR, IT'S ONLY SOMETHING YOU CAN EARN.
I WILL TEACH YOU HOW TO DO THAT.

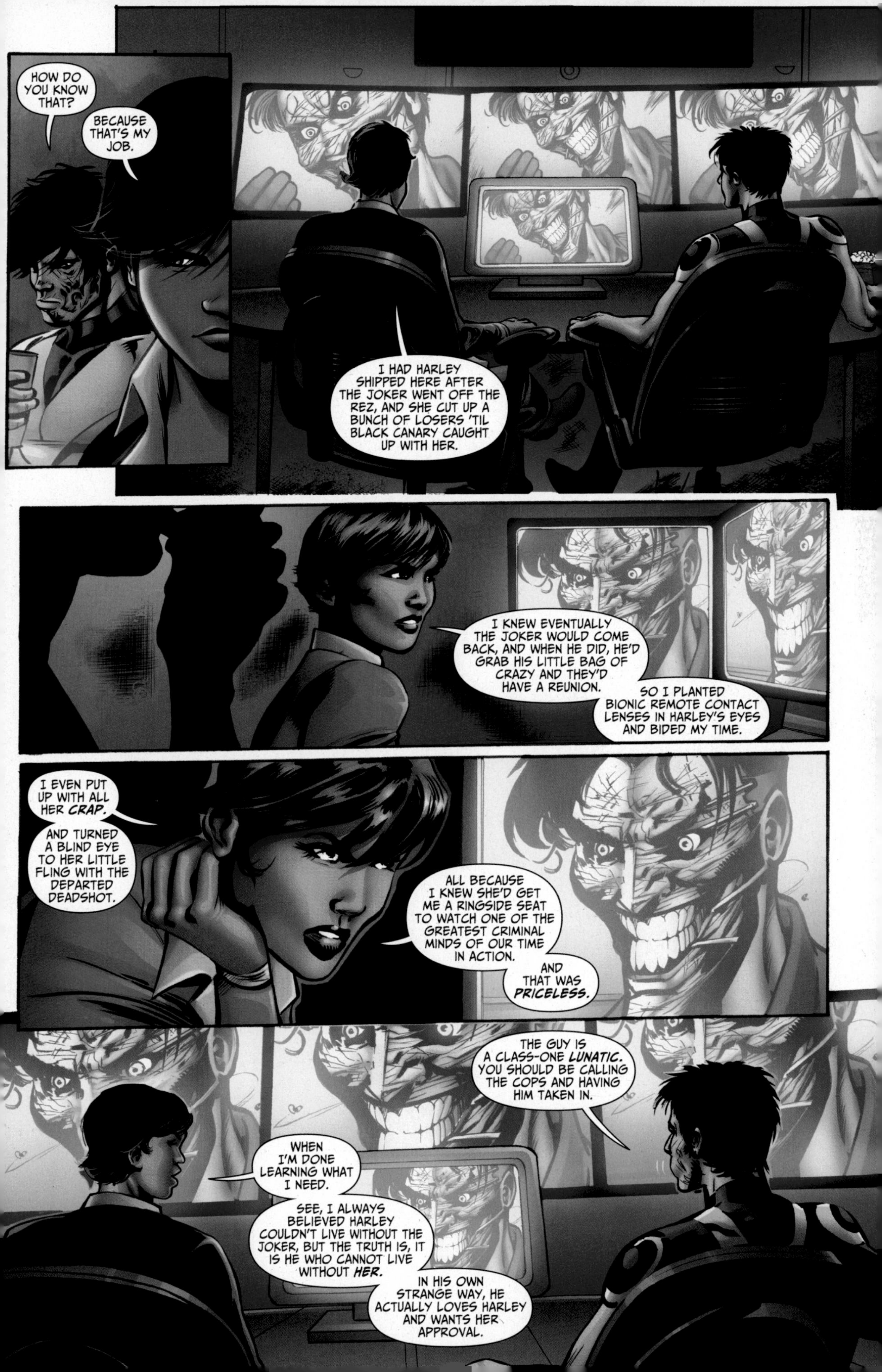

HOW DO YOU KNOW THAT?
BECAUSE THAT'S MY JOB.
I HAD HARLEY SHIPPED HERE AFTER THE JOKER WENT OFF THE REZ, AND SHE CUT UP A BUNCH OF LOSERS 'TIL BLACK CANARY CAUGHT UP WITH HER.
I KNEW EVENTUALLY THE JOKER WOULD COME BACK, AND WHEN HE DID, HE'D GRAB HIS LITTLE BAG OF CRAZY AND THEY'D HAVE A REUNION.
SO I PLANTED BIONIC REMOTE CONTACT LENSES IN HARLEY'S EYES AND BIDED MY TIME.
I EVEN PUT UP WITH ALL HER *CRAP.*
AND TURNED A BLIND EYE TO HER LITTLE FLING WITH THE DEPARTED DEADSHOT.
ALL BECAUSE I KNEW SHE'D GET ME A RINGSIDE SEAT TO WATCH ONE OF THE GREATEST CRIMINAL MINDS OF OUR TIME IN ACTION.
AND THAT WAS *PRICELESS.*
THE GUY IS A CLASS-ONE *LUNATIC.* YOU SHOULD BE CALLING THE COPS AND HAVING HIM TAKEN IN.
WHEN I'M DONE LEARNING WHAT I NEED.
SEE, I ALWAYS BELIEVED HARLEY COULDN'T LIVE WITHOUT THE JOKER, BUT THE TRUTH IS, IT IS HE WHO CANNOT LIVE WITHOUT *HER.*
IN HIS OWN STRANGE WAY, HE ACTUALLY LOVES HARLEY AND WANTS HER APPROVAL.

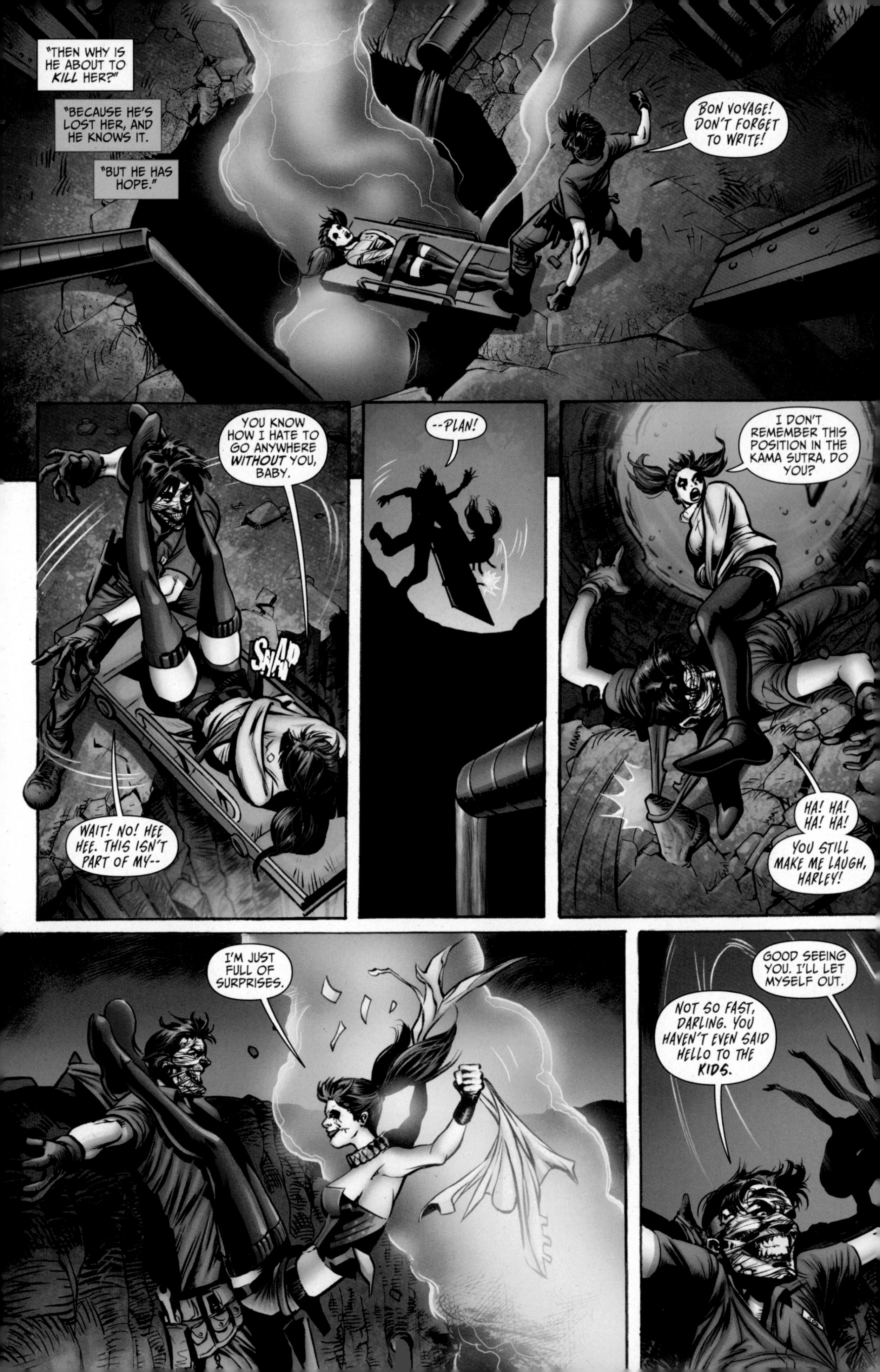
"THEN WHY IS HE ABOUT TO KILL HER?"
"BECAUSE HE'S LOST HER, AND HE KNOWS IT.
"BUT HE HAS HOPE."
BON VOYAGE! DON'T FORGET TO WRITE!
YOU KNOW HOW I HATE TO GO ANYWHERE WITHOUT YOU, BABY.
SNAP
WAIT! NO! HEE HEE. THIS ISN'T PART OF MY--
--PLAN!
I DON'T REMEMBER THIS POSITION IN THE KAMA SUTRA, DO YOU?
HA! HA! HA! HA!
YOU STILL MAKE ME LAUGH, HARLEY!
I'M JUST FULL OF SURPRISES.
GOOD SEEING YOU. I'LL LET MYSELF OUT.
NOT SO FAST, DARLING. YOU HAVEN'T EVEN SAID HELLO TO THE KIDS.

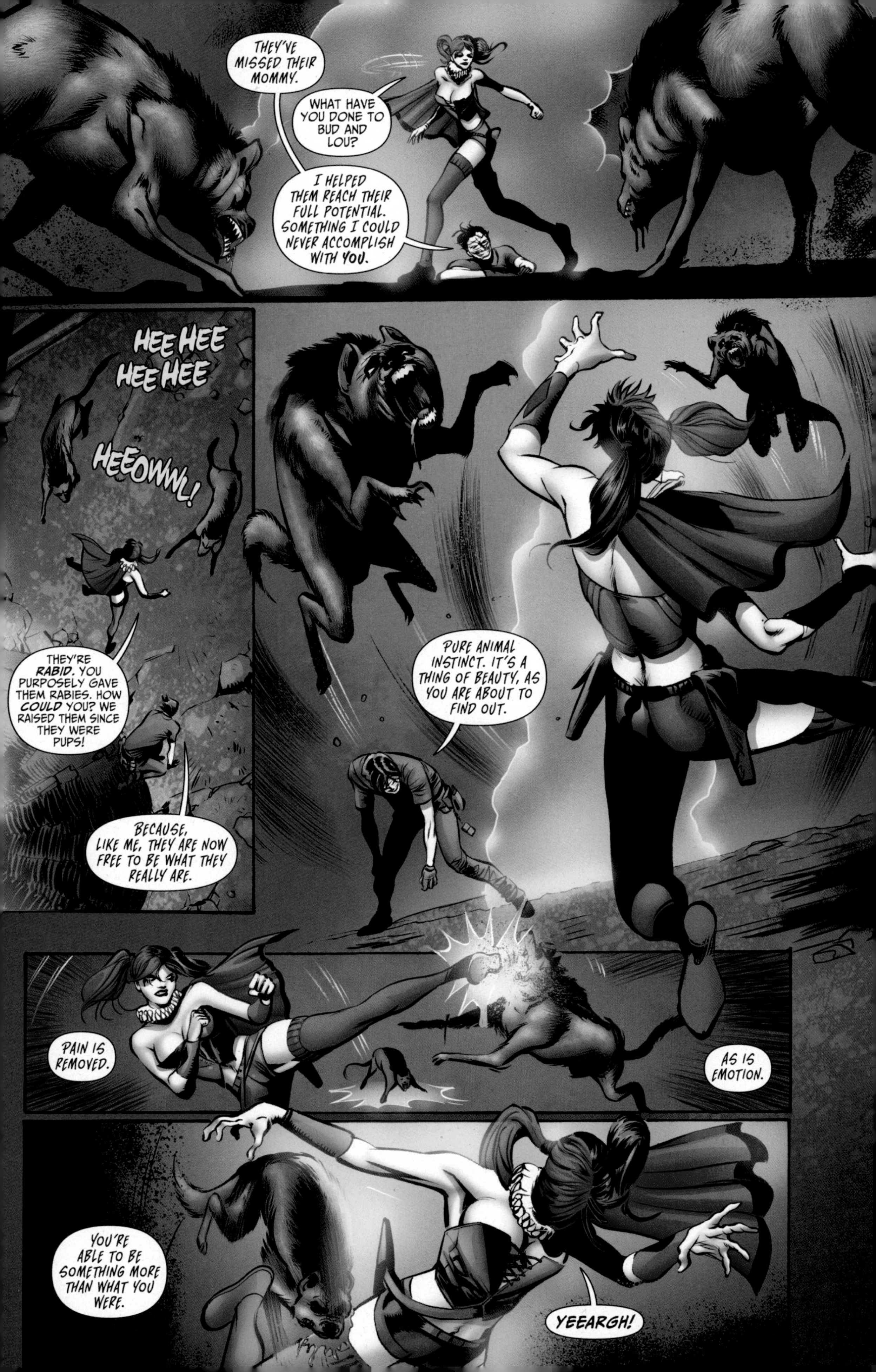
THEY'VE MISSED THEIR MOMMY.
WHAT HAVE YOU DONE TO BUD AND LOU?
I HELPED THEM REACH THEIR FULL POTENTIAL. SOMETHING I COULD NEVER ACCOMPLISH WITH YOU.
HEE HEE HEE HEE
HEEOWWL!
THEY'RE RABID. YOU PURPOSELY GAVE THEM RABIES. HOW COULD YOU? WE RAISED THEM SINCE THEY WERE PUPS!
BECAUSE, LIKE ME, THEY ARE NOW FREE TO BE WHAT THEY REALLY ARE.
PURE ANIMAL INSTINCT. IT'S A THING OF BEAUTY, AS YOU ARE ABOUT TO FIND OUT.
PAIN IS REMOVED.
AS IS EMOTION.
YOU'RE ABLE TO BE SOMETHING MORE THAN WHAT YOU WERE.
YEEARGH!

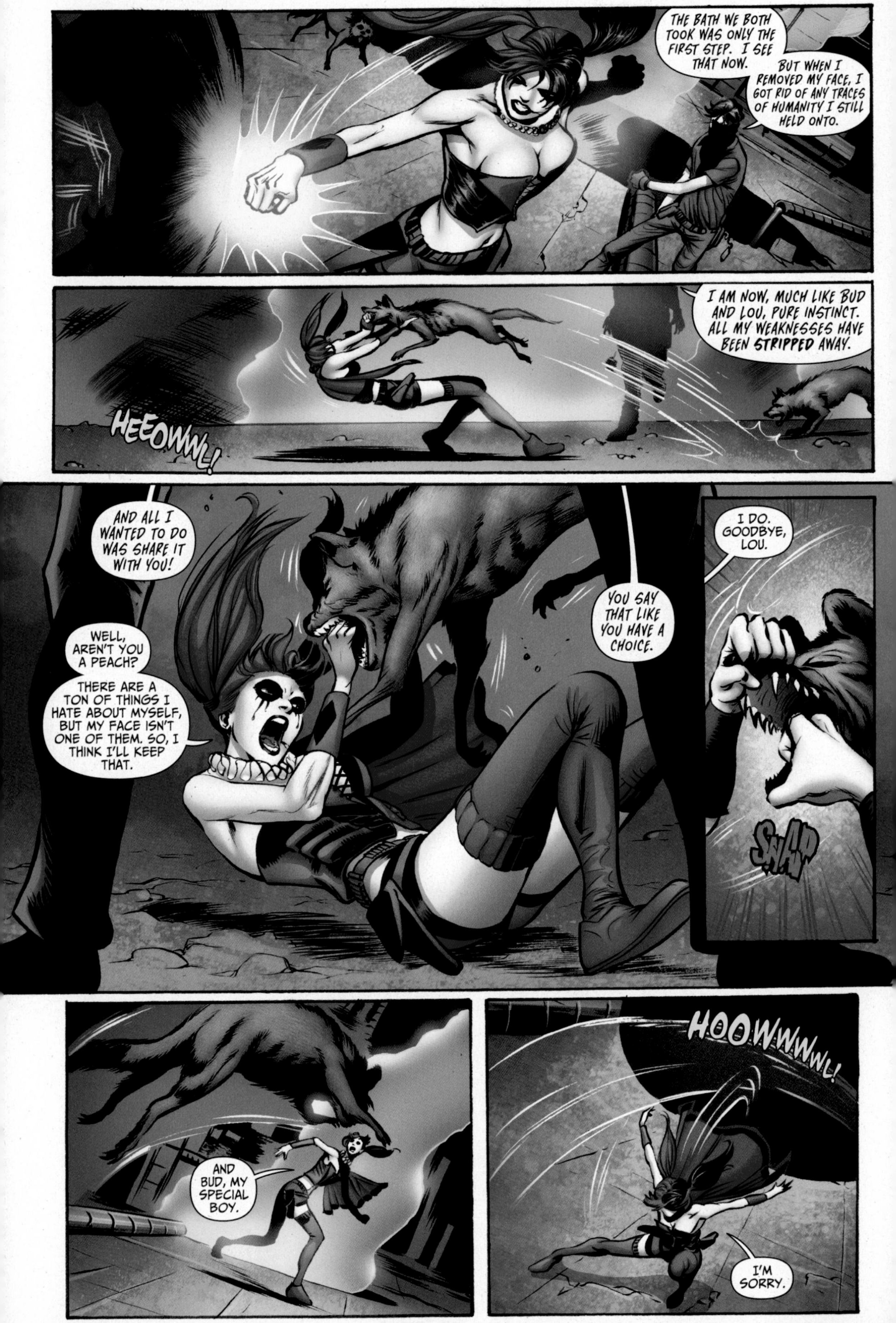
THE BATH WE BOTH TOOK WAS ONLY THE FIRST STEP. I SEE THAT NOW.
BUT WHEN I REMOVED MY FACE, I GOT RID OF ANY TRACES OF HUMANITY I STILL HELD ONTO.
I AM NOW, MUCH LIKE BUD AND LOU, PURE INSTINCT. ALL MY WEAKNESSES HAVE BEEN STRIPPED AWAY.
HEEOWWL!
AND ALL I WANTED TO DO WAS SHARE IT WITH YOU!
WELL, AREN'T YOU A PEACH?
THERE ARE A TON OF THINGS I HATE ABOUT MYSELF, BUT MY FACE ISN'T ONE OF THEM. SO, I THINK I'LL KEEP THAT.
YOU SAY THAT LIKE YOU HAVE A CHOICE.
I DO. GOODBYE, LOU.
SNAP
AND BUD, MY SPECIAL BOY.
HOOWWWWL!
I'M SORRY.

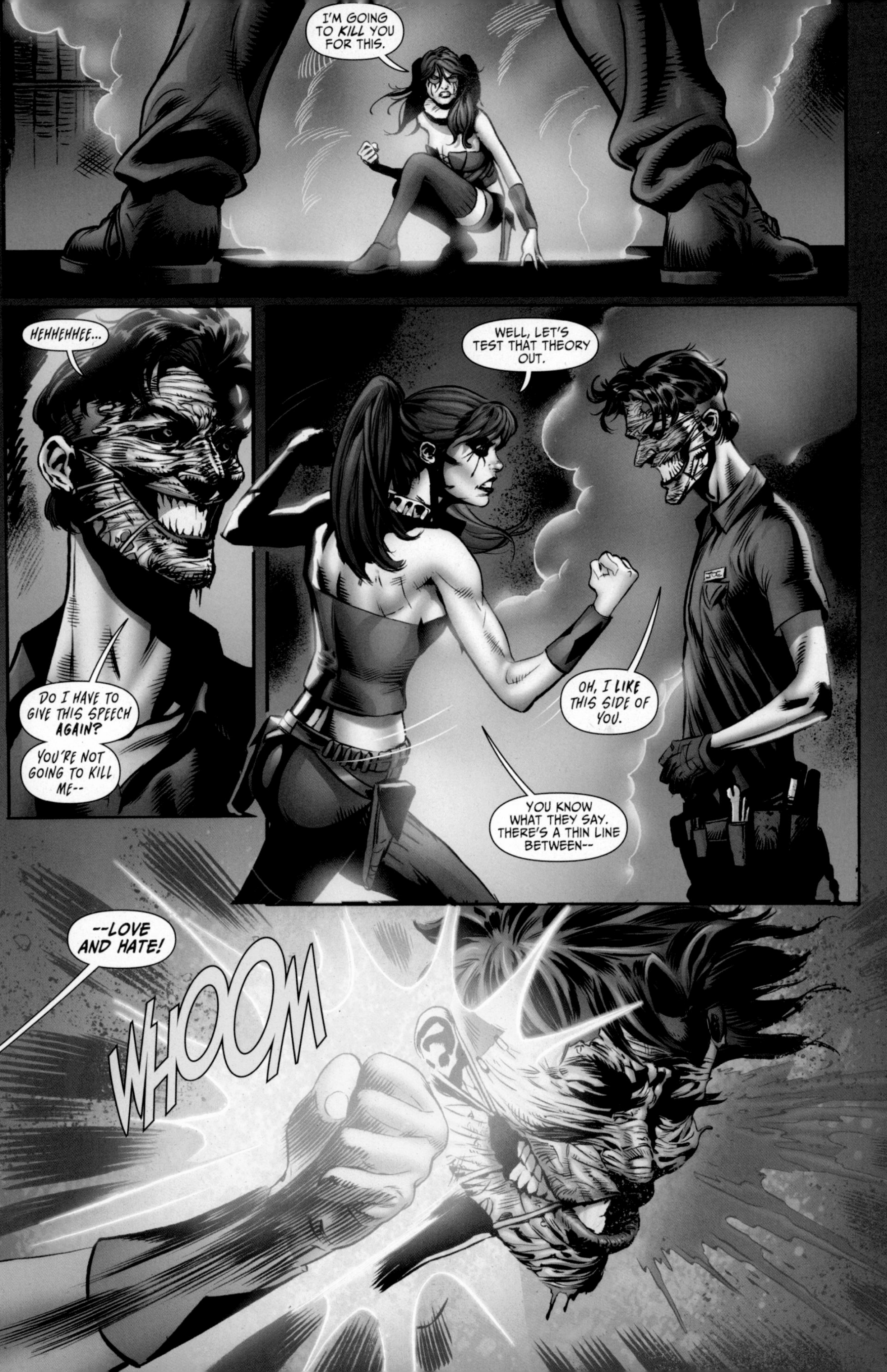
I'M GOING TO KILL YOU FOR THIS.
HEHHEHHEE...
DO I HAVE TO GIVE THIS SPEECH AGAIN?
YOU'RE NOT GOING TO KILL ME--
WELL, LET'S TEST THAT THEORY OUT.
OH, I LIKE THIS SIDE OF YOU.
YOU KNOW WHAT THEY SAY. THERE'S A THIN LINE BETWEEN--
--LOVE AND HATE!
WHOOM

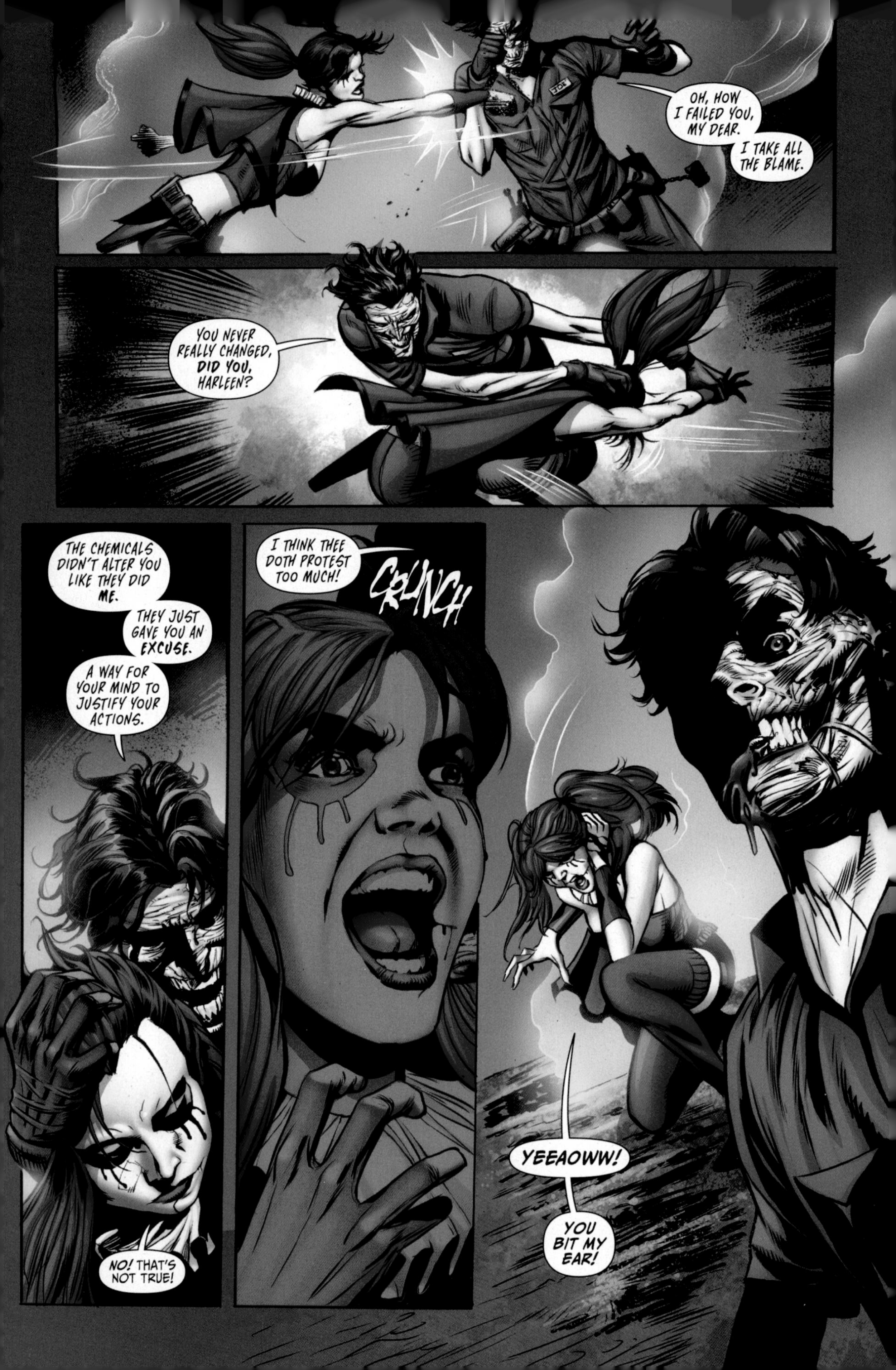
OH, HOW I FAILED YOU, MY DEAR.
I TAKE ALL THE BLAME.
YOU NEVER REALLY CHANGED, DID YOU, HARLEEN?
THE CHEMICALS DIDN'T ALTER YOU LIKE THEY DID ME.
THEY JUST GAVE YOU AN EXCUSE.
A WAY FOR YOUR MIND TO JUSTIFY YOUR ACTIONS.
NO! THAT'S NOT TRUE!
I THINK THEE DOTH PROTEST TOO MUCH!
CRUNCH
YEEAOWW!
YOU BIT MY EAR!

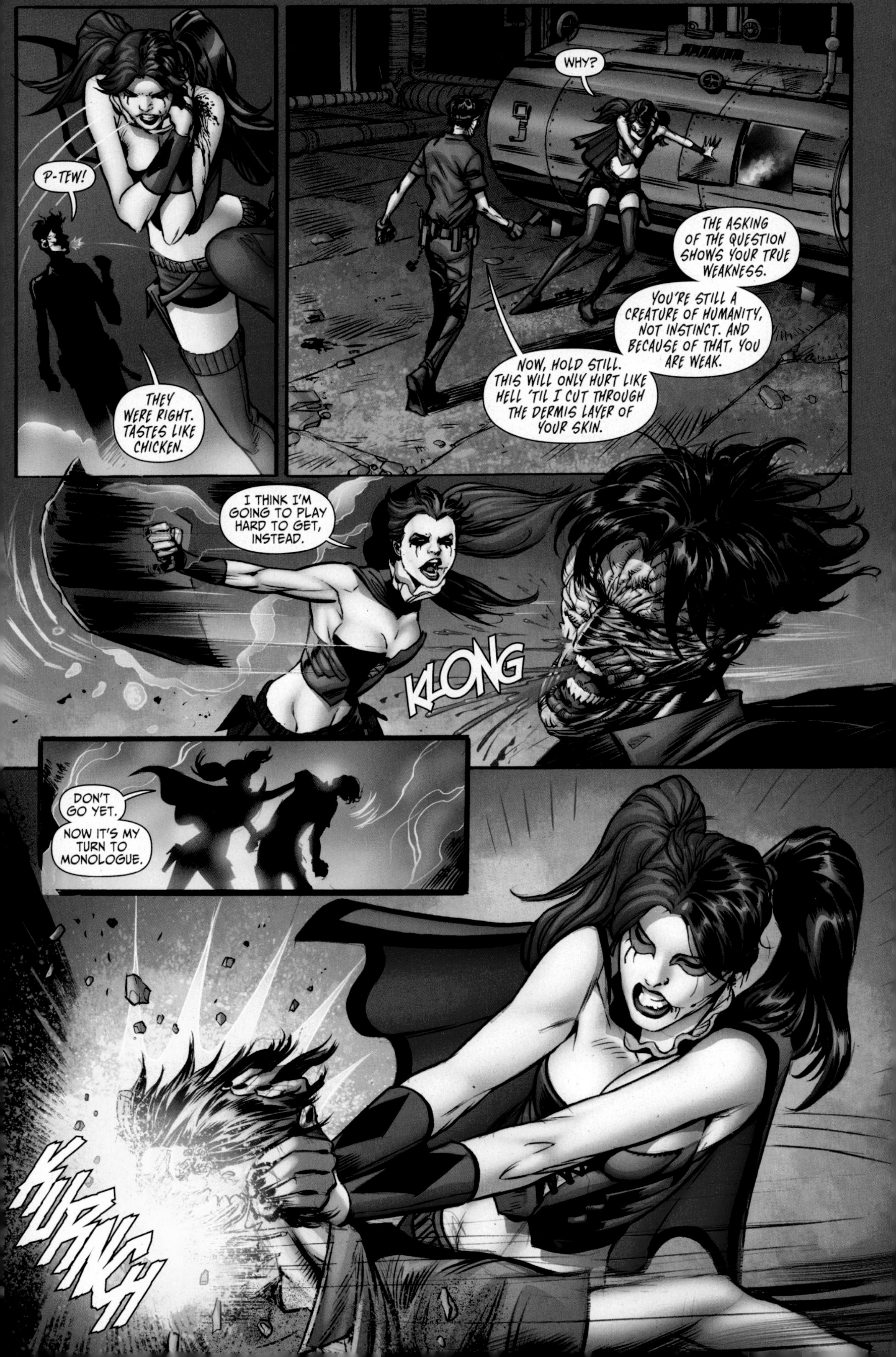
P-TEW!
THEY WERE RIGHT. TASTES LIKE CHICKEN.
WHY?
THE ASKING OF THE QUESTION SHOWS YOUR TRUE WEAKNESS.
YOU'RE STILL A CREATURE OF HUMANITY, NOT INSTINCT. AND BECAUSE OF THAT, YOU ARE WEAK.
NOW, HOLD STILL. THIS WILL ONLY HURT LIKE HELL 'TIL I CUT THROUGH THE DERMIS LAYER OF YOUR SKIN.
I THINK I'M GOING TO PLAY HARD TO GET, INSTEAD.
KLONG
DON'T GO YET.
NOW IT'S MY TURN TO MONOLOGUE.
KRUNCH

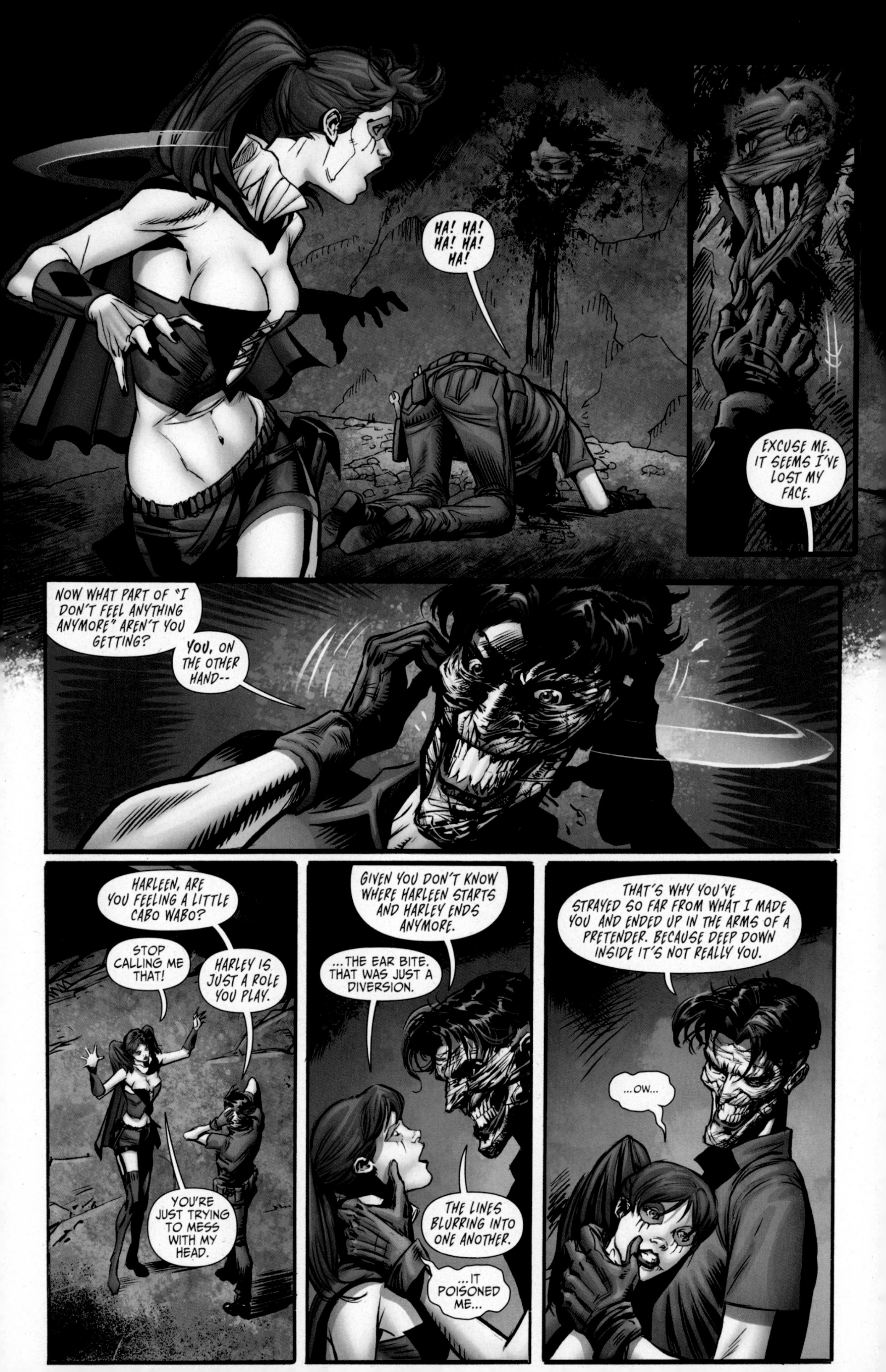
HA! HA! HA! HA! HA!
EXCUSE ME. IT SEEMS I'VE LOST MY FACE.
NOW WHAT PART OF "I DON'T FEEL ANYTHING ANYMORE" AREN'T YOU GETTING?
YOU, ON THE OTHER HAND--
HARLEEN, ARE YOU FEELING A LITTLE CABO WABO?
STOP CALLING ME THAT!
HARLEY IS JUST A ROLE YOU PLAY.
YOU'RE JUST TRYING TO MESS WITH MY HEAD.
GIVEN YOU DON'T KNOW WHERE HARLEEN STARTS AND HARLEY ENDS ANYMORE.
...THE EAR BITE. THAT WAS JUST A DIVERSION.
THE LINES BLURRING INTO ONE ANOTHER.
...IT POISONED ME...
THAT'S WHY YOU'VE STRAYED SO FAR FROM WHAT I MADE YOU AND ENDED UP IN THE ARMS OF A PRETENDER. BECAUSE DEEP DOWN INSIDE IT'S NOT REALLY YOU.
...OW...

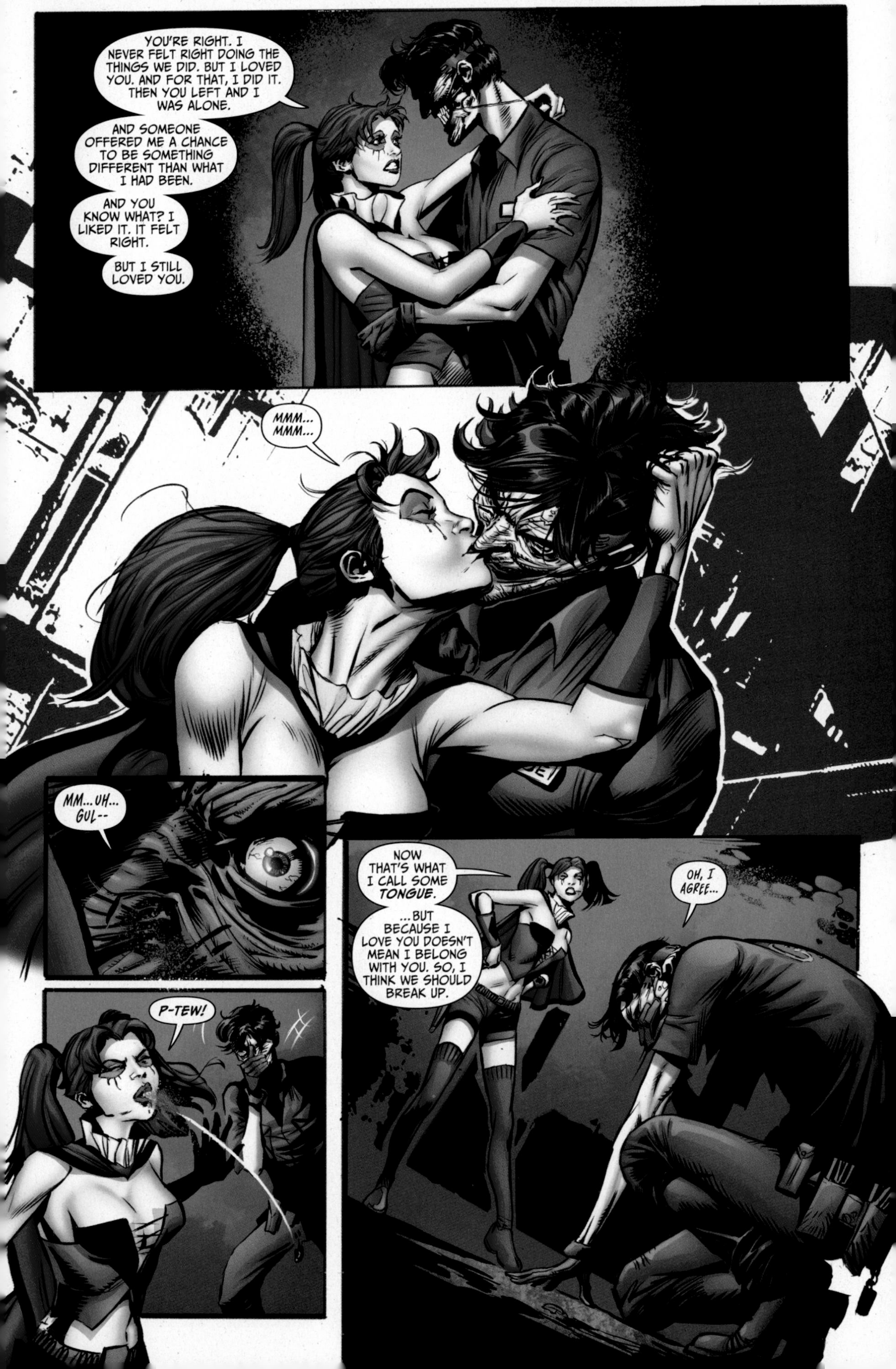
YOU'RE RIGHT. I NEVER FELT RIGHT DOING THE THINGS WE DID. BUT I LOVED YOU. AND FOR THAT, I DID IT. THEN YOU LEFT AND I WAS ALONE.
AND SOMEONE OFFERED ME A CHANCE TO BE SOMETHING DIFFERENT THAN WHAT I HAD BEEN.
AND YOU KNOW WHAT? I LIKED IT. IT FELT RIGHT.
BUT I STILL LOVED YOU.
MMM... MMM...
MM...UH... GUL--
P-TEW!
NOW THAT'S WHAT I CALL SOME *TONGUE*.
...BUT BECAUSE I LOVE YOU DOESN'T MEAN I BELONG WITH YOU. SO, I THINK WE SHOULD BREAK UP.
OH, I AGREE...

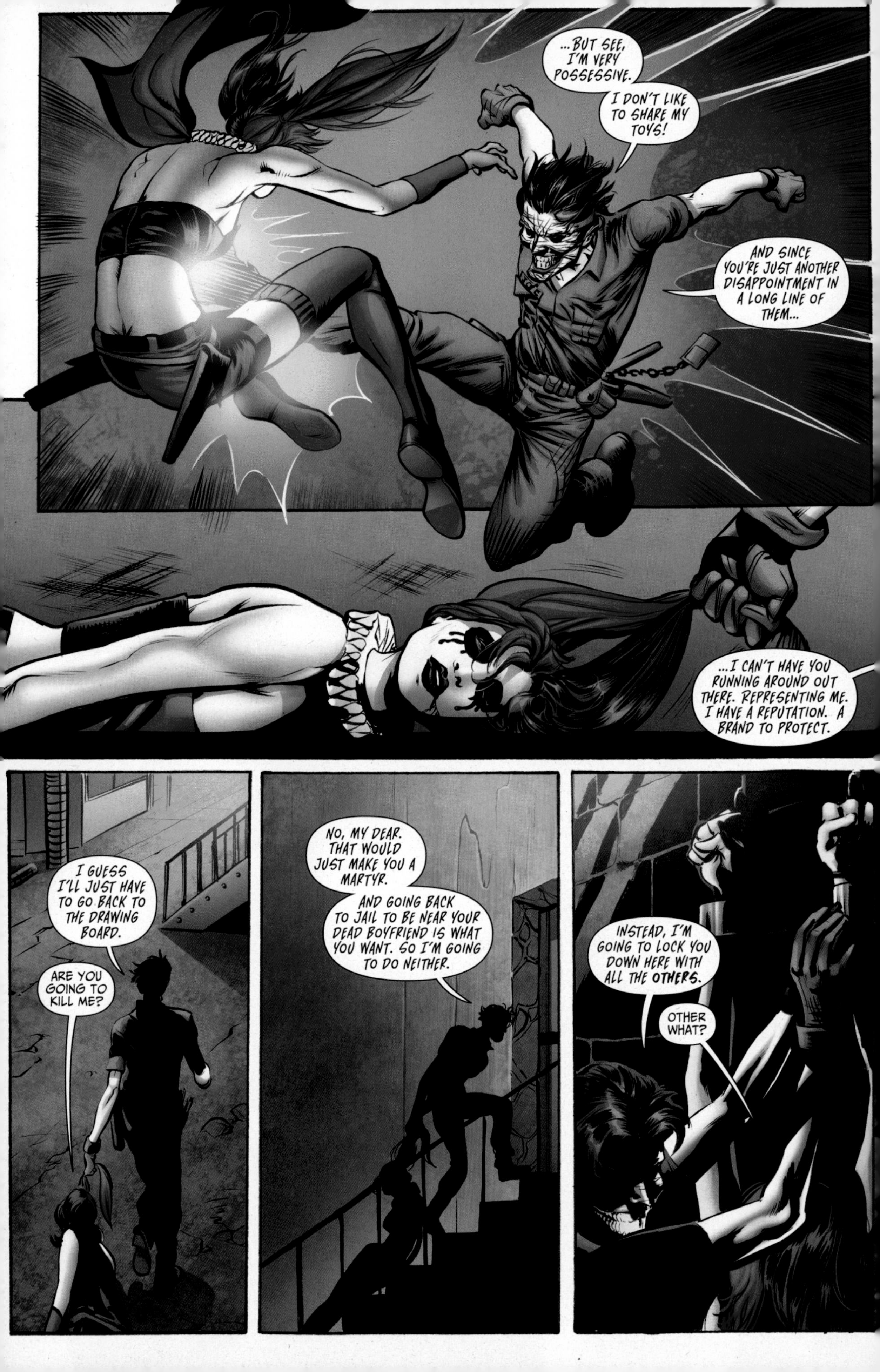
...BUT SEE, I'M VERY POSSESSIVE.
I DON'T LIKE TO SHARE MY TOYS!
AND SINCE YOU'RE JUST ANOTHER DISAPPOINTMENT IN A LONG LINE OF THEM...
...I CAN'T HAVE YOU RUNNING AROUND OUT THERE. REPRESENTING ME. I HAVE A REPUTATION. A BRAND TO PROTECT.
I GUESS I'LL JUST HAVE TO GO BACK TO THE DRAWING BOARD.
ARE YOU GOING TO KILL ME?
NO, MY DEAR. THAT WOULD JUST MAKE YOU A MARTYR.
AND GOING BACK TO JAIL TO BE NEAR YOUR DEAD BOYFRIEND IS WHAT YOU WANT. SO I'M GOING TO DO NEITHER.
INSTEAD, I'M GOING TO LOCK YOU DOWN HERE WITH ALL THE OTHERS.
OTHER WHAT?

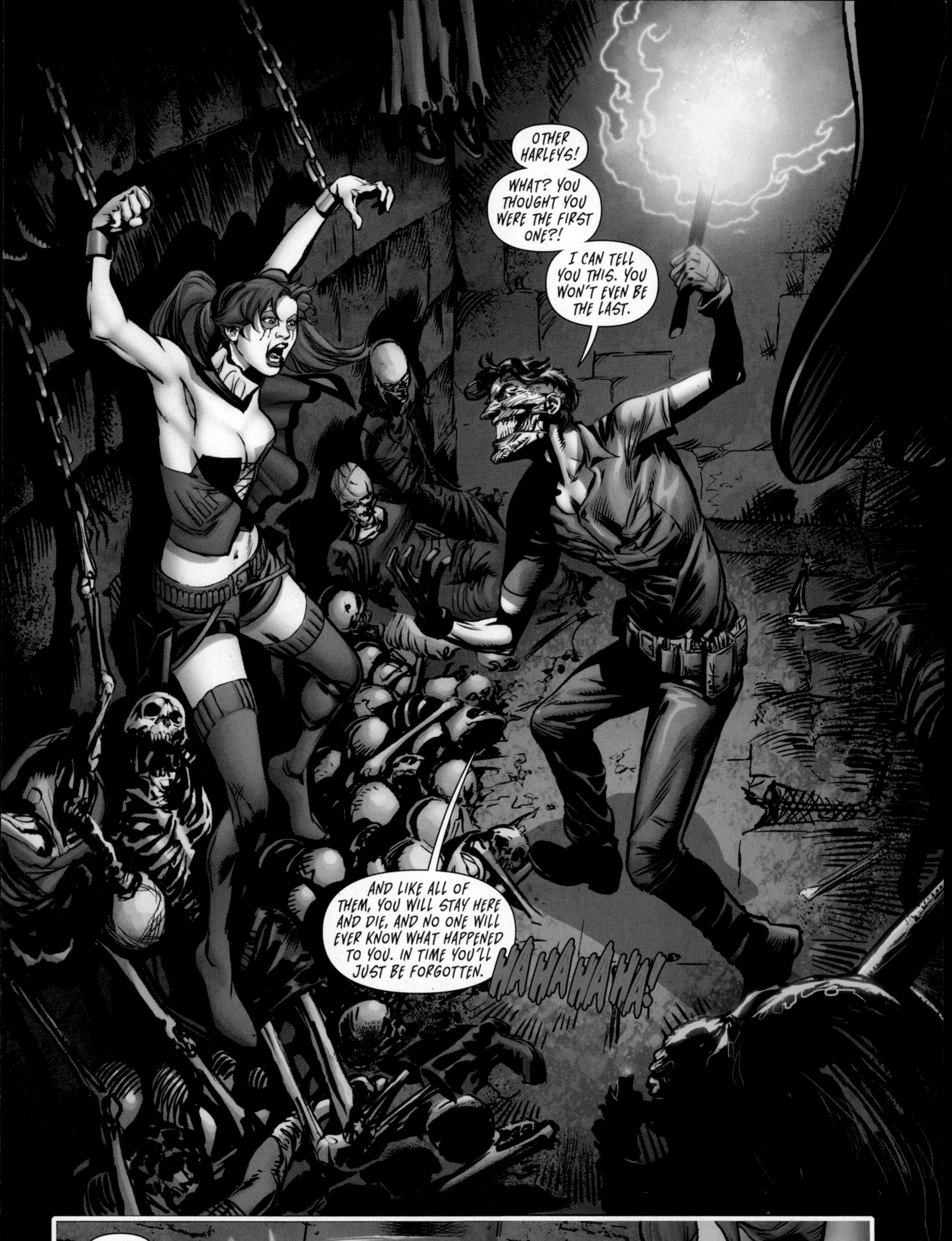
OTHER HARLEYS!
WHAT? YOU THOUGHT YOU WERE THE FIRST ONE?!
I CAN TELL YOU THIS. YOU WON'T EVEN BE THE LAST.
AND LIKE ALL OF THEM, YOU WILL STAY HERE AND DIE, AND NO ONE WILL EVER KNOW WHAT HAPPENED TO YOU. IN TIME YOU'LL JUST BE FORGOTTEN.
HAHAHAHAHA!

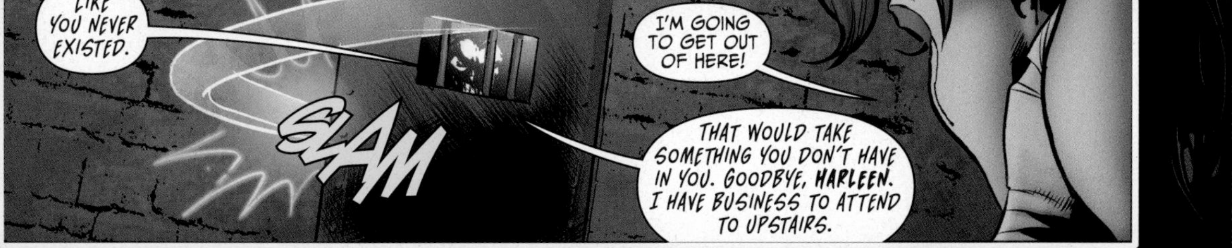
LIKE YOU NEVER EXISTED.
SLAM
I'M GOING TO GET OUT OF HERE!
THAT WOULD TAKE SOMETHING YOU DON'T HAVE IN YOU. GOODBYE, **HARLEEN**. I HAVE BUSINESS TO ATTEND TO UPSTAIRS.

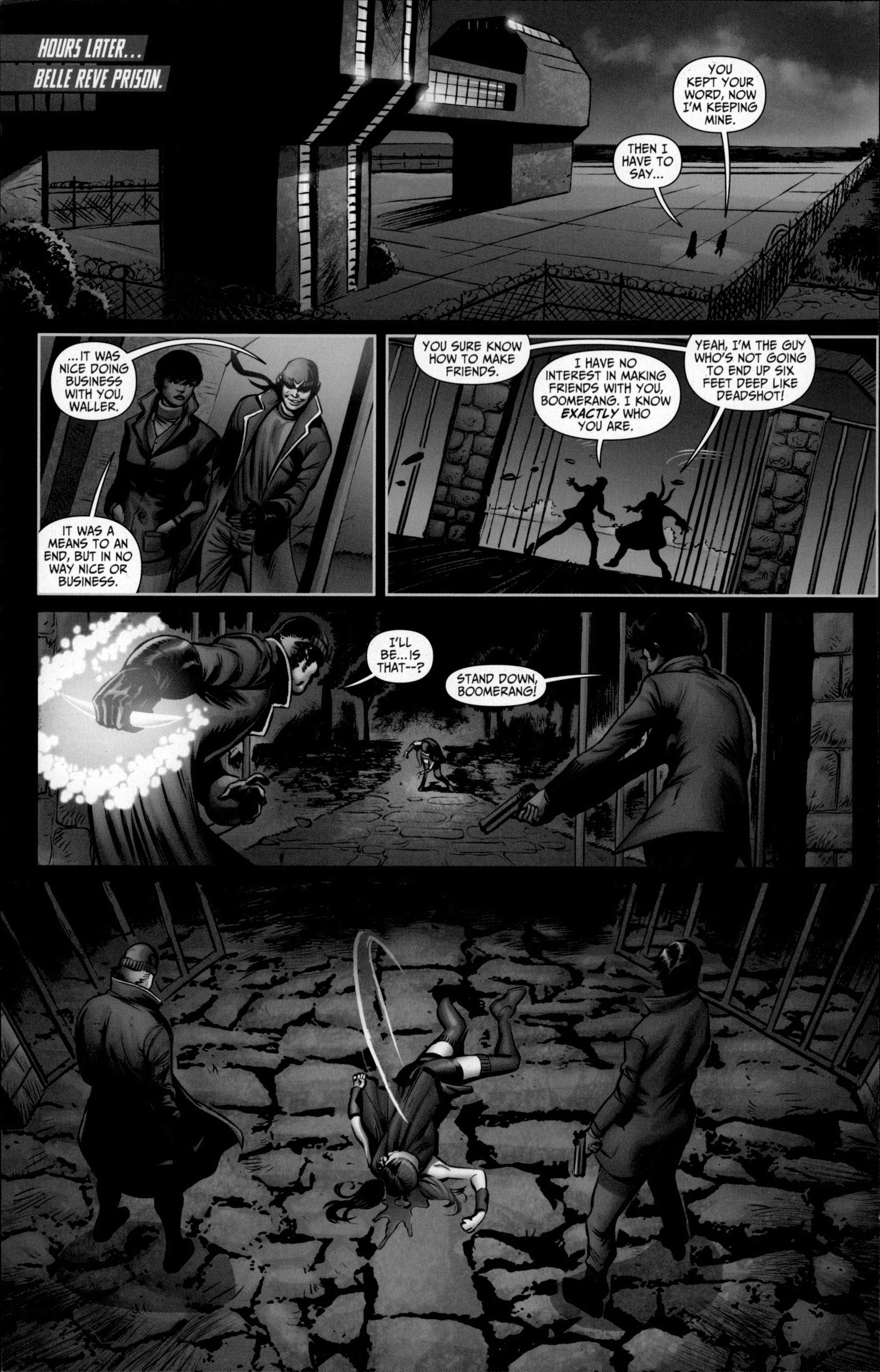
HOURS LATER... BELLE REVE PRISON.
YOU KEPT YOUR WORD, NOW I'M KEEPING MINE.
THEN I HAVE TO SAY...
...IT WAS NICE DOING BUSINESS WITH YOU, WALLER.
IT WAS A MEANS TO AN END, BUT IN NO WAY NICE OR BUSINESS.
YOU SURE KNOW HOW TO MAKE FRIENDS.
I HAVE NO INTEREST IN MAKING FRIENDS WITH YOU, BOOMERANG. I KNOW EXACTLY WHO YOU ARE.
YEAH, I'M THE GUY WHO'S NOT GOING TO END UP SIX FEET DEEP LIKE DEADSHOT!
I'LL BE...IS THAT--?
STAND DOWN, BOOMERANG!

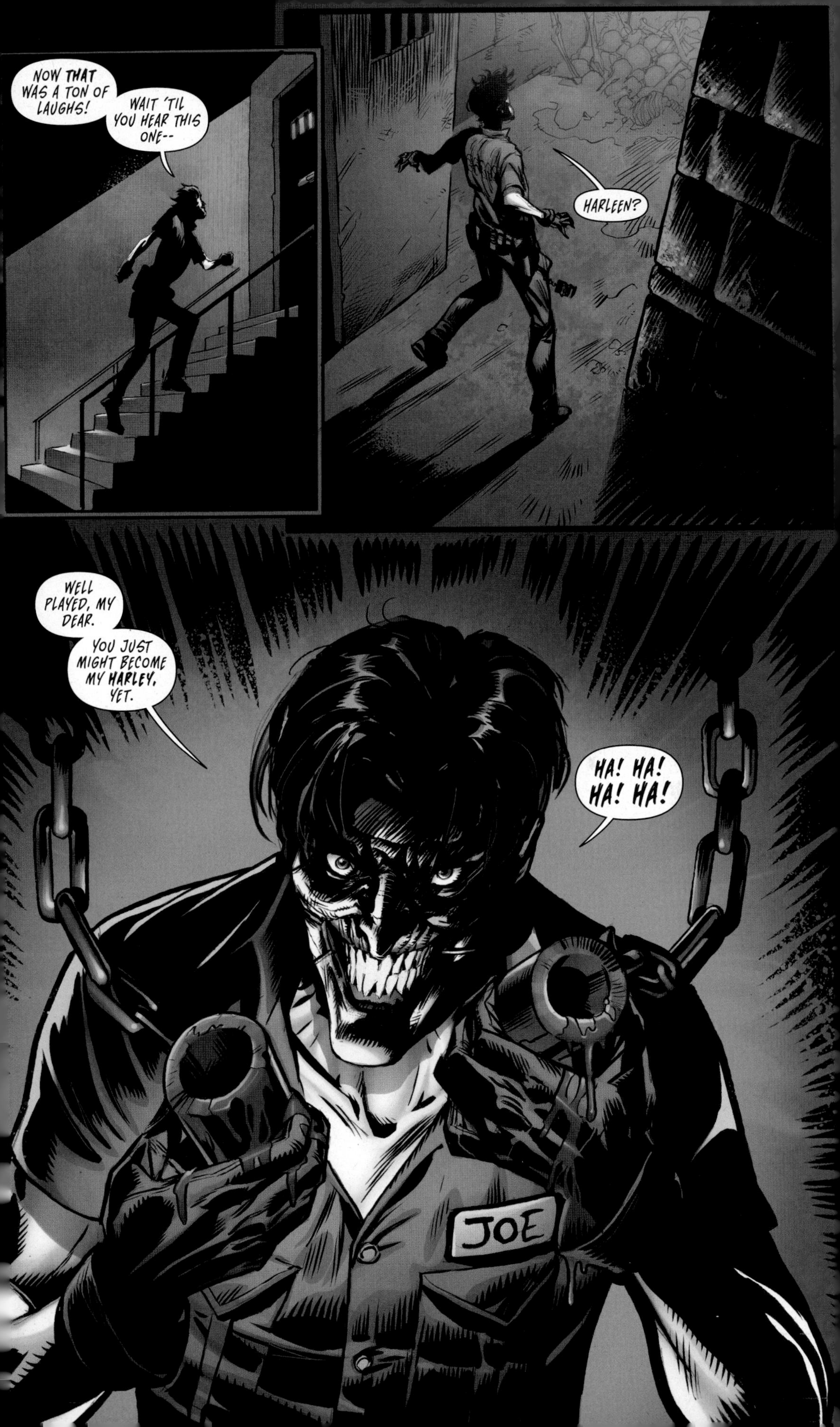
NOW **THAT** WAS A TON OF LAUGHS!
WAIT 'TIL YOU HEAR THIS ONE--
HARLEEN?
WELL PLAYED, MY DEAR.
YOU JUST MIGHT BECOME MY **HARLEY**, YET.
HA! HA! HA! HA!
JOE

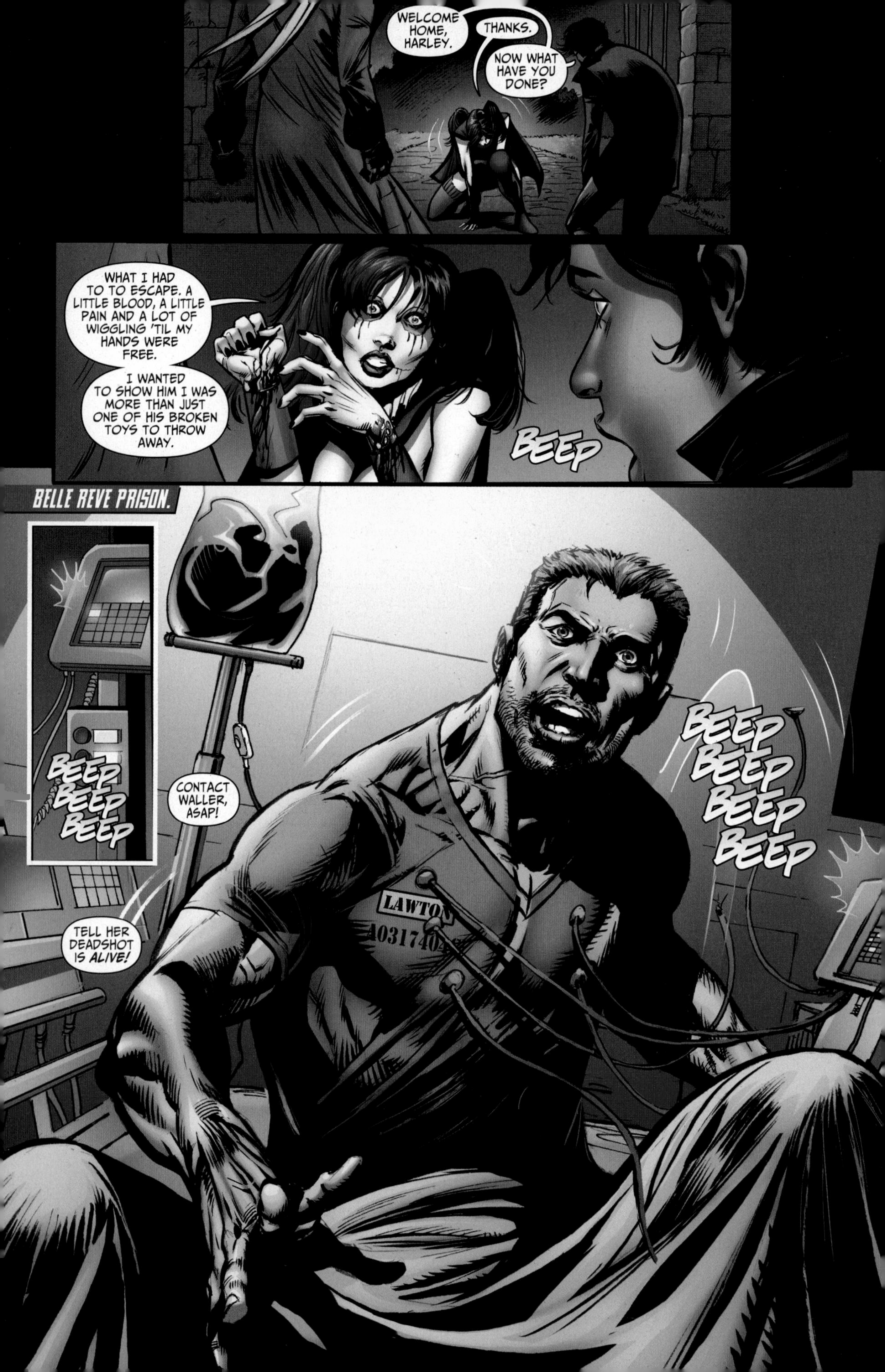
WELCOME HOME, HARLEY.
THANKS.
NOW WHAT HAVE YOU DONE?
WHAT I HAD TO TO ESCAPE. A LITTLE BLOOD, A LITTLE PAIN AND A LOT OF WIGGLING 'TIL MY HANDS WERE FREE.
I WANTED TO SHOW HIM I WAS MORE THAN JUST ONE OF HIS BROKEN TOYS TO THROW AWAY.
BEEP
BELLE REVE PRISON.
BEEP BEEP BEEP
CONTACT WALLER, ASAP!
BEEP BEEP BEEP BEEP
TELL HER DEADSHOT IS ALIVE!
LAWTON
A0317404

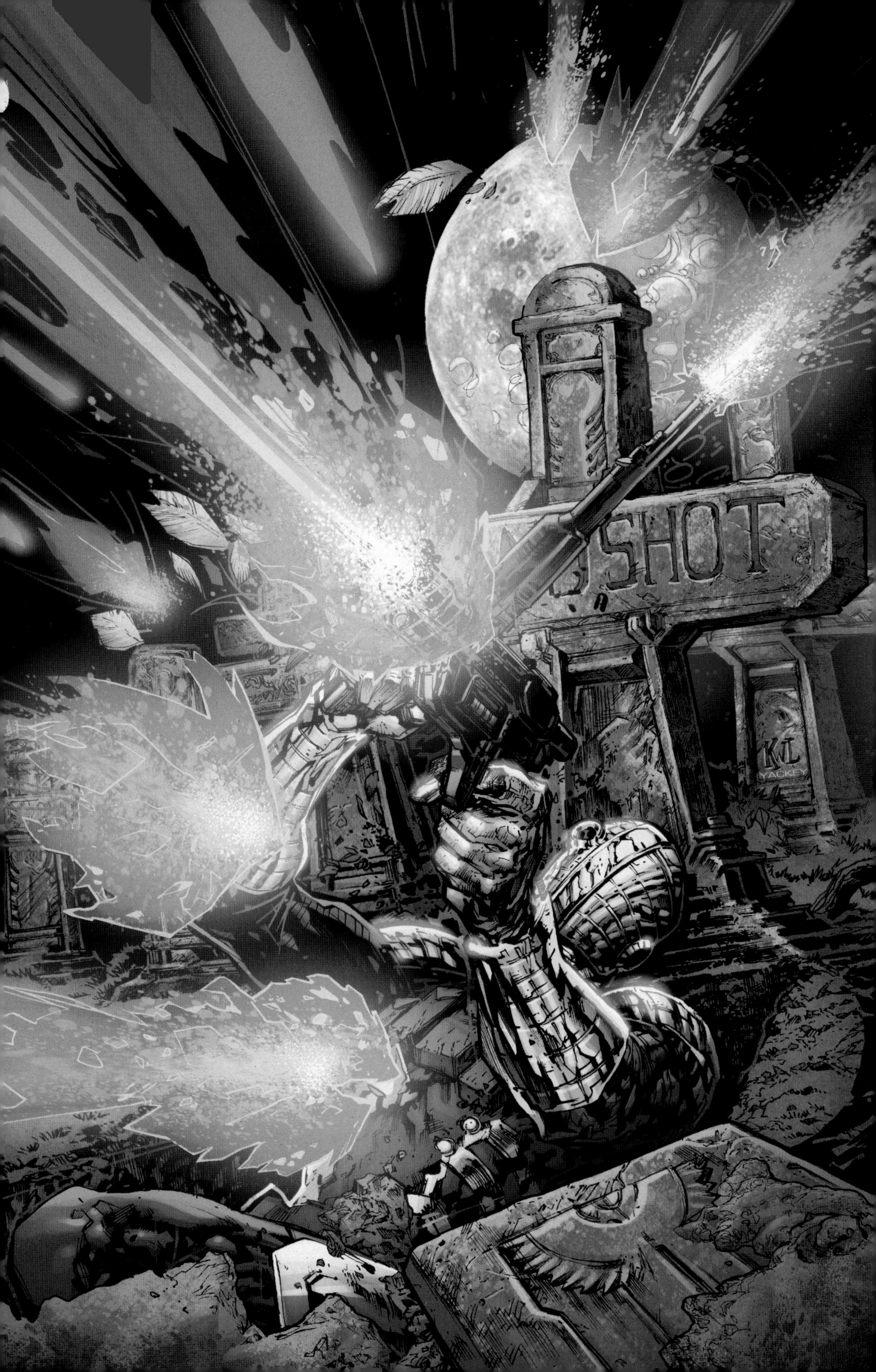
SHOT
KL
YACKEY

KILLING IN THE NAME OF...

ADAM GLASS writer HENRIK JONSSON penciller SANDU FLOREA inker cover art by KEN LASHLEY & MATT YACKEY

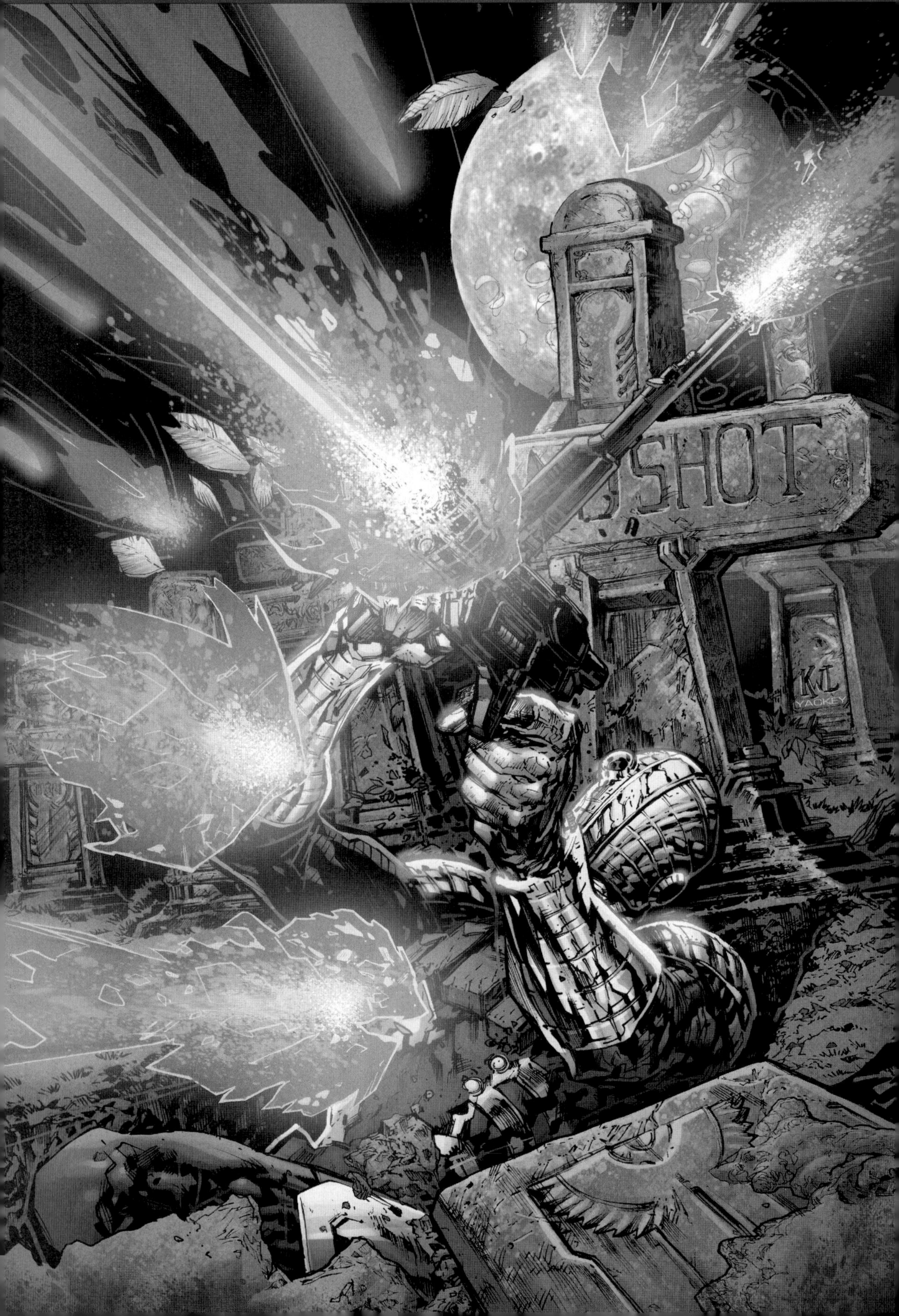
SHOT
KL
YACKEY

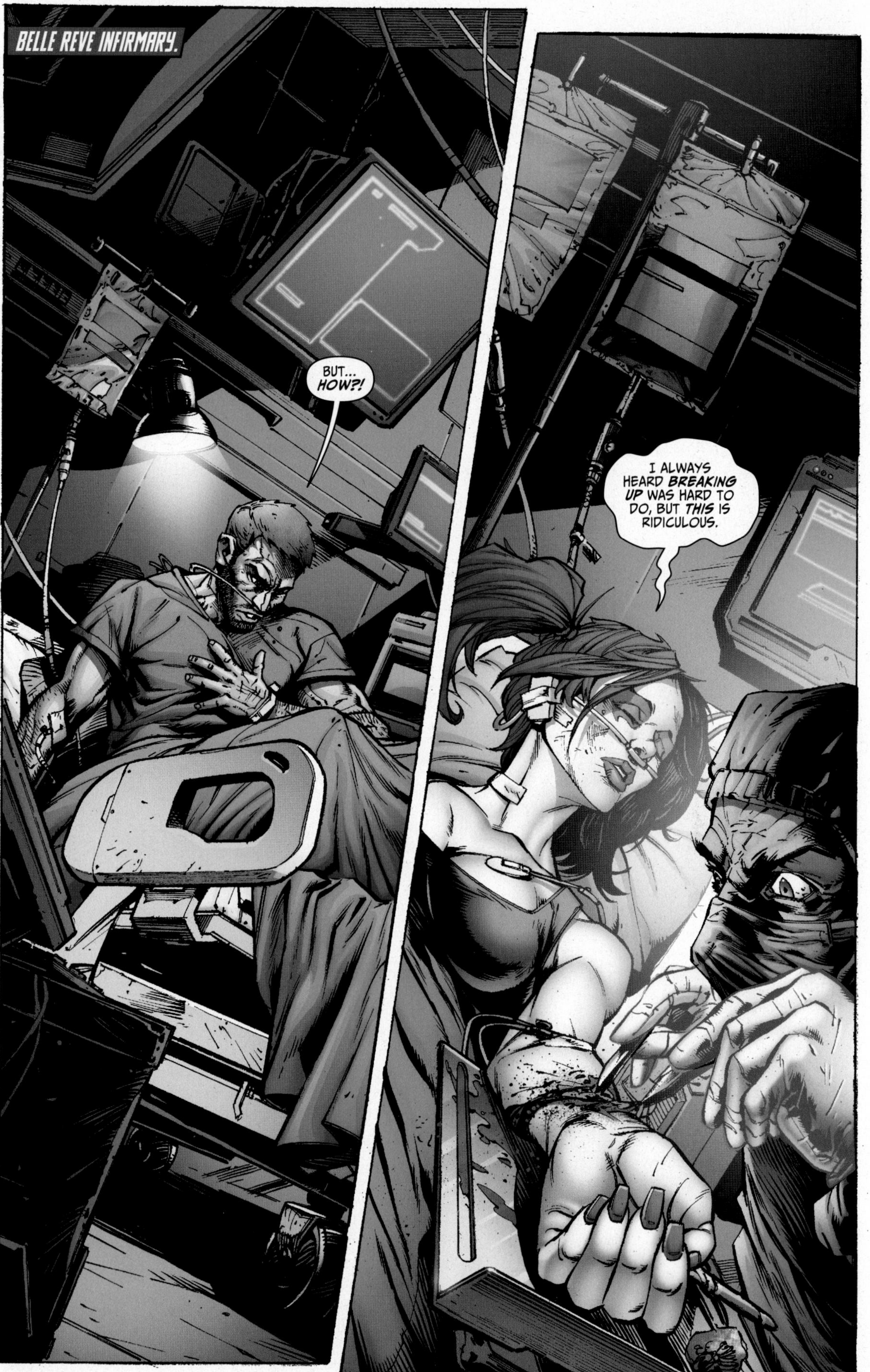
BELLE REVE INFIRMARY.
BUT... HOW?!
I ALWAYS HEARD BREAKING UP WAS HARD TO DO, BUT THIS IS RIDICULOUS.

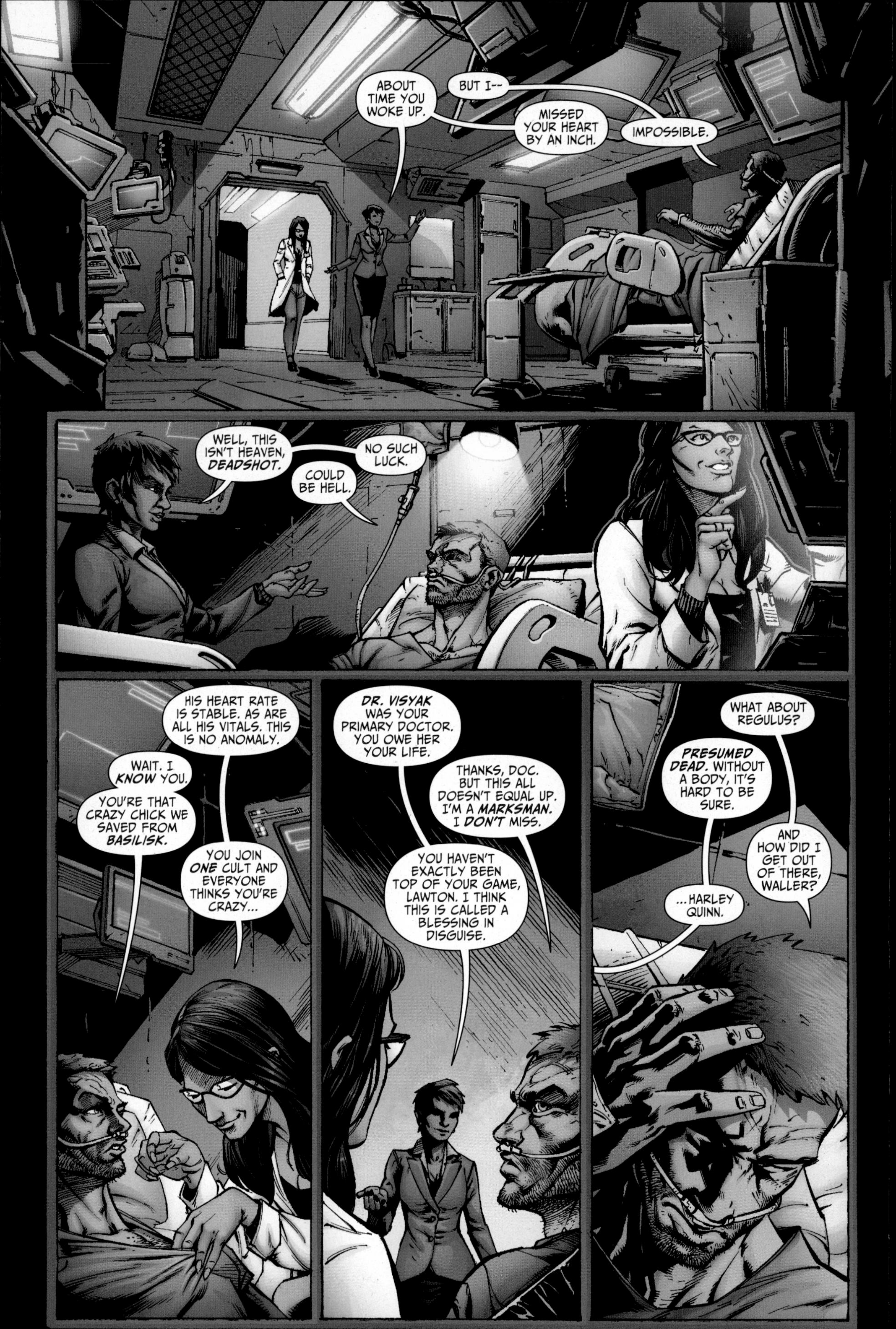
ABOUT TIME YOU WOKE UP.
BUT I--
MISSED YOUR HEART BY AN INCH.
IMPOSSIBLE.
WELL, THIS ISN'T HEAVEN, DEADSHOT.
NO SUCH LUCK.
COULD BE HELL.
HIS HEART RATE IS STABLE. AS ARE ALL HIS VITALS. THIS IS NO ANOMALY.
WAIT. I KNOW YOU.
YOU'RE THAT CRAZY CHICK WE SAVED FROM BASILISK.
YOU JOIN ONE CULT AND EVERYONE THINKS YOU'RE CRAZY...
DR. VISYAK WAS YOUR PRIMARY DOCTOR. YOU OWE HER YOUR LIFE.
THANKS, DOC. BUT THIS ALL DOESN'T EQUAL UP. I'M A MARKSMAN. I DON'T MISS.
YOU HAVEN'T EXACTLY BEEN TOP OF YOUR GAME, LAWTON. I THINK THIS IS CALLED A BLESSING IN DISGUISE.
WHAT ABOUT REGULUS?
PRESUMED DEAD. WITHOUT A BODY, IT'S HARD TO BE SURE.
AND HOW DID I GET OUT OF THERE, WALLER?
...HARLEY QUINN.

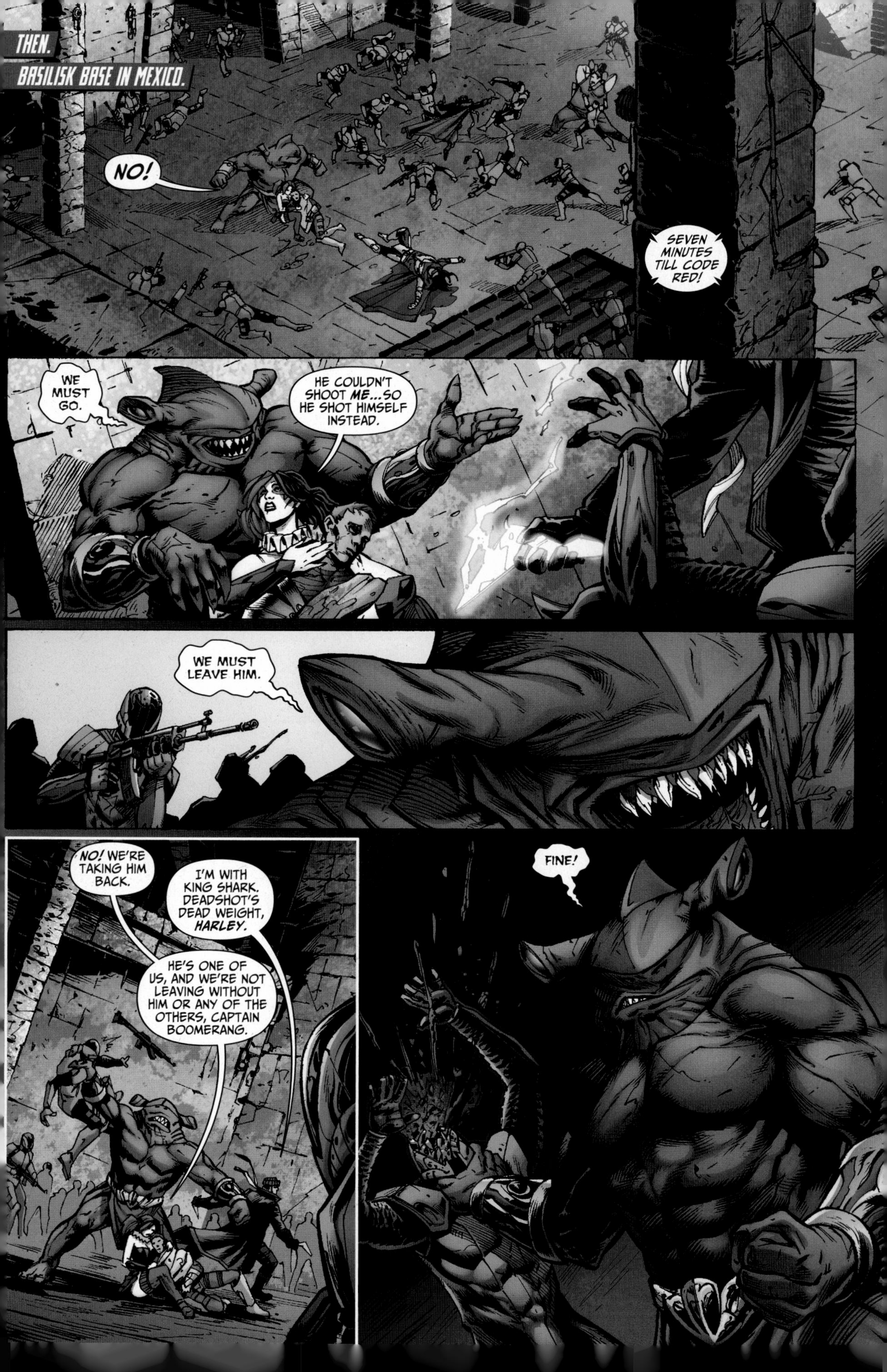
THEN.
BASILISK BASE IN MEXICO.
NO!
SEVEN MINUTES TILL CODE RED!
WE MUST GO.
HE COULDN'T SHOOT ME...SO HE SHOT HIMSELF INSTEAD.
WE MUST LEAVE HIM.
NO! WE'RE TAKING HIM BACK.
I'M WITH KING SHARK. DEADSHOT'S DEAD WEIGHT, HARLEY.
HE'S ONE OF US, AND WE'RE NOT LEAVING WITHOUT HIM OR ANY OF THE OTHERS, CAPTAIN BOOMERANG.
FINE!

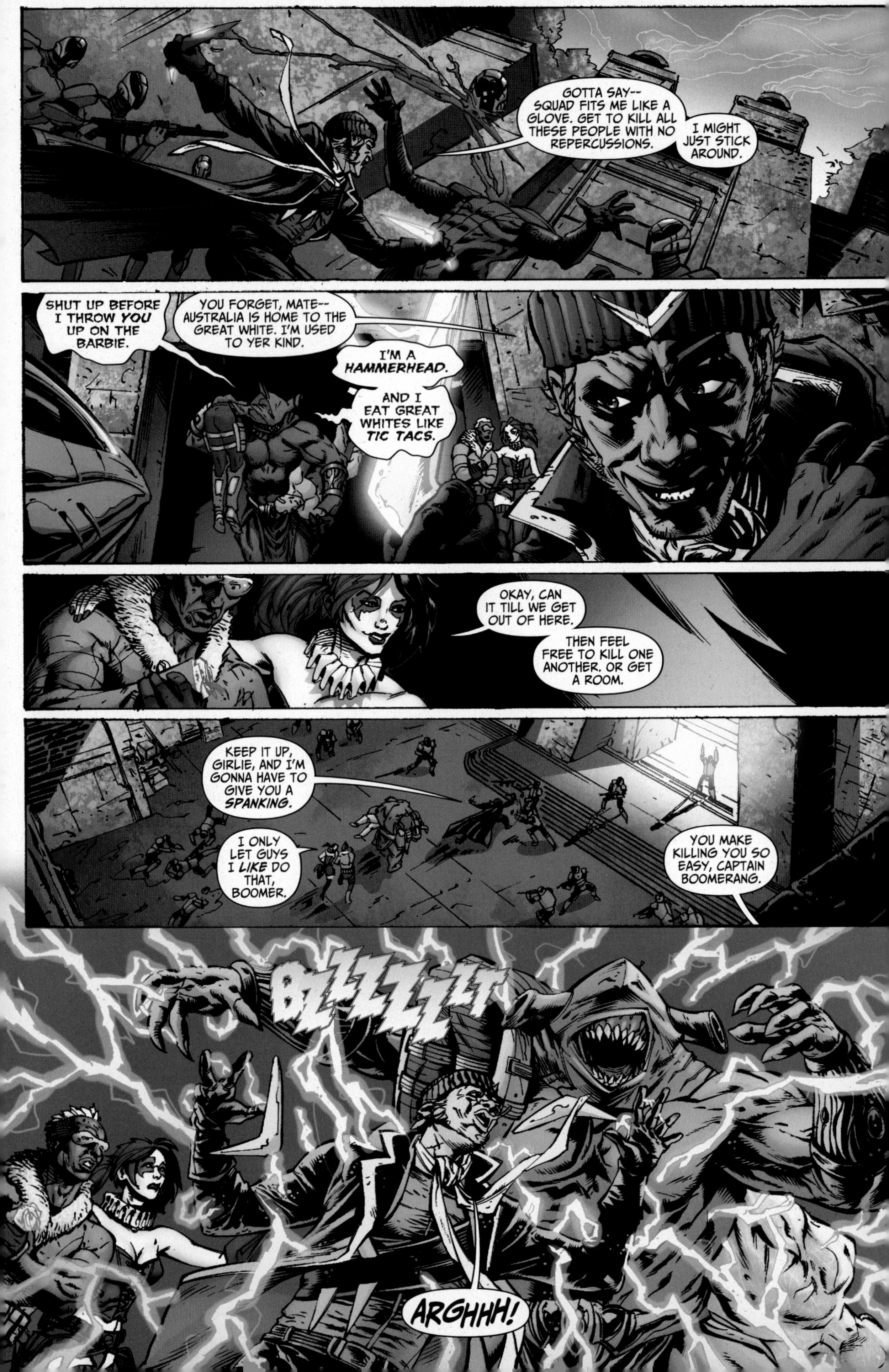
GOTTA SAY-- SQUAD FITS ME LIKE A GLOVE. GET TO KILL ALL THESE PEOPLE WITH NO REPERCUSSIONS.
I MIGHT JUST STICK AROUND.
SHUT UP BEFORE I THROW YOU UP ON THE BARBIE.
YOU FORGET, MATE-- AUSTRALIA IS HOME TO THE GREAT WHITE. I'M USED TO YER KIND.
I'M A HAMMERHEAD.
AND I EAT GREAT WHITES LIKE TIC TACS.
OKAY, CAN IT TILL WE GET OUT OF HERE.
THEN FEEL FREE TO KILL ONE ANOTHER. OR GET A ROOM.
KEEP IT UP, GIRLIE, AND I'M GONNA HAVE TO GIVE YOU A SPANKING.
I ONLY LET GUYS I LIKE DO THAT, BOOMER.
YOU MAKE KILLING YOU SO EASY, CAPTAIN BOOMERANG.
BZZZZZZZT
ARGHHH!

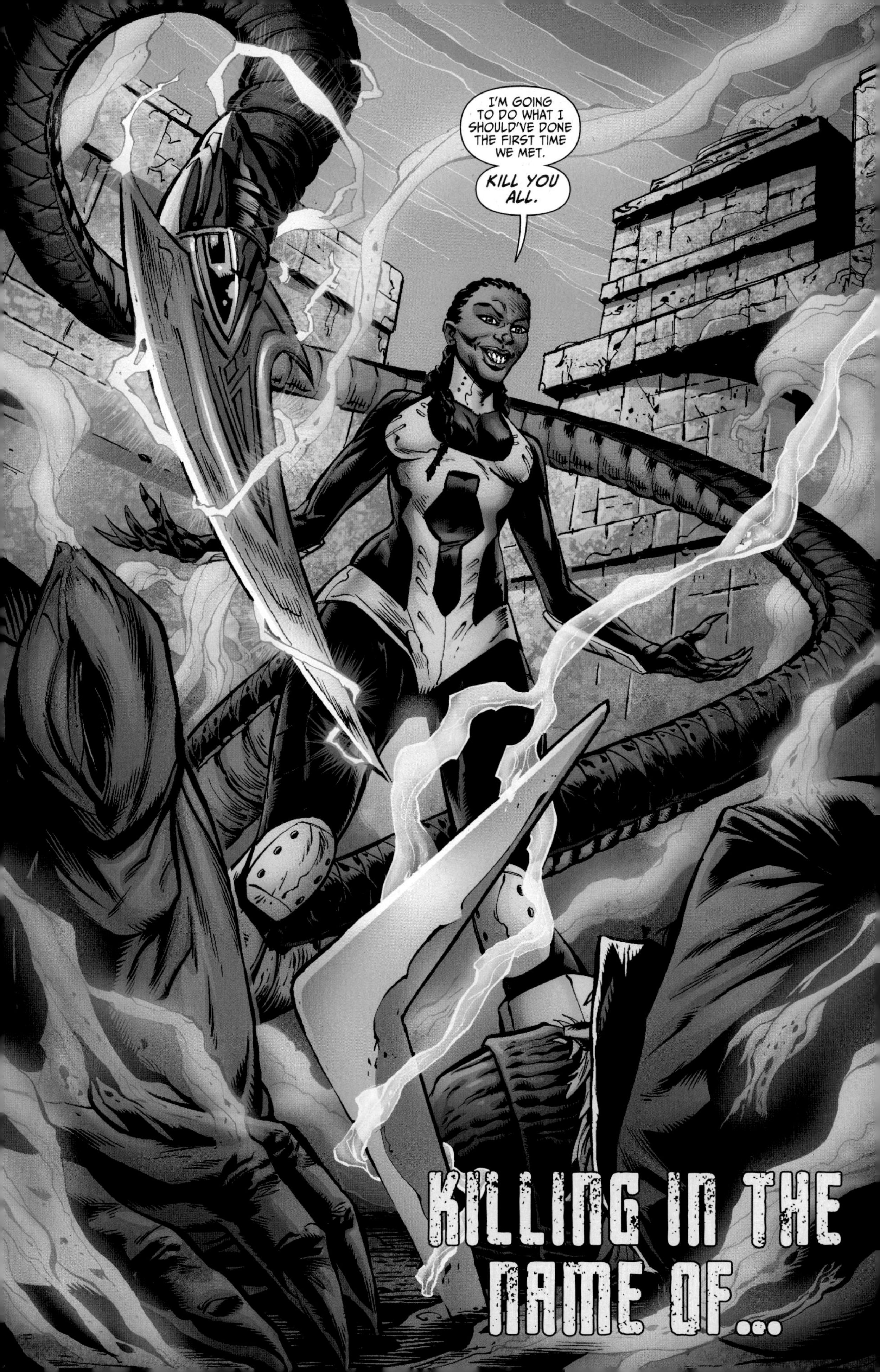
I'M GOING TO DO WHAT I SHOULD'VE DONE THE FIRST TIME WE MET.
KILL YOU ALL.
KILLING IN THE NAME OF...

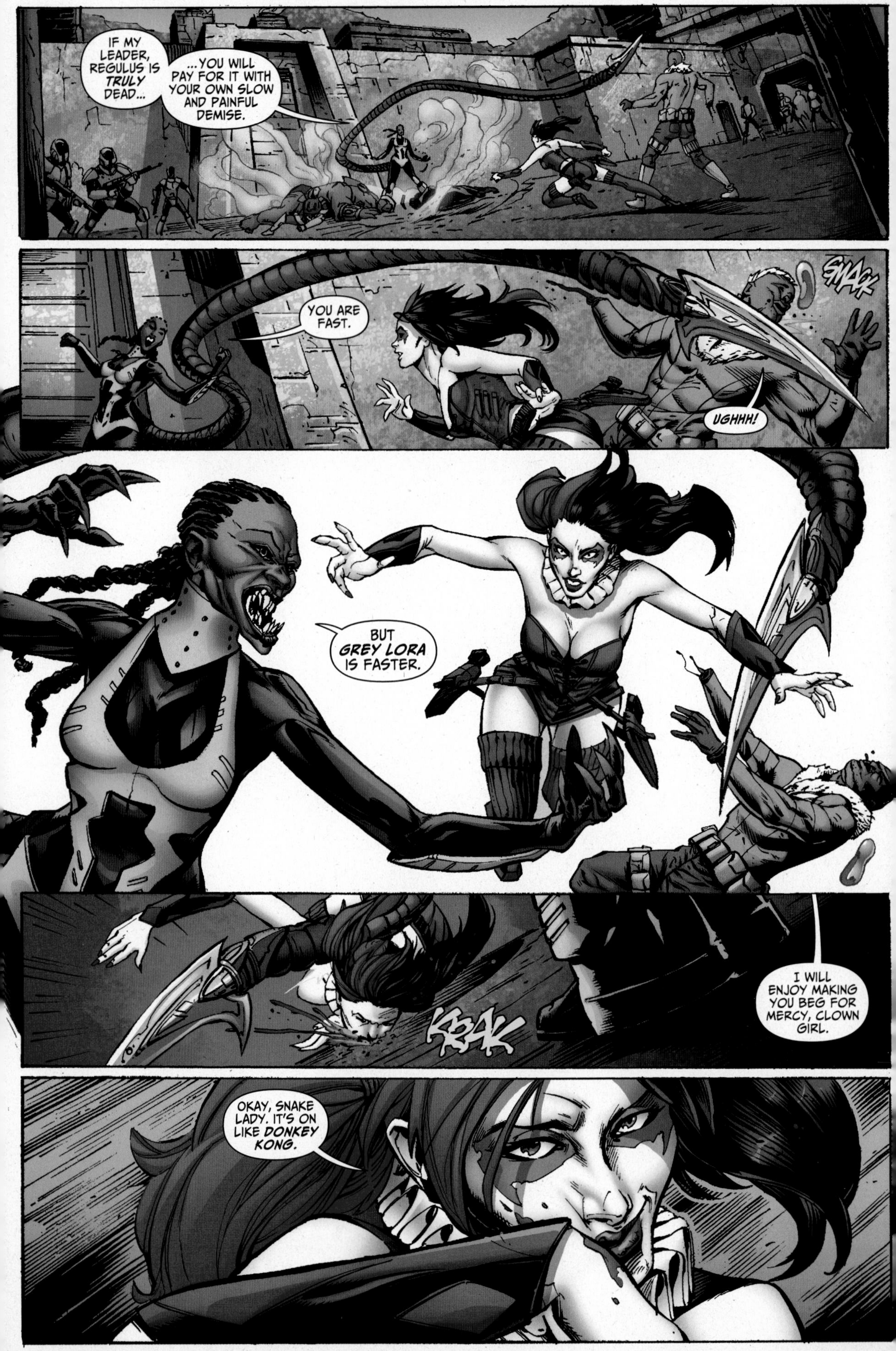
IF MY LEADER, REGULUS IS TRULY DEAD...
...YOU WILL PAY FOR IT WITH YOUR OWN SLOW AND PAINFUL DEMISE.
YOU ARE FAST.
SMACK
UGHHH!
BUT GREY LORA IS FASTER.
KRAK
I WILL ENJOY MAKING YOU BEG FOR MERCY, CLOWN GIRL.
OKAY, SNAKE LADY. IT'S ON LIKE DONKEY KONG.

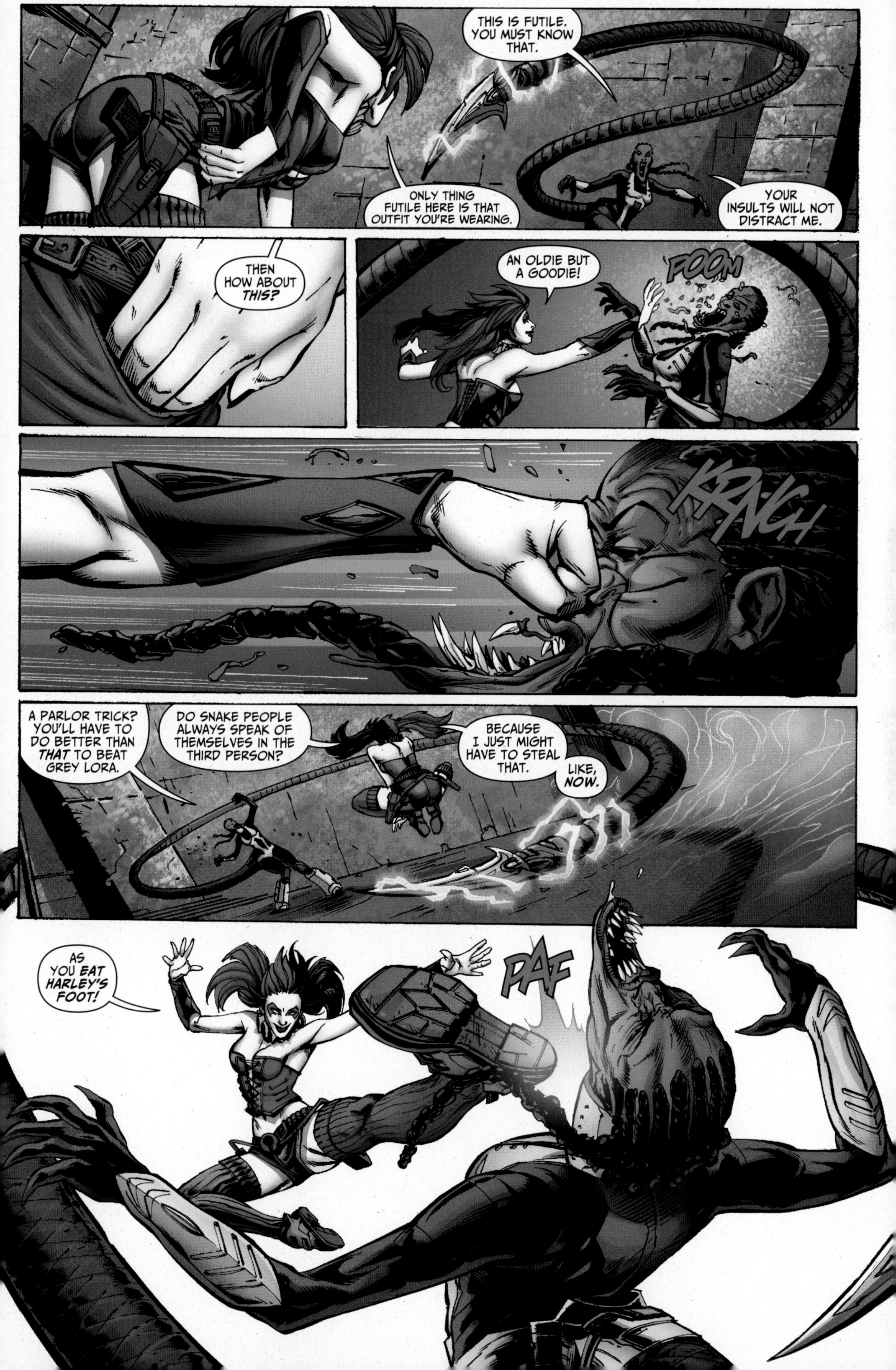
THIS IS FUTILE. YOU MUST KNOW THAT.
ONLY THING FUTILE HERE IS THAT OUTFIT YOU'RE WEARING.
YOUR INSULTS WILL NOT DISTRACT ME.
THEN HOW ABOUT *THIS?*
AN OLDIE BUT A GOODIE!
FOOM
KRNCH
A PARLOR TRICK? YOU'LL HAVE TO DO BETTER THAN *THAT* TO BEAT GREY LORA.
DO SNAKE PEOPLE ALWAYS SPEAK OF THEMSELVES IN THE THIRD PERSON?
BECAUSE I JUST MIGHT HAVE TO STEAL THAT.
LIKE, *NOW.*
AS YOU *EAT HARLEY'S FOOT!*
PAF

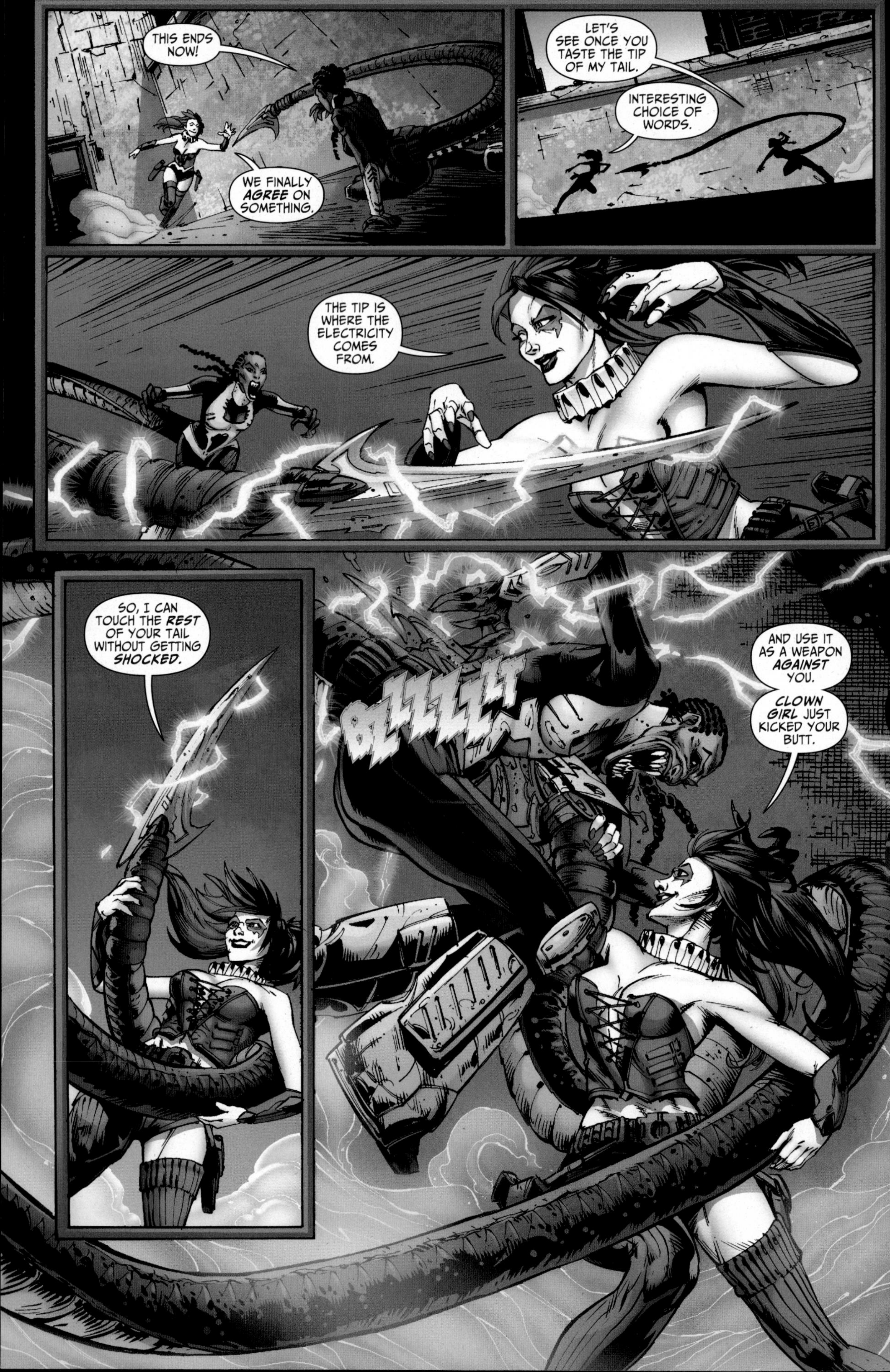
THIS ENDS NOW!
WE FINALLY AGREE ON SOMETHING.
LET'S SEE ONCE YOU TASTE THE TIP OF MY TAIL.
INTERESTING CHOICE OF WORDS.
THE TIP IS WHERE THE ELECTRICITY COMES FROM.
SO, I CAN TOUCH THE REST OF YOUR TAIL WITHOUT GETTING SHOCKED.
BZZZZZZT
AND USE IT AS A WEAPON AGAINST YOU.
CLOWN GIRL JUST KICKED YOUR BUTT.

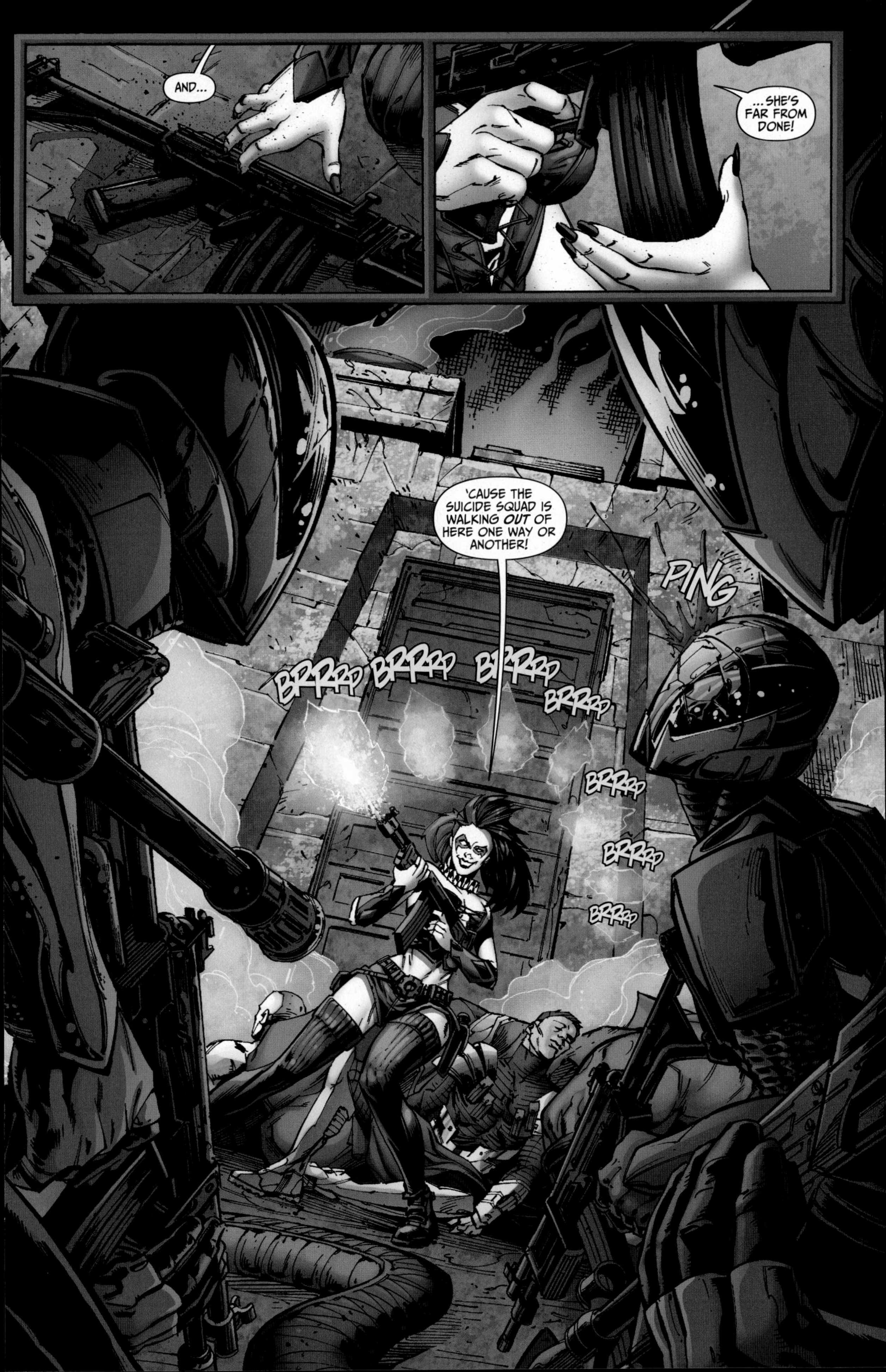

AND...
...SHE'S FAR FROM DONE!
'CAUSE THE SUICIDE SQUAD IS WALKING OUT OF HERE ONE WAY OR ANOTHER!
PING
BRRRRP BRRRRP BRRRRP BRRRRP
BRRRRP
BRRRRP
BRRRRP

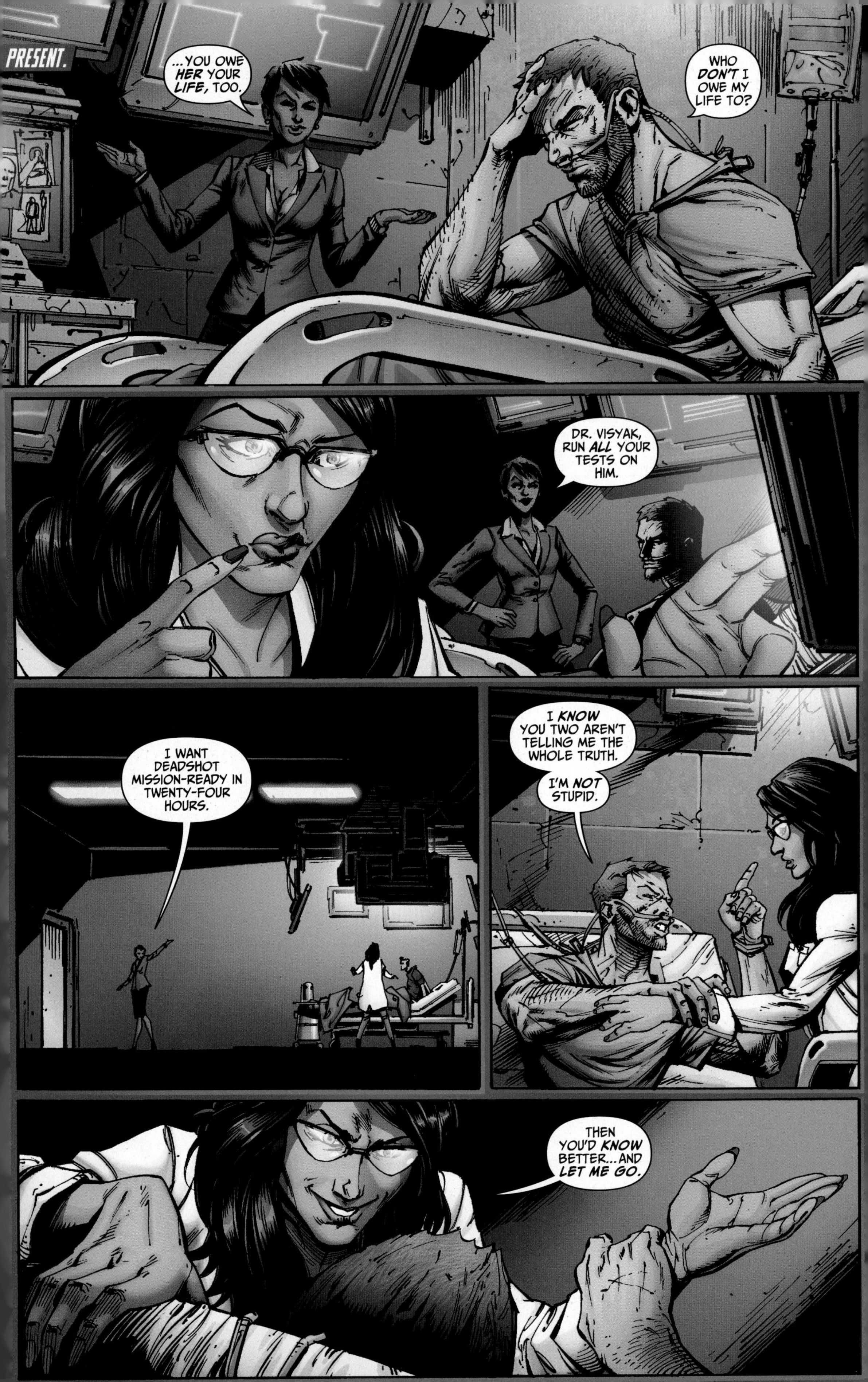
PRESENT.
...YOU OWE HER YOUR LIFE, TOO.
WHO DON'T I OWE MY LIFE TO?
DR. VISYAK, RUN ALL YOUR TESTS ON HIM.
I WANT DEADSHOT MISSION-READY IN TWENTY-FOUR HOURS.
I KNOW YOU TWO AREN'T TELLING ME THE WHOLE TRUTH.
I'M NOT STUPID.
THEN YOU'D KNOW BETTER...AND LET ME GO.

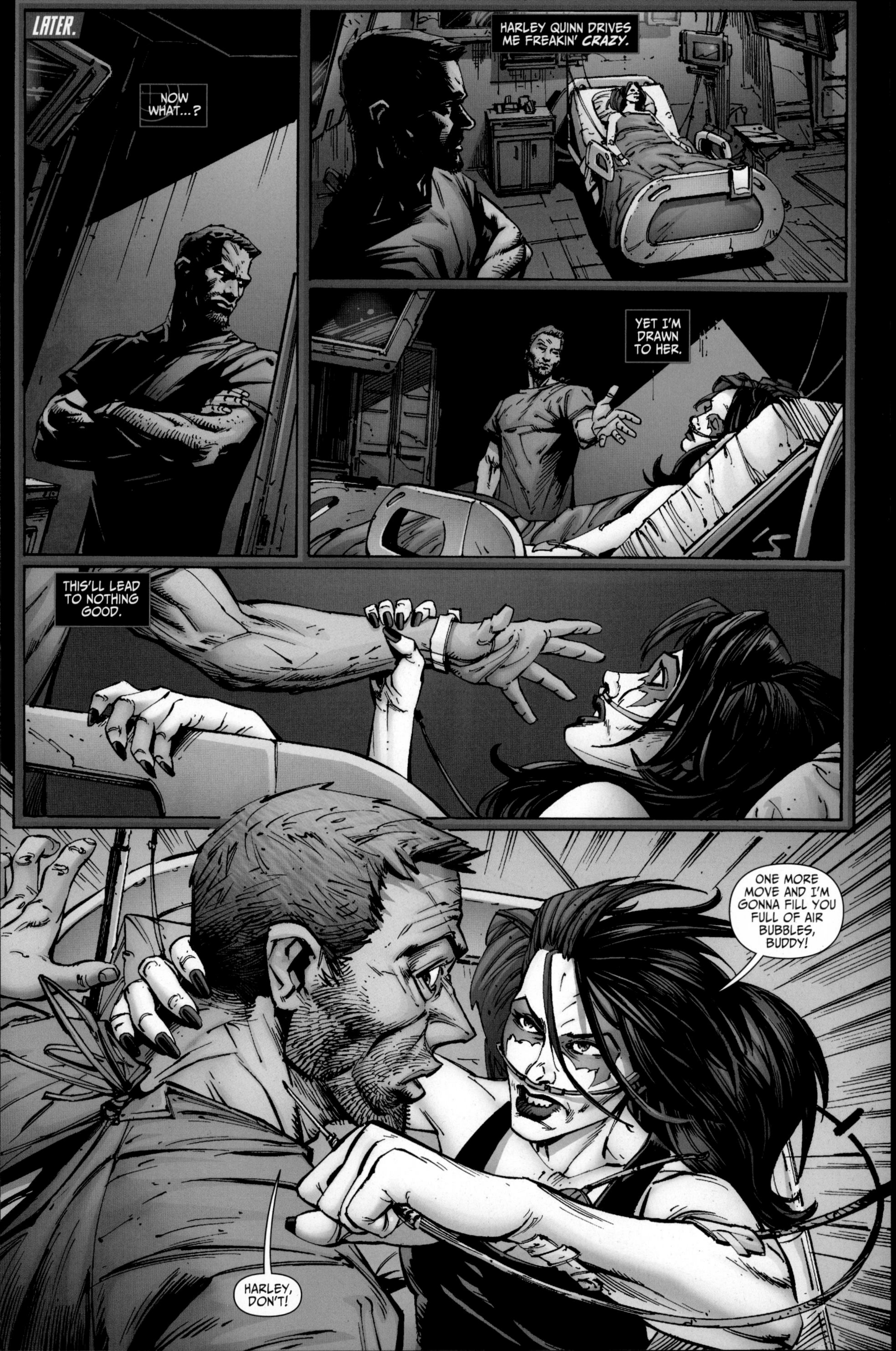

LATER.
NOW WHAT...?
HARLEY QUINN DRIVES ME FREAKIN' CRAZY.
YET I'M DRAWN TO HER.
THIS'LL LEAD TO NOTHING GOOD.
ONE MORE MOVE AND I'M GONNA FILL YOU FULL OF AIR BUBBLES, BUDDY!
HARLEY, DON'T!

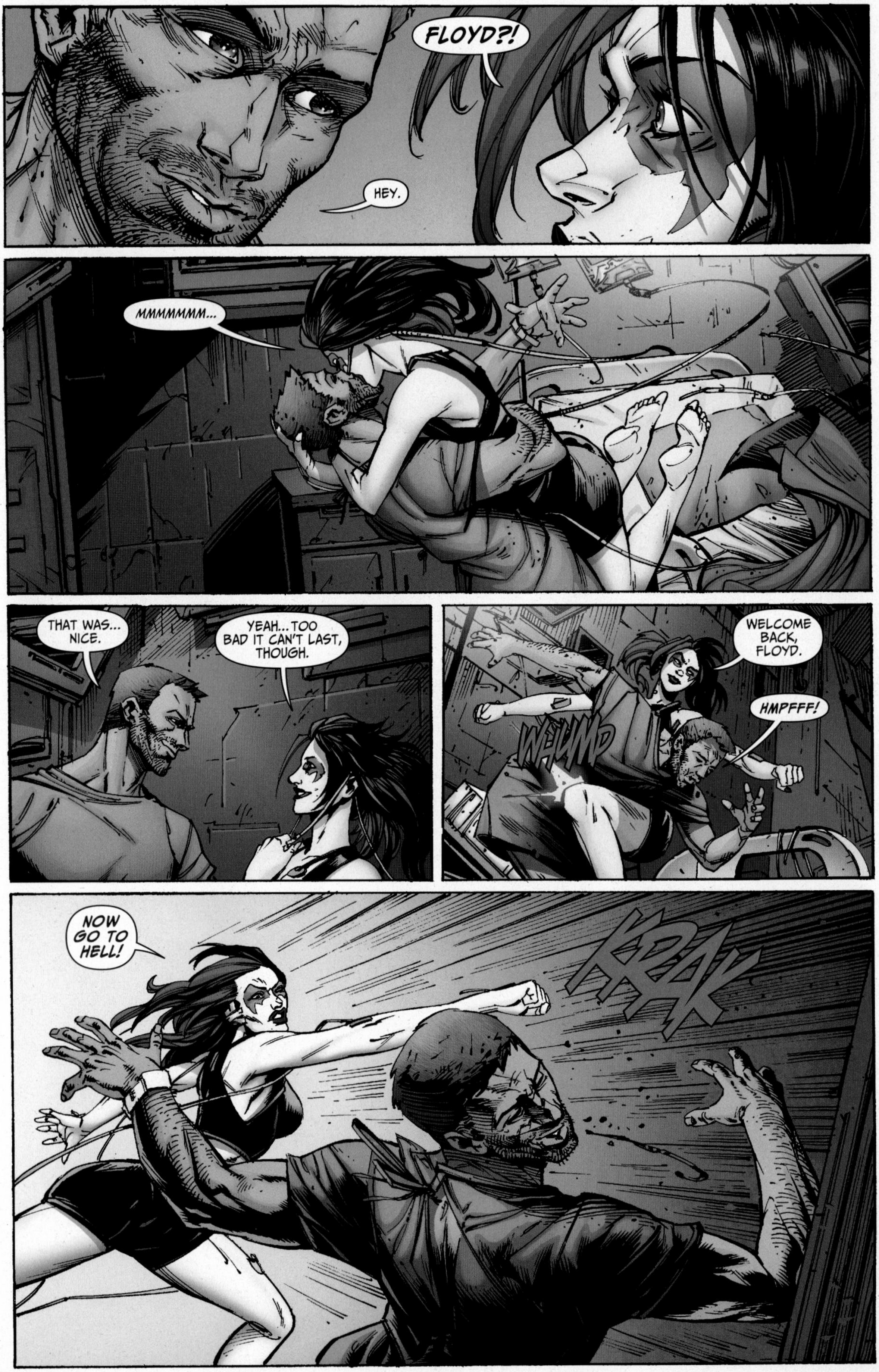
FLOYD?!
HEY.
MMMMMMM...
THAT WAS... NICE.
YEAH... TOO BAD IT CAN'T LAST, THOUGH.
WELCOME BACK, FLOYD.
HMPFFF!
WHUMP
NOW GO TO HELL!
KRAK

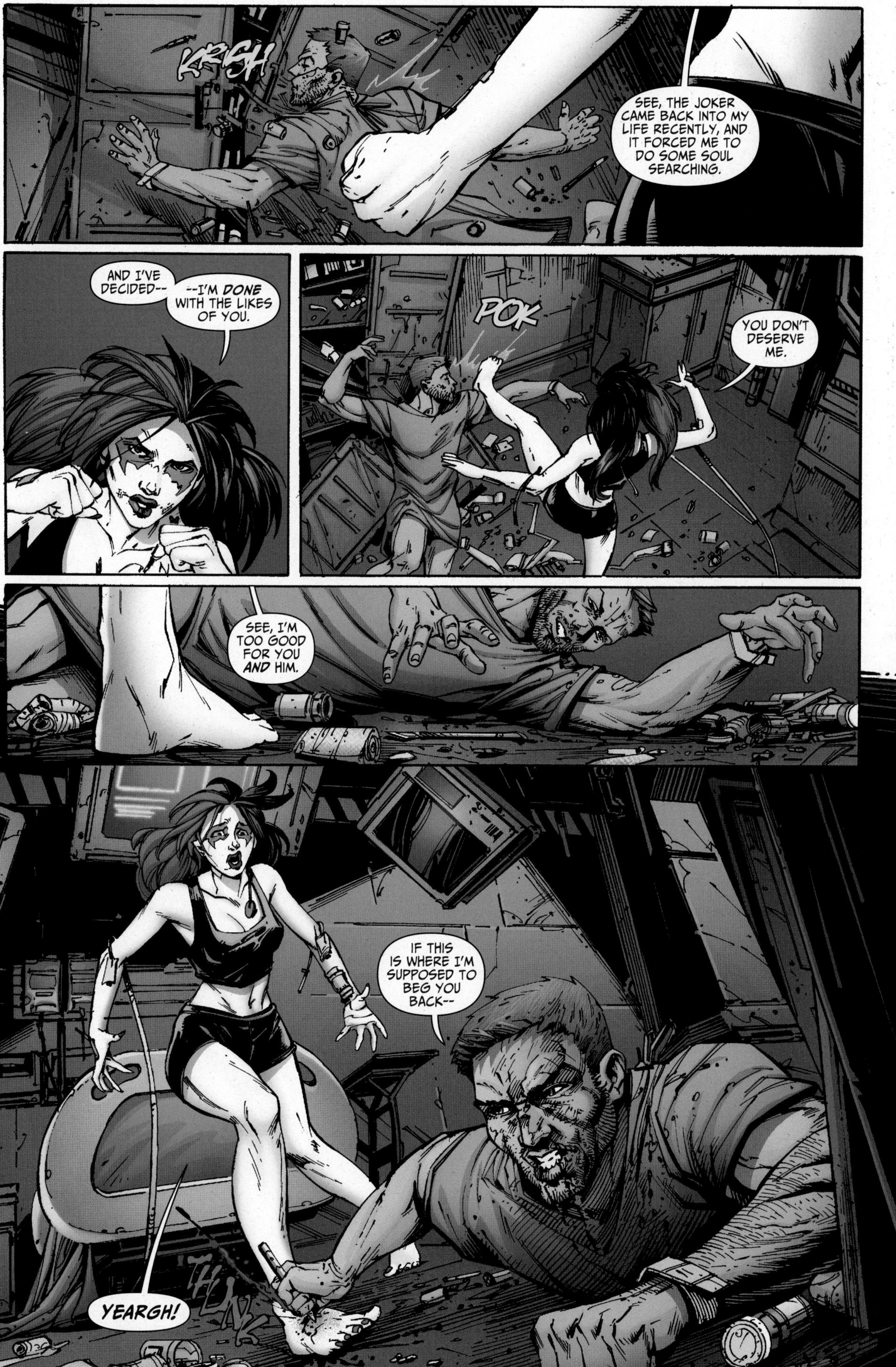
KRISH
SEE, THE JOKER CAME BACK INTO MY LIFE RECENTLY, AND IT FORCED ME TO DO SOME SOUL SEARCHING.
AND I'VE DECIDED--
--I'M DONE WITH THE LIKES OF YOU.
POK
YOU DON'T DESERVE ME.
SEE, I'M TOO GOOD FOR YOU AND HIM.
IF THIS IS WHERE I'M SUPPOSED TO BEG YOU BACK--
YEARGH!
THUNK

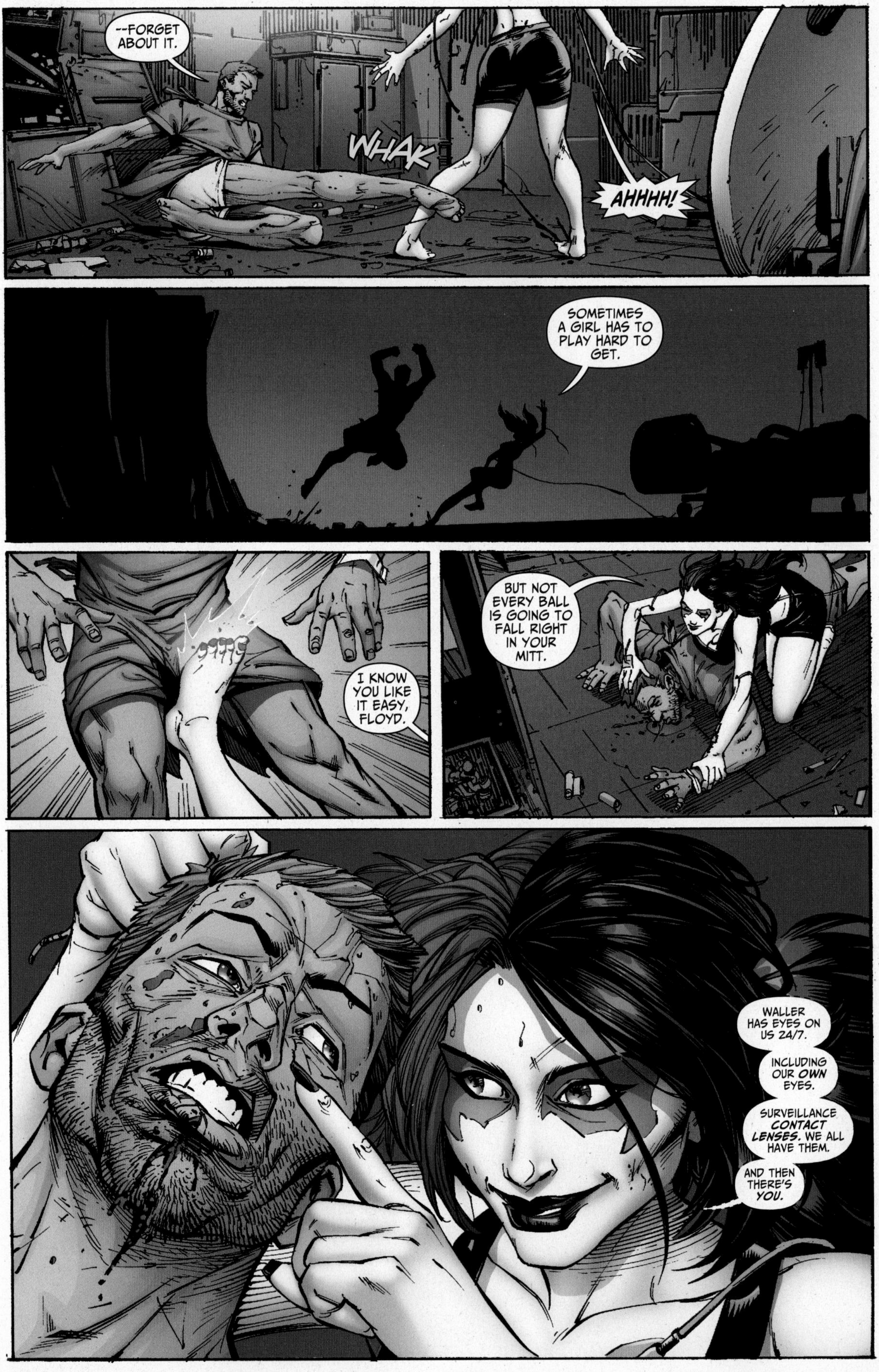
--FORGET ABOUT IT.
WHAK
AHHHH!
SOMETIMES A GIRL HAS TO PLAY HARD TO GET.
I KNOW YOU LIKE IT EASY, FLOYD.
BUT NOT EVERY BALL IS GOING TO FALL RIGHT IN YOUR MITT.
WALLER HAS EYES ON US 24/7.
INCLUDING OUR OWN EYES.
SURVEILLANCE CONTACT LENSES. WE ALL HAVE THEM.
AND THEN THERE'S YOU.

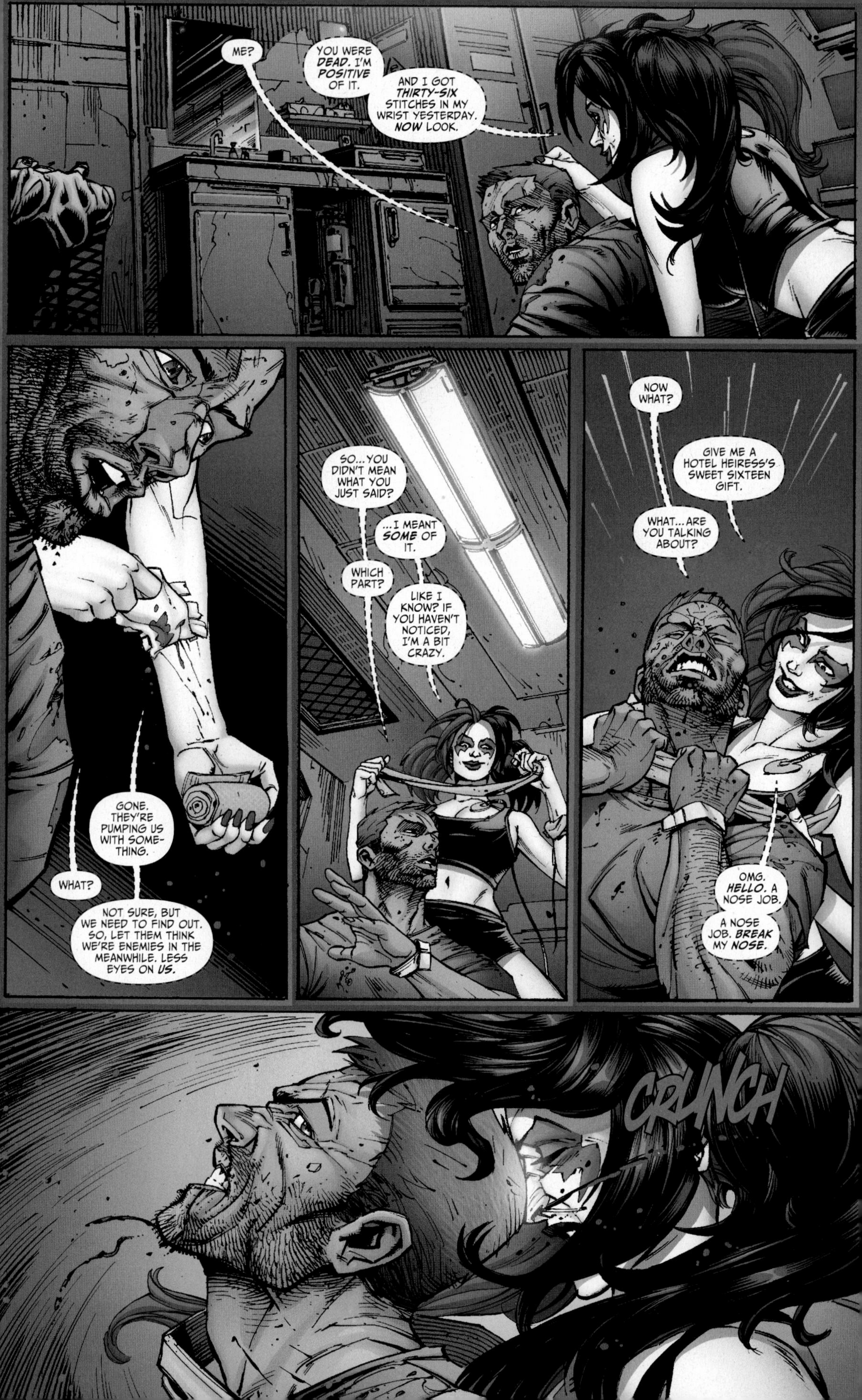

ME?
YOU WERE DEAD. I'M POSITIVE OF IT.
AND I GOT THIRTY-SIX STITCHES IN MY WRIST YESTERDAY. NOW LOOK.
GONE. THEY'RE PUMPING US WITH SOME-THING.
WHAT?
NOT SURE, BUT WE NEED TO FIND OUT. SO, LET THEM THINK WE'RE ENEMIES IN THE MEANWHILE. LESS EYES ON US.
SO...YOU DIDN'T MEAN WHAT YOU JUST SAID?
...I MEANT SOME OF IT.
WHICH PART?
LIKE I KNOW? IF YOU HAVEN'T NOTICED, I'M A BIT CRAZY.
NOW WHAT?
GIVE ME A HOTEL HEIRESS'S SWEET SIXTEEN GIFT.
WHAT...ARE YOU TALKING ABOUT?
OMG. HELLO. A NOSE JOB.
A NOSE JOB. BREAK MY NOSE.
CRUNCH

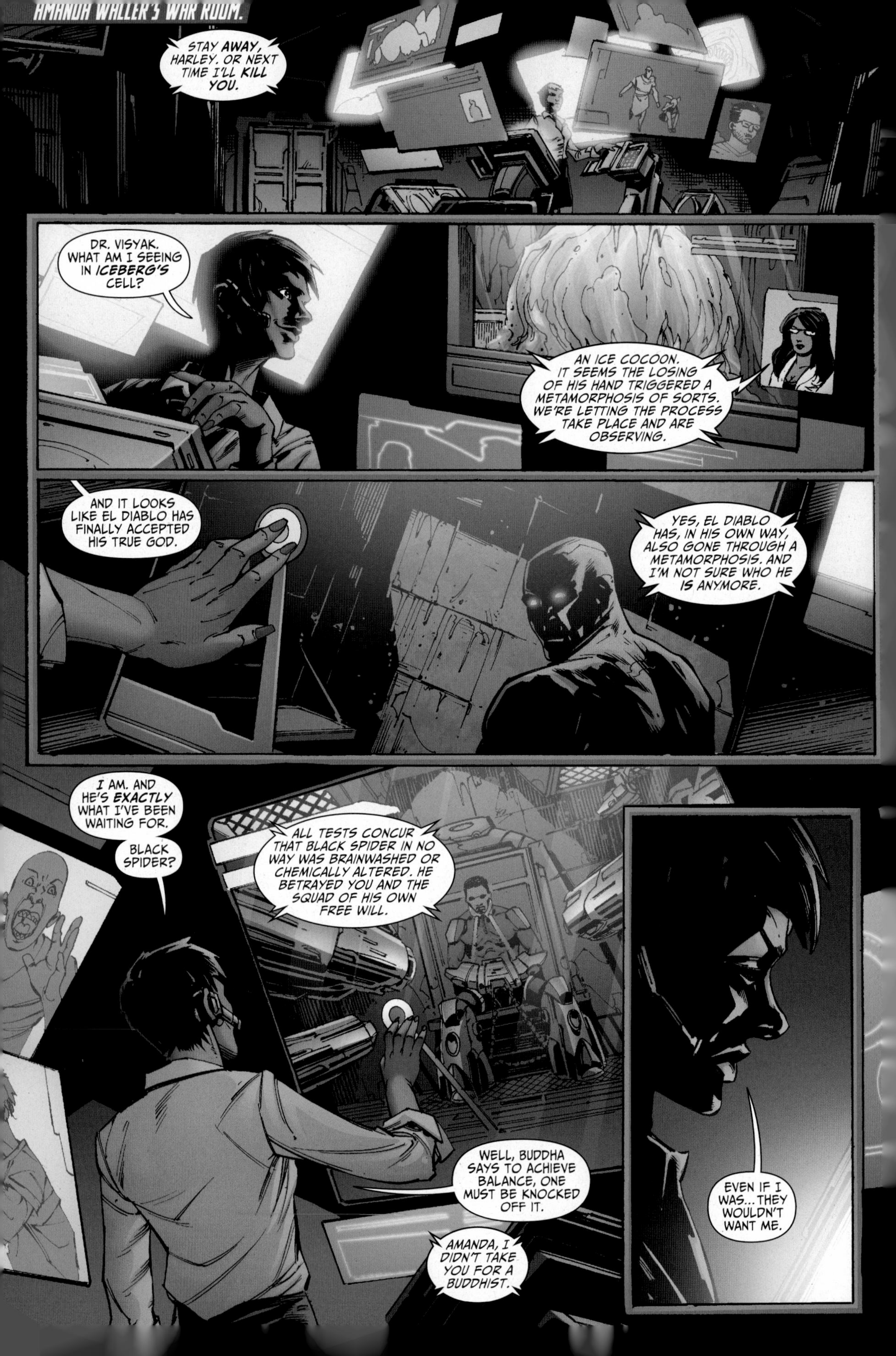
AMANDA WALLER'S WAR ROOM.
STAY AWAY, HARLEY. OR NEXT TIME I'LL KILL YOU.
DR. VISYAK. WHAT AM I SEEING IN ICEBERG'S CELL?
AN ICE COCOON. IT SEEMS THE LOSING OF HIS HAND TRIGGERED A METAMORPHOSIS OF SORTS. WE'RE LETTING THE PROCESS TAKE PLACE AND ARE OBSERVING.
AND IT LOOKS LIKE EL DIABLO HAS FINALLY ACCEPTED HIS TRUE GOD.
YES, EL DIABLO HAS, IN HIS OWN WAY, ALSO GONE THROUGH A METAMORPHOSIS. AND I'M NOT SURE WHO HE IS ANYMORE.
I AM. AND HE'S EXACTLY WHAT I'VE BEEN WAITING FOR.
BLACK SPIDER?
ALL TESTS CONCUR THAT BLACK SPIDER IN NO WAY WAS BRAINWASHED OR CHEMICALLY ALTERED. HE BETRAYED YOU AND THE SQUAD OF HIS OWN FREE WILL.
WELL, BUDDHA SAYS TO ACHIEVE BALANCE, ONE MUST BE KNOCKED OFF IT.
AMANDA, I DIDN'T TAKE YOU FOR A BUDDHIST.
EVEN IF I WAS...THEY WOULDN'T WANT ME.

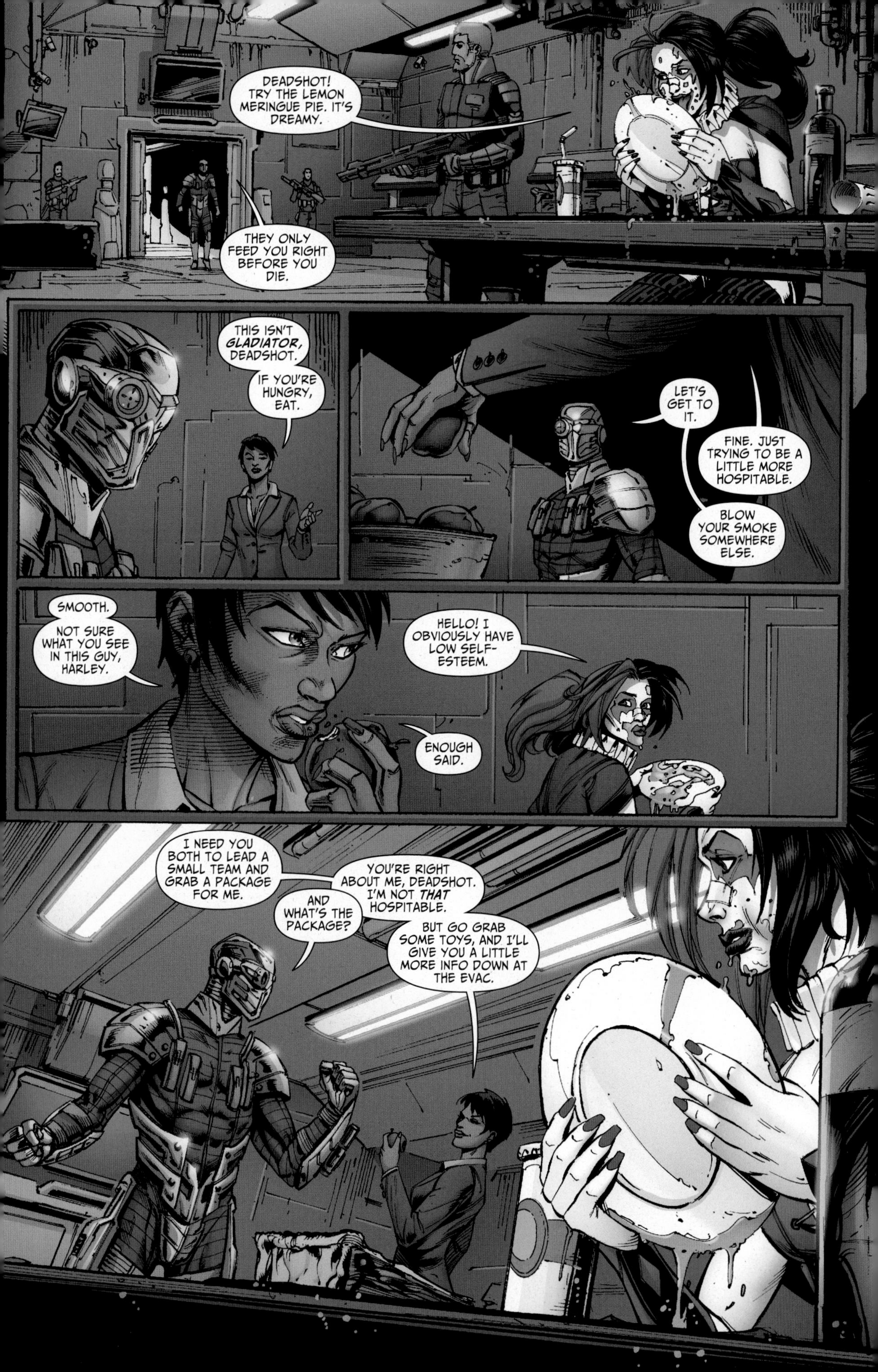

DEADSHOT! TRY THE LEMON MERINGUE PIE. IT'S DREAMY.
THEY ONLY FEED YOU RIGHT BEFORE YOU DIE.
THIS ISN'T GLADIATOR, DEADSHOT.
IF YOU'RE HUNGRY, EAT.
LET'S GET TO IT.
FINE. JUST TRYING TO BE A LITTLE MORE HOSPITABLE.
BLOW YOUR SMOKE SOMEWHERE ELSE.
SMOOTH.
NOT SURE WHAT YOU SEE IN THIS GUY, HARLEY.
HELLO! I OBVIOUSLY HAVE LOW SELF-ESTEEM.
ENOUGH SAID.
I NEED YOU BOTH TO LEAD A SMALL TEAM AND GRAB A PACKAGE FOR ME.
YOU'RE RIGHT ABOUT ME, DEADSHOT. I'M NOT THAT HOSPITABLE.
AND WHAT'S THE PACKAGE?
BUT GO GRAB SOME TOYS, AND I'LL GIVE YOU A LITTLE MORE INFO DOWN AT THE EVAC.

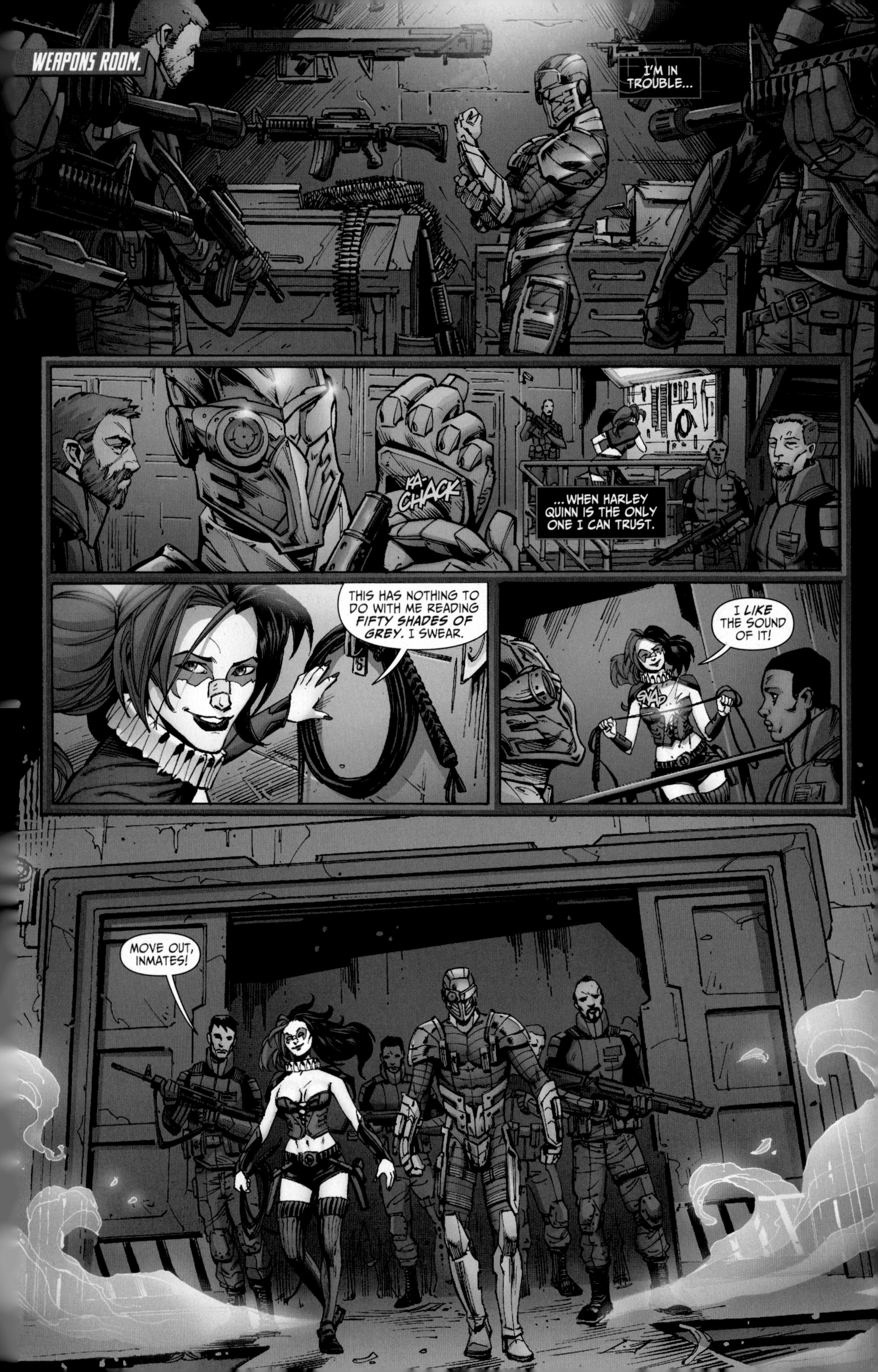
WEAPONS ROOM.
I'M IN TROUBLE...
KA-CHACK
...WHEN HARLEY QUINN IS THE ONLY ONE I CAN TRUST.
THIS HAS NOTHING TO DO WITH ME READING FIFTY SHADES OF GREY. I SWEAR.
SNAP
I LIKE THE SOUND OF IT!
MOVE OUT, INMATES!

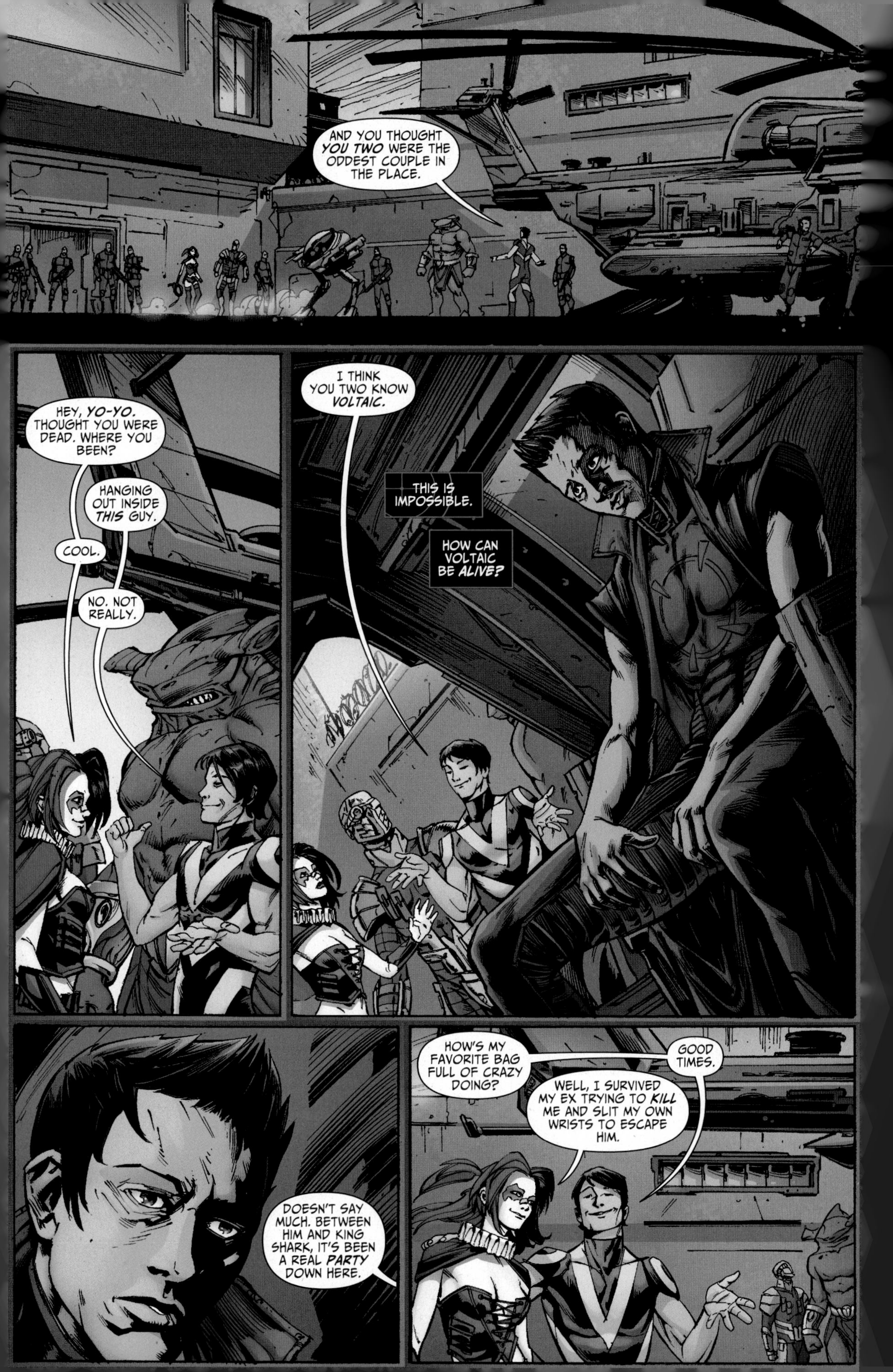
AND YOU THOUGHT YOU TWO WERE THE ODDEST COUPLE IN THE PLACE.
HEY, YO-YO. THOUGHT YOU WERE DEAD. WHERE YOU BEEN?
HANGING OUT INSIDE THIS GUY.
COOL.
NO. NOT REALLY.
I THINK YOU TWO KNOW VOLTAIC.
THIS IS IMPOSSIBLE.
HOW CAN VOLTAIC BE ALIVE?
DOESN'T SAY MUCH. BETWEEN HIM AND KING SHARK, IT'S BEEN A REAL PARTY DOWN HERE.
HOW'S MY FAVORITE BAG FULL OF CRAZY DOING?
GOOD TIMES.
WELL, I SURVIVED MY EX TRYING TO KILL ME AND SLIT MY OWN WRISTS TO ESCAPE HIM.

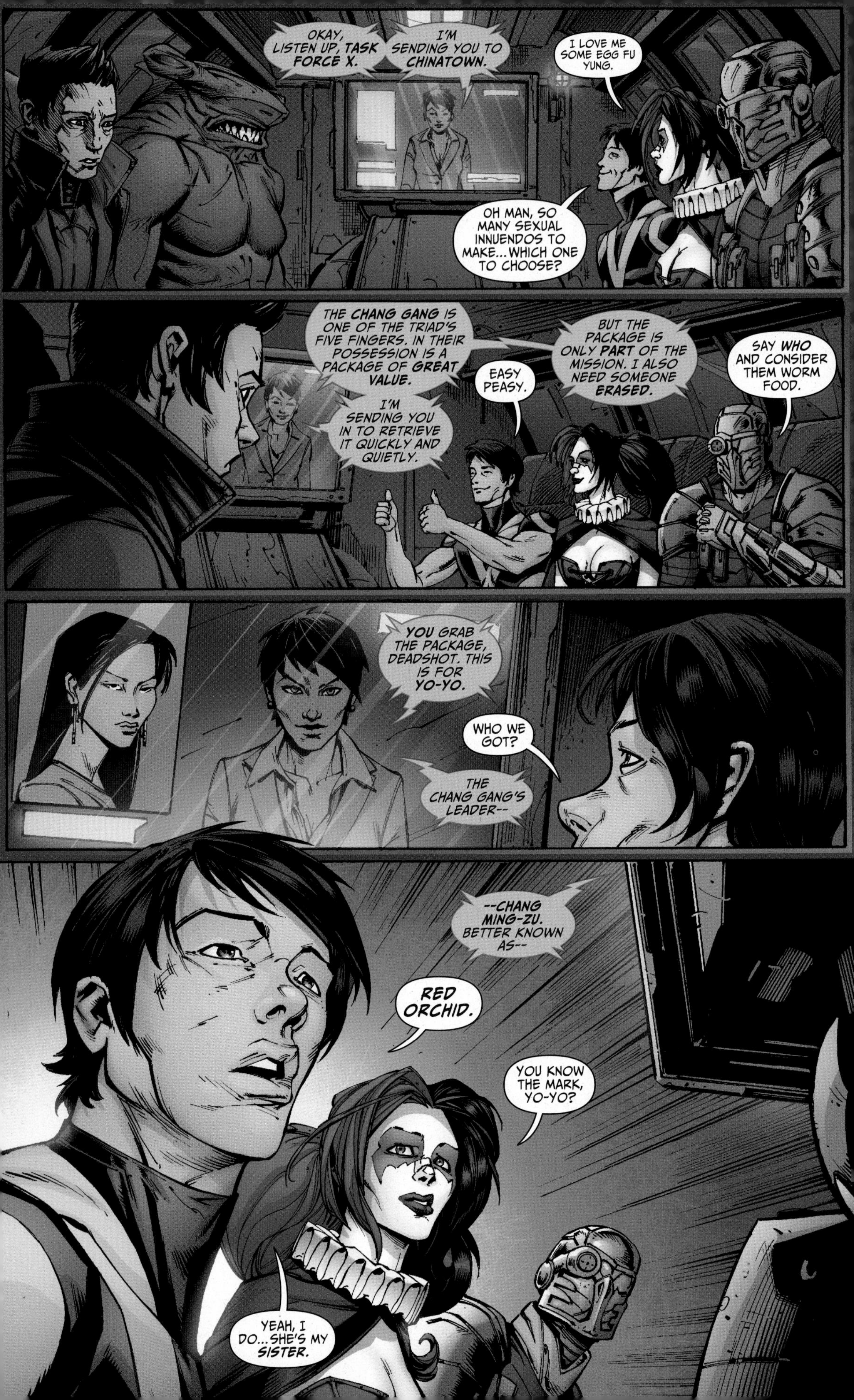
OKAY, LISTEN UP, TASK FORCE X.
I'M SENDING YOU TO CHINATOWN.
I LOVE ME SOME EGG FU YUNG.
OH MAN, SO MANY SEXUAL INNUENDOS TO MAKE...WHICH ONE TO CHOOSE?
THE CHANG GANG IS ONE OF THE TRIAD'S FIVE FINGERS. IN THEIR POSSESSION IS A PACKAGE OF GREAT VALUE.
I'M SENDING YOU IN TO RETRIEVE IT QUICKLY AND QUIETLY.
EASY PEASY.
BUT THE PACKAGE IS ONLY PART OF THE MISSION. I ALSO NEED SOMEONE ERASED.
SAY WHO AND CONSIDER THEM WORM FOOD.
YOU GRAB THE PACKAGE, DEADSHOT. THIS IS FOR YO-YO.
WHO WE GOT?
THE CHANG GANG'S LEADER--
--CHANG MING-ZU. BETTER KNOWN AS--
RED ORCHID.
YOU KNOW THE MARK, YO-YO?
YEAH, I DO...SHE'S MY SISTER.

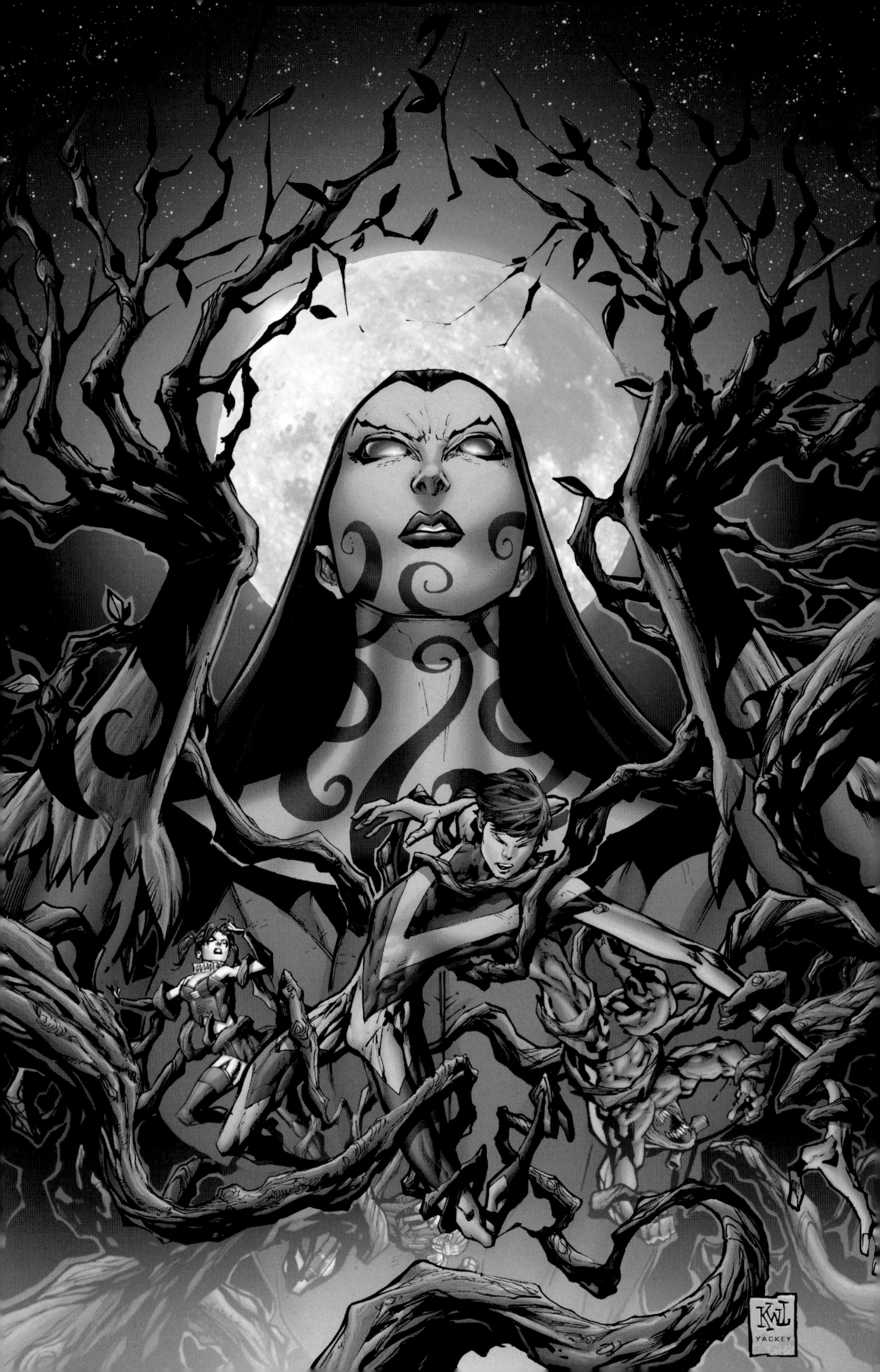
YACKEY

BAD MOON RISING

ADAM GLASS writer **HENRIK JONSSON** penciller **SANDU FLOREA** inker cover art by **KEN LASHLEY & MATT YACKEY**

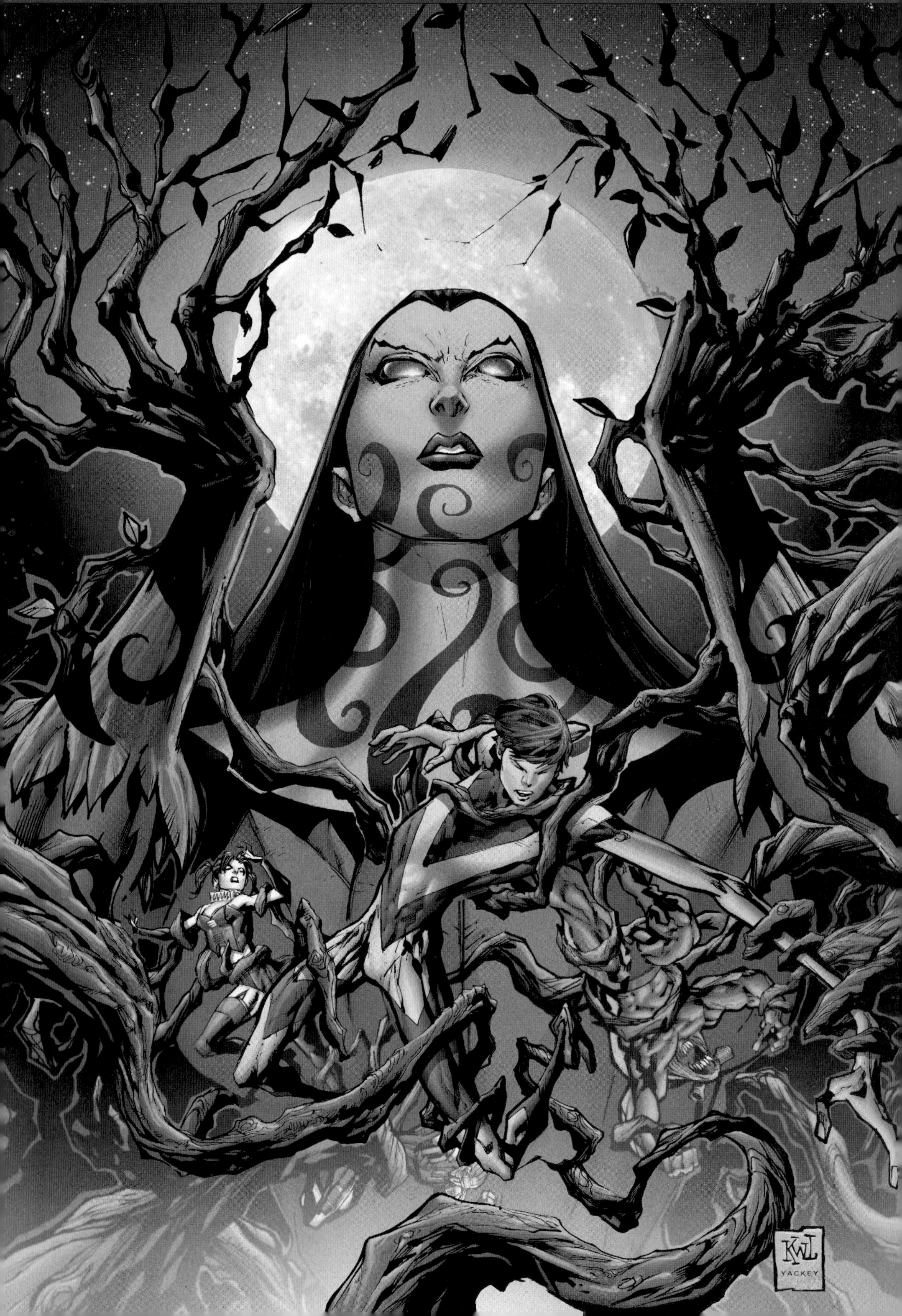

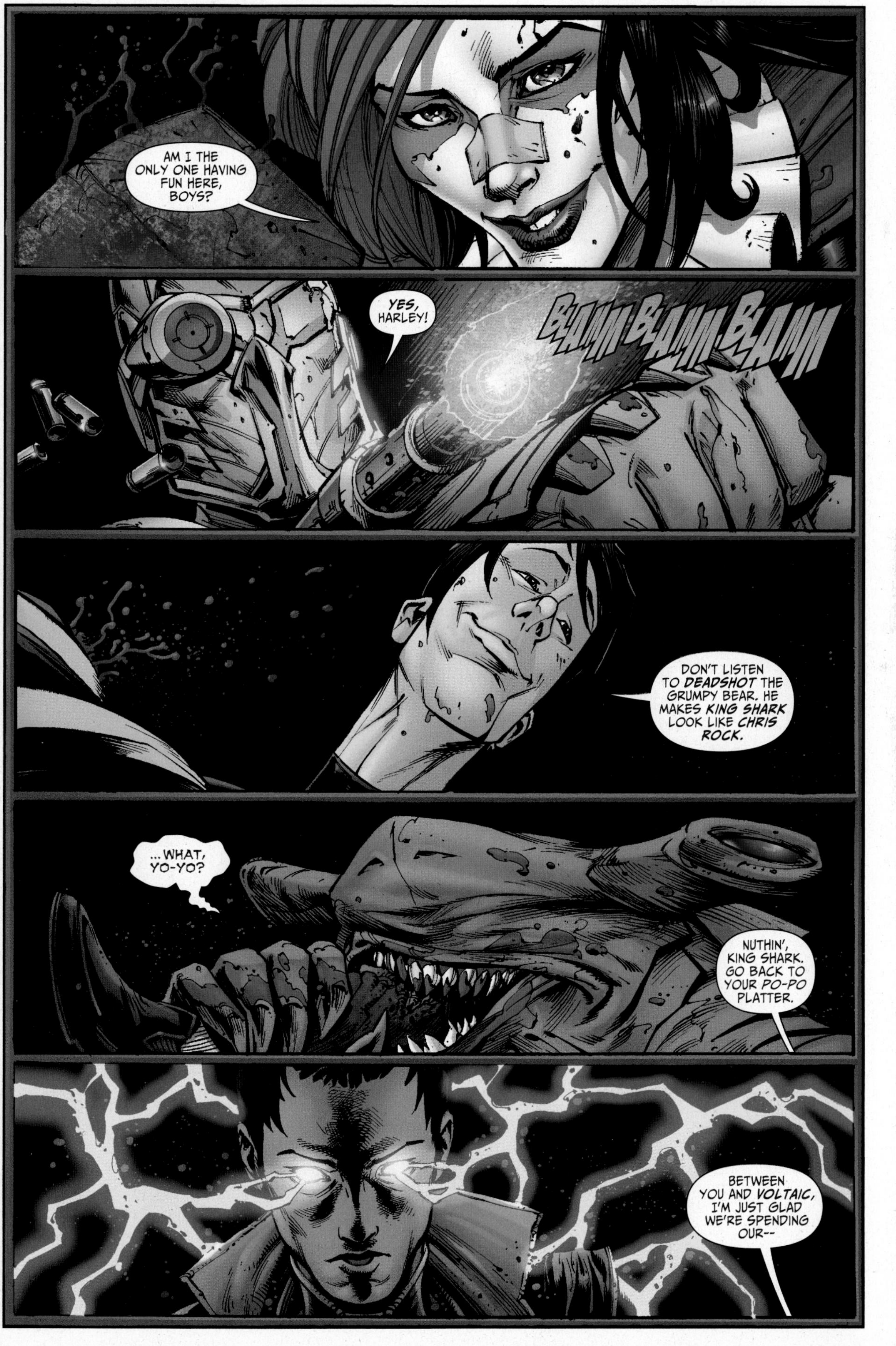

AM I THE ONLY ONE HAVING FUN HERE, BOYS?
YES, HARLEY!
BLAM BLAM BLAM
DON'T LISTEN TO **DEADSHOT** THE GRUMPY BEAR. HE MAKES **KING SHARK** LOOK LIKE **CHRIS ROCK.**
...WHAT, YO-YO?
NUTHIN', KING SHARK. GO BACK TO YOUR **PO-PO** PLATTER.
BETWEEN YOU AND **VOLTAIC**, I'M JUST GLAD WE'RE SPENDING OUR--

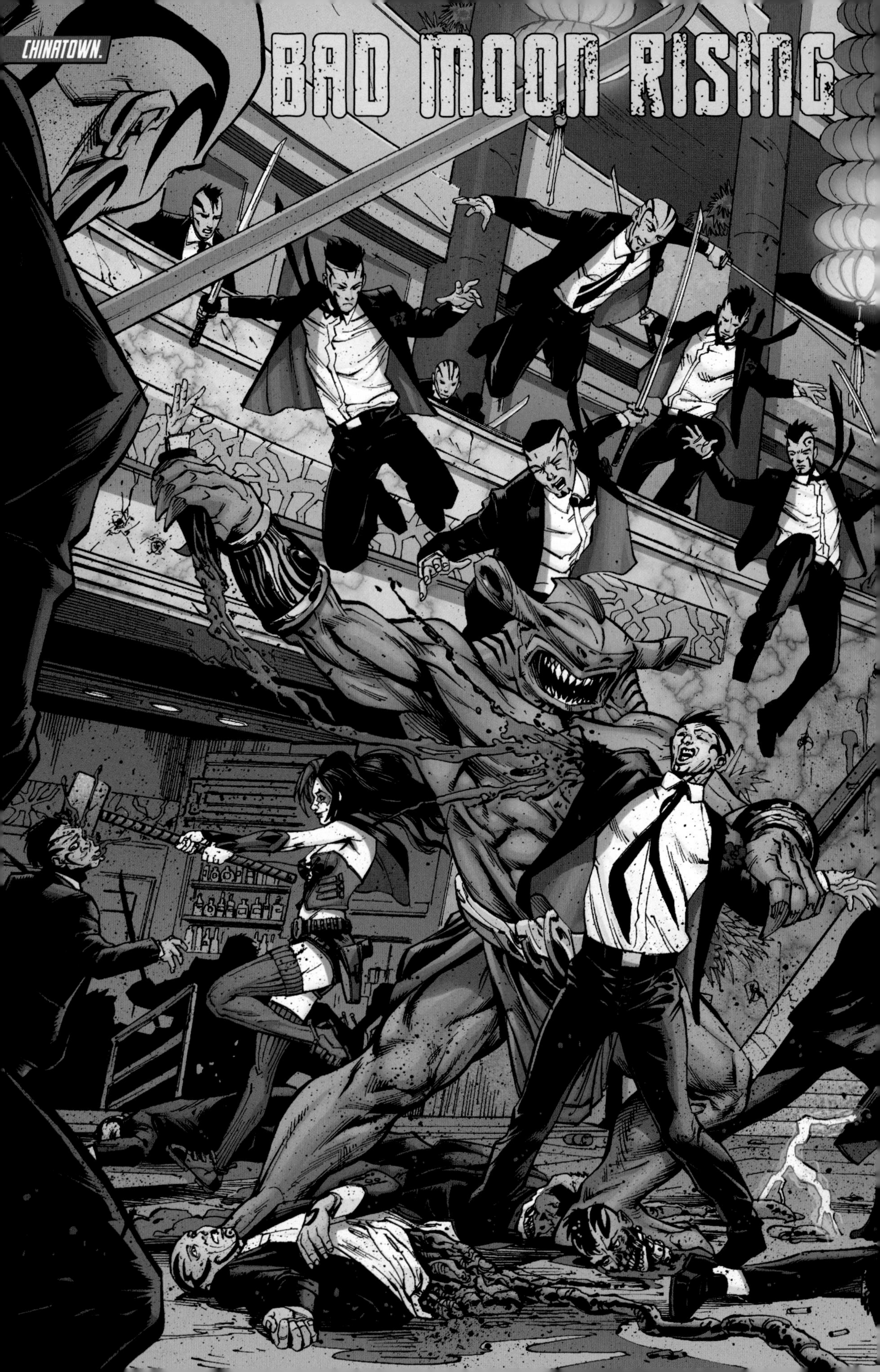
CHINATOWN.
BAD MOON RISING

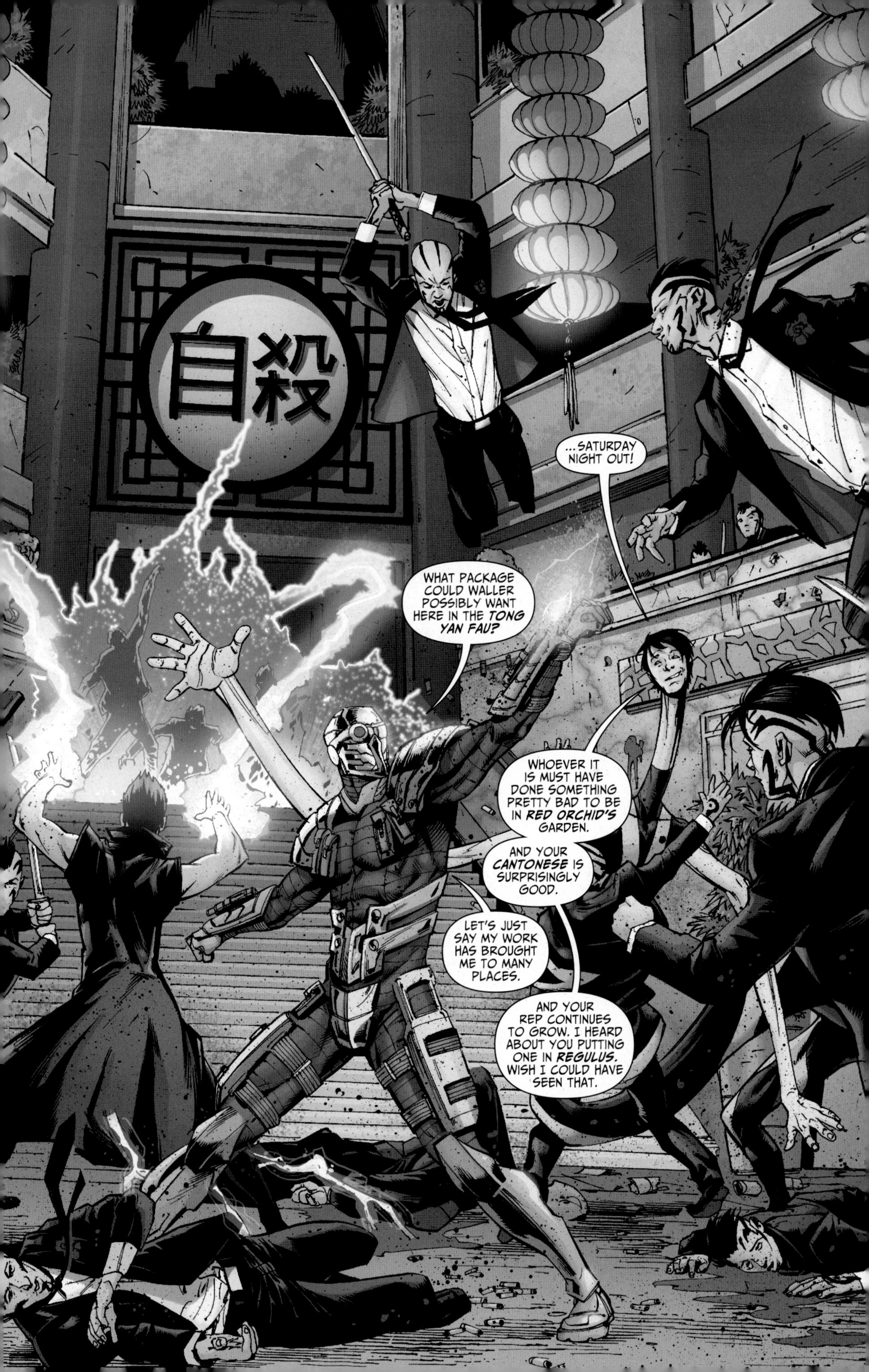

自殺
...SATURDAY NIGHT OUT!
WHAT PACKAGE COULD WALLER POSSIBLY WANT HERE IN THE TONG YAN FAU?
WHOEVER IT IS MUST HAVE DONE SOMETHING PRETTY BAD TO BE IN RED ORCHID'S GARDEN.
AND YOUR CANTONESE IS SURPRISINGLY GOOD.
LET'S JUST SAY MY WORK HAS BROUGHT ME TO MANY PLACES.
AND YOUR REP CONTINUES TO GROW. I HEARD ABOUT YOU PUTTING ONE IN REGULUS. WISH I COULD HAVE SEEN THAT.

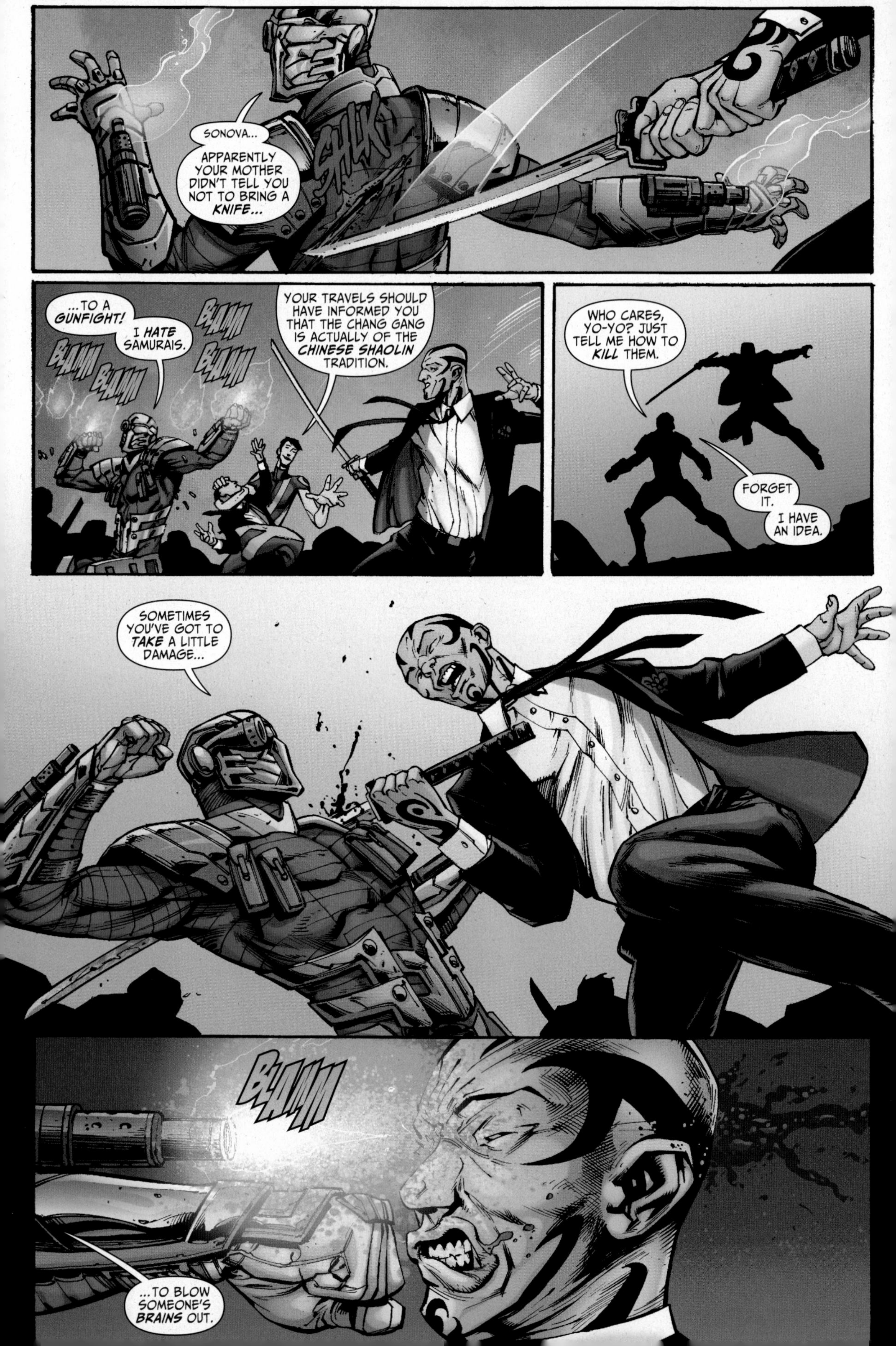
SHUK
SONOVA...
APPARENTLY YOUR MOTHER DIDN'T TELL YOU NOT TO BRING A *KNIFE*...
...TO A *GUNFIGHT!*
I *HATE* SAMURAIS.
BLAMM BLAMM
BLAMM BLAMM
YOUR TRAVELS SHOULD HAVE INFORMED YOU THAT THE CHANG GANG IS ACTUALLY OF THE *CHINESE SHAOLIN* TRADITION.
WHO CARES, YO-YO? JUST TELL ME HOW TO *KILL* THEM.
FORGET IT.
I HAVE AN IDEA.
SOMETIMES YOU'VE GOT TO *TAKE* A LITTLE DAMAGE...
BLAMM
...TO BLOW SOMEONE'S *BRAINS* OUT.

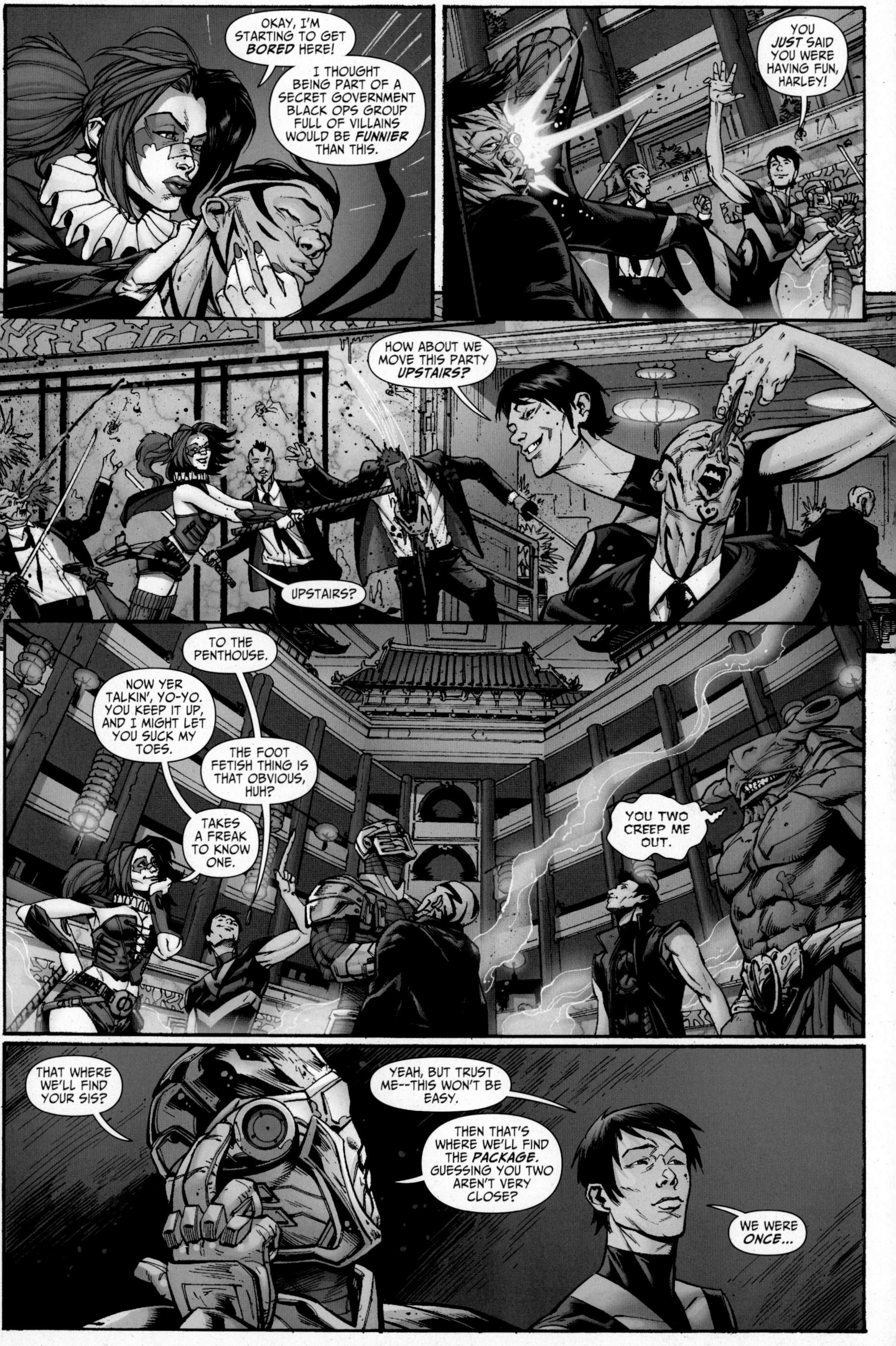
OKAY, I'M STARTING TO GET BORED HERE!
I THOUGHT BEING PART OF A SECRET GOVERNMENT BLACK OPS GROUP FULL OF VILLAINS WOULD BE FUNNIER THAN THIS.
YOU JUST SAID YOU WERE HAVING FUN, HARLEY!
HOW ABOUT WE MOVE THIS PARTY UPSTAIRS?
UPSTAIRS?
TO THE PENTHOUSE.
NOW YER TALKIN', YO-YO. YOU KEEP IT UP, AND I MIGHT LET YOU SUCK MY TOES.
THE FOOT FETISH THING IS THAT OBVIOUS, HUH?
TAKES A FREAK TO KNOW ONE.
YOU TWO CREEP ME OUT.
THAT WHERE WE'LL FIND YOUR SIS?
YEAH, BUT TRUST ME--THIS WON'T BE EASY.
THEN THAT'S WHERE WE'LL FIND THE PACKAGE. GUESSING YOU TWO AREN'T VERY CLOSE?
WE WERE ONCE...

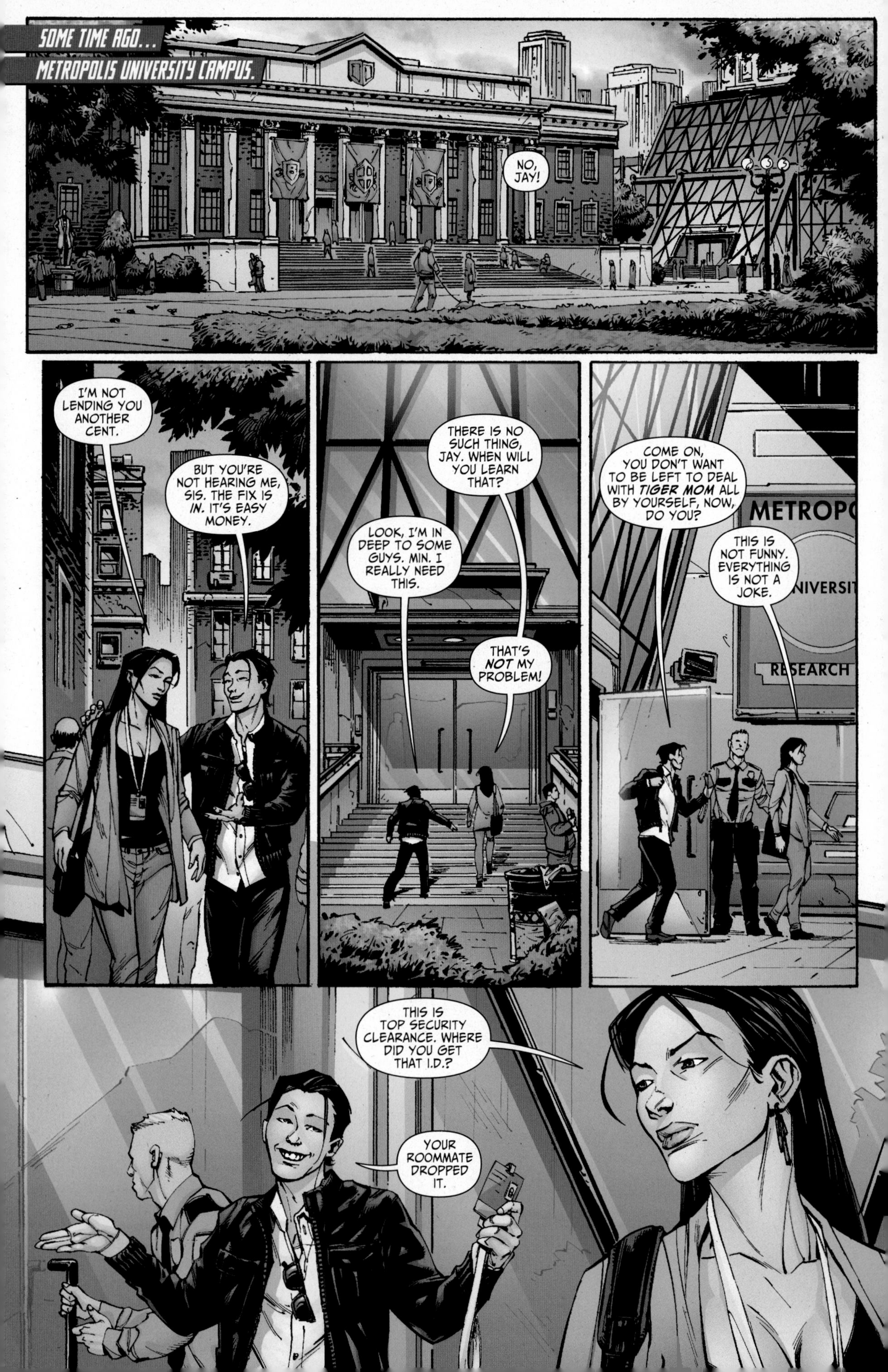
SOME TIME AGO...
METROPOLIS UNIVERSITY CAMPUS.
NO, JAY!
I'M NOT LENDING YOU ANOTHER CENT.
BUT YOU'RE NOT HEARING ME, SIS. THE FIX IS IN. IT'S EASY MONEY.
THERE IS NO SUCH THING, JAY. WHEN WILL YOU LEARN THAT?
LOOK, I'M IN DEEP TO SOME GUYS. MIN. I REALLY NEED THIS.
THAT'S NOT MY PROBLEM!
COME ON, YOU DON'T WANT TO BE LEFT TO DEAL WITH TIGER MOM ALL BY YOURSELF, NOW, DO YOU?
METROPO
THIS IS NOT FUNNY. EVERYTHING IS NOT A JOKE.
UNIVERSIT
RESEARCH
THIS IS TOP SECURITY CLEARANCE. WHERE DID YOU GET THAT I.D.?
YOUR ROOMMATE DROPPED IT.

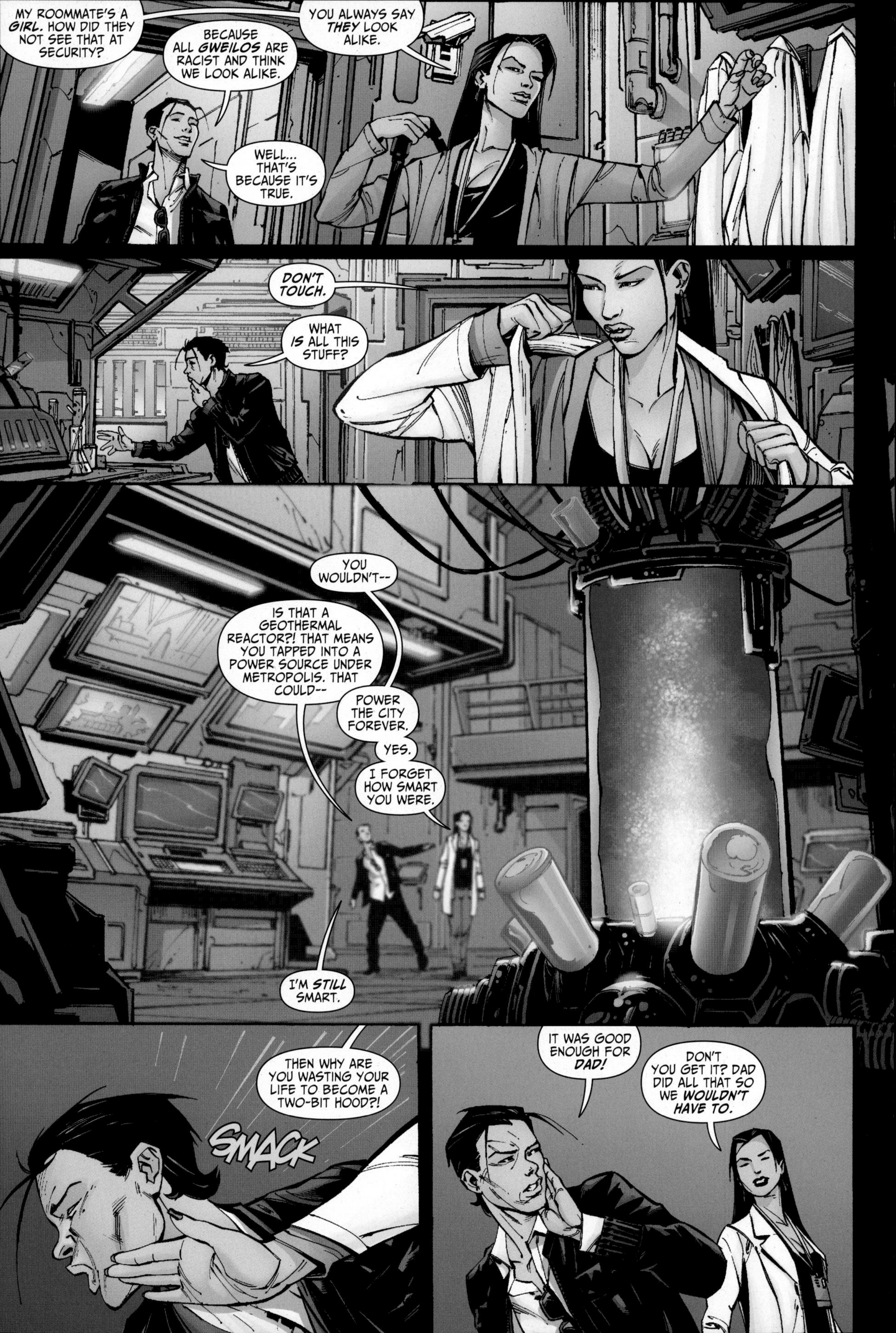
MY ROOMMATE'S A GIRL. HOW DID THEY NOT SEE THAT AT SECURITY?
BECAUSE ALL GWEILOS ARE RACIST AND THINK WE LOOK ALIKE.
YOU ALWAYS SAY THEY LOOK ALIKE.
WELL... THAT'S BECAUSE IT'S TRUE.
DON'T TOUCH.
WHAT IS ALL THIS STUFF?
YOU WOULDN'T--
IS THAT A GEOTHERMAL REACTOR?! THAT MEANS YOU TAPPED INTO A POWER SOURCE UNDER METROPOLIS. THAT COULD--
POWER THE CITY FOREVER.
YES.
I FORGET HOW SMART YOU WERE.
I'M STILL SMART.
THEN WHY ARE YOU WASTING YOUR LIFE TO BECOME A TWO-BIT HOOD?!
SMACK
IT WAS GOOD ENOUGH FOR DAD!
DON'T YOU GET IT? DAD DID ALL THAT SO WE WOULDN'T HAVE TO.

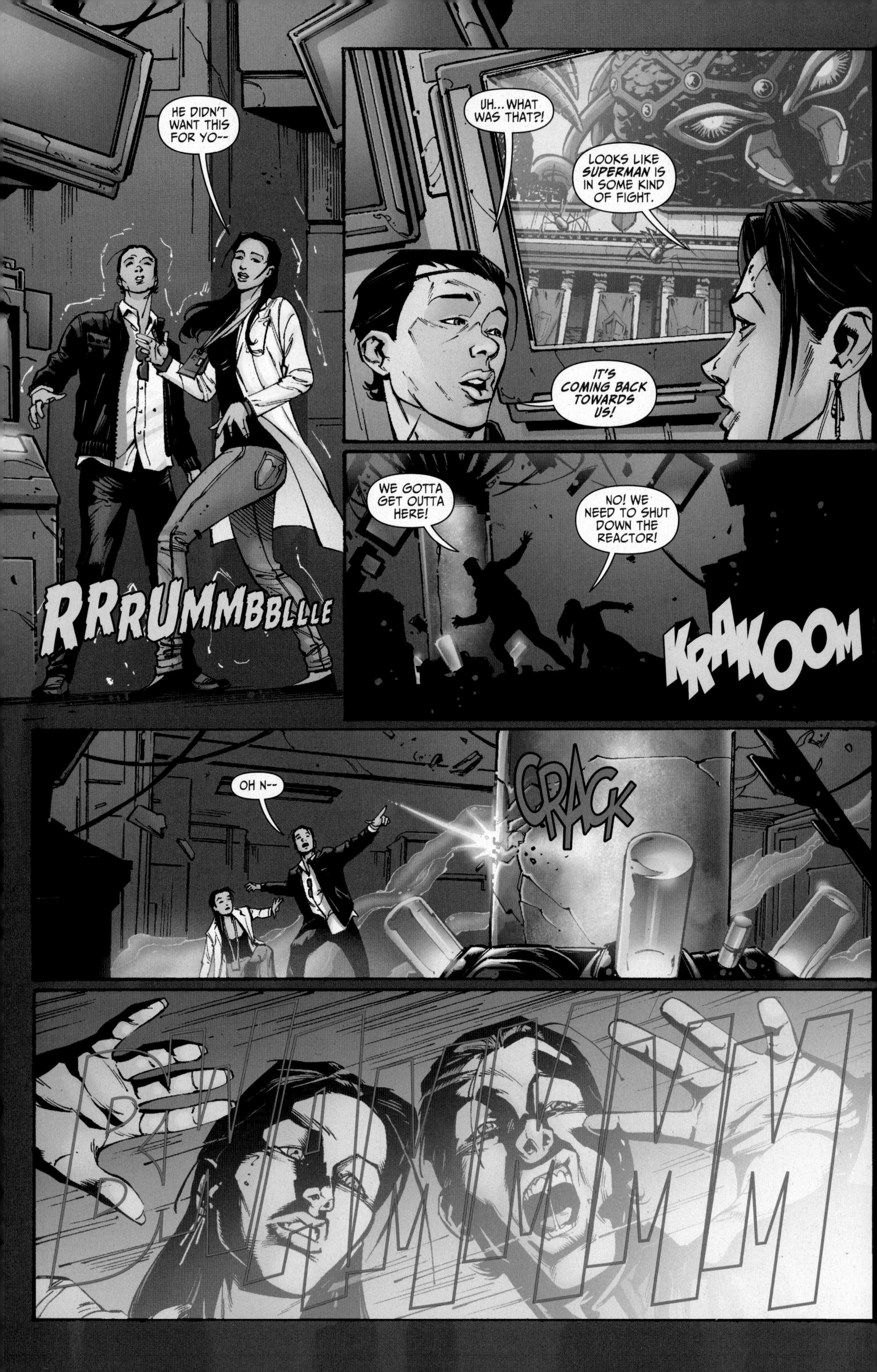
HE DIDN'T WANT THIS FOR YO--
RRRUMMBBLLLE
UH... WHAT WAS THAT?!
LOOKS LIKE SUPERMAN IS IN SOME KIND OF FIGHT.
IT'S COMING BACK TOWARDS US!
WE GOTTA GET OUTTA HERE!
NO! WE NEED TO SHUT DOWN THE REACTOR!
KRAKOOM
OH N--
CRACK

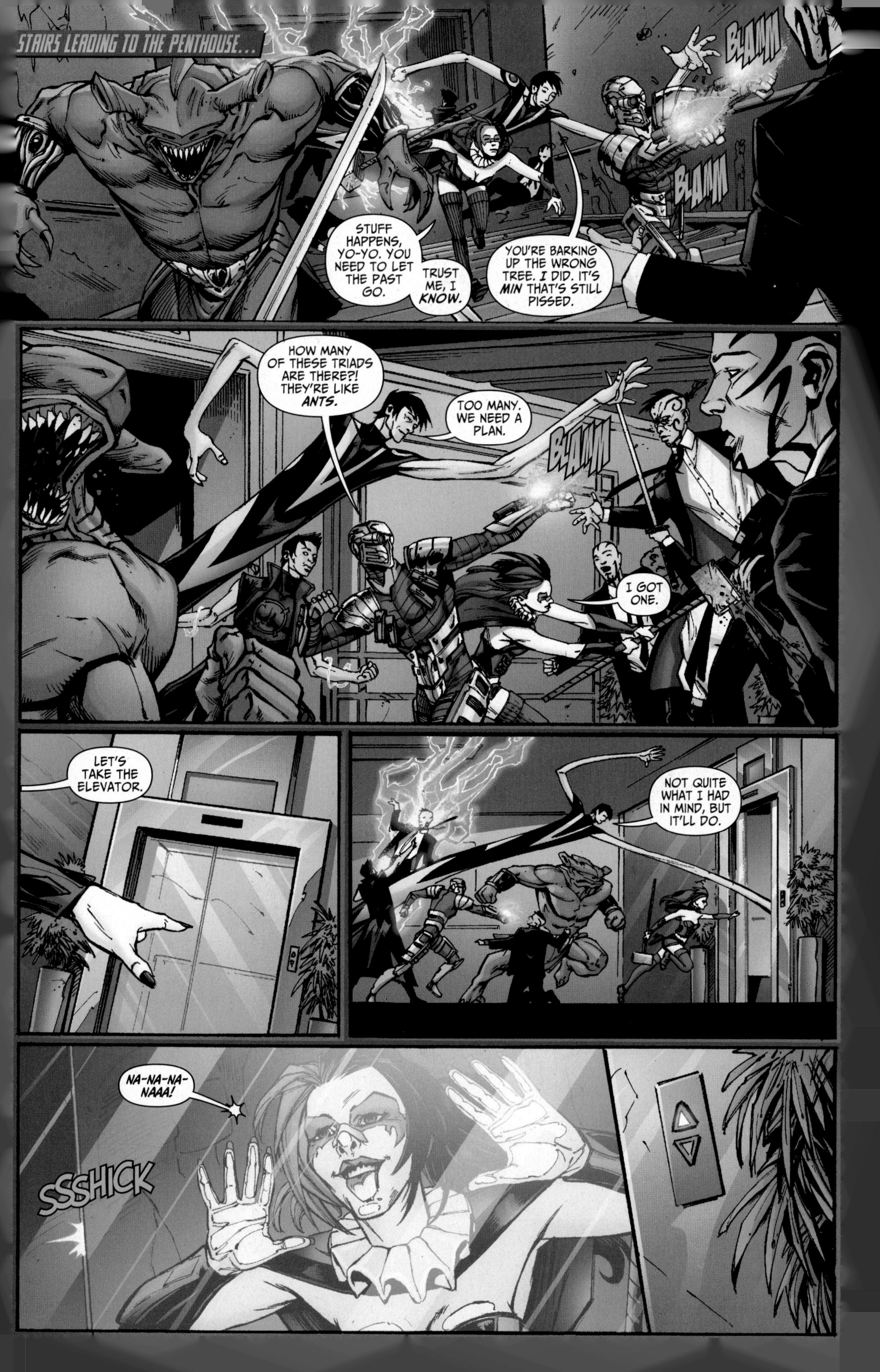
STAIRS LEADING TO THE PENTHOUSE...
BLAMM
BLAMM
STUFF HAPPENS, YO-YO. YOU NEED TO LET THE PAST GO.
TRUST ME, I KNOW.
YOU'RE BARKING UP THE WRONG TREE. I DID. IT'S MIN THAT'S STILL PISSED.
HOW MANY OF THESE TRIADS ARE THERE?! THEY'RE LIKE ANTS.
TOO MANY. WE NEED A PLAN.
BLAMM
I GOT ONE.
LET'S TAKE THE ELEVATOR.
NOT QUITE WHAT I HAD IN MIND, BUT IT'LL DO.
NA-NA-NA-NAAA!
SSSHICK

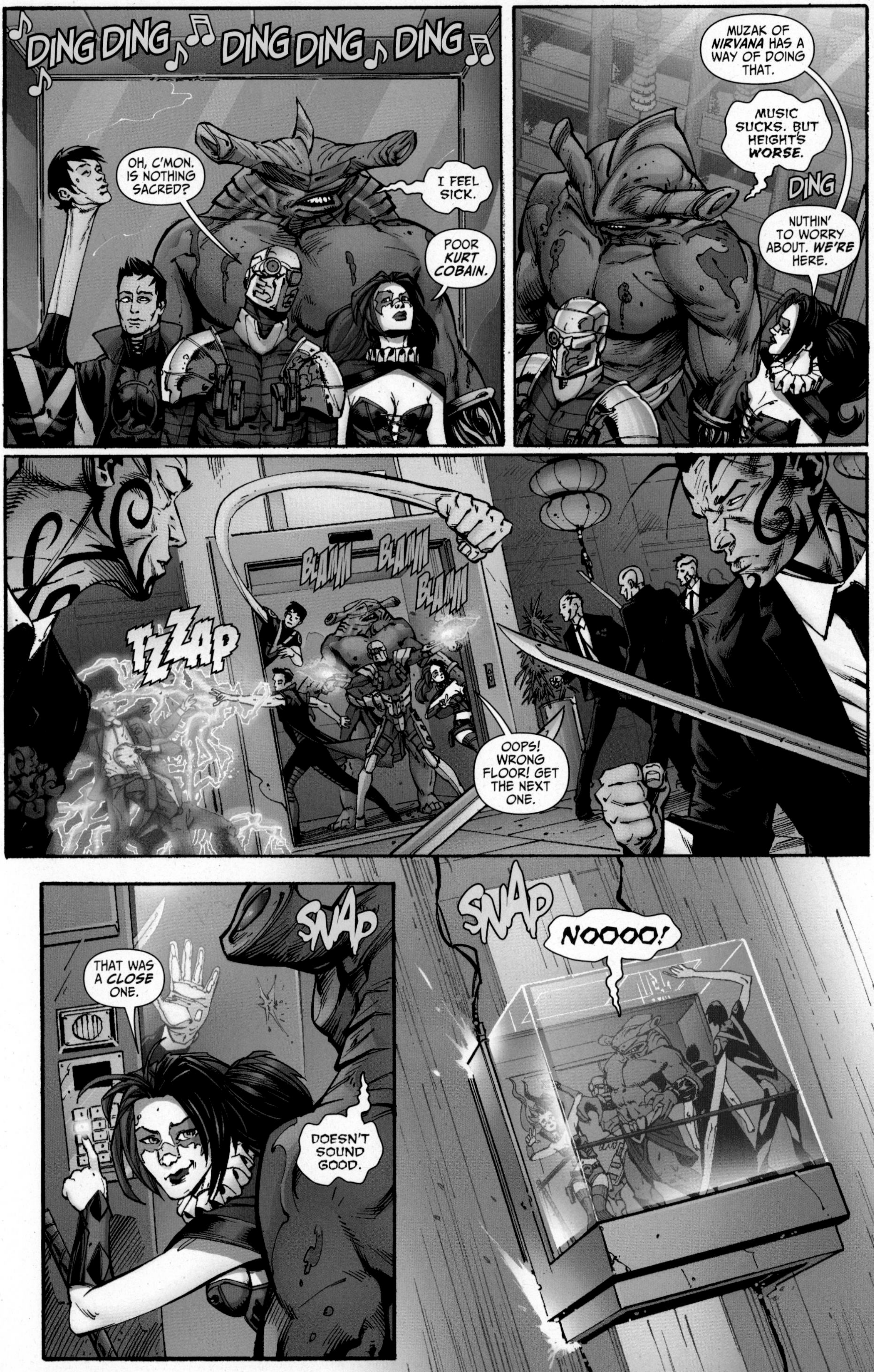
DING DING DING DING DING
OH, C'MON. IS NOTHING SACRED?
I FEEL SICK.
POOR KURT COBAIN.
MUZAK OF NIRVANA HAS A WAY OF DOING THAT.
MUSIC SUCKS. BUT HEIGHT'S WORSE.
DING
NUTHIN' TO WORRY ABOUT. WE'RE HERE.
BLAMM BLAMM BLAMM
TZZAP
OOPS! WRONG FLOOR! GET THE NEXT ONE.
SNAP
THAT WAS A CLOSE ONE.
DOESN'T SOUND GOOD.
SNAP
NOOOO!

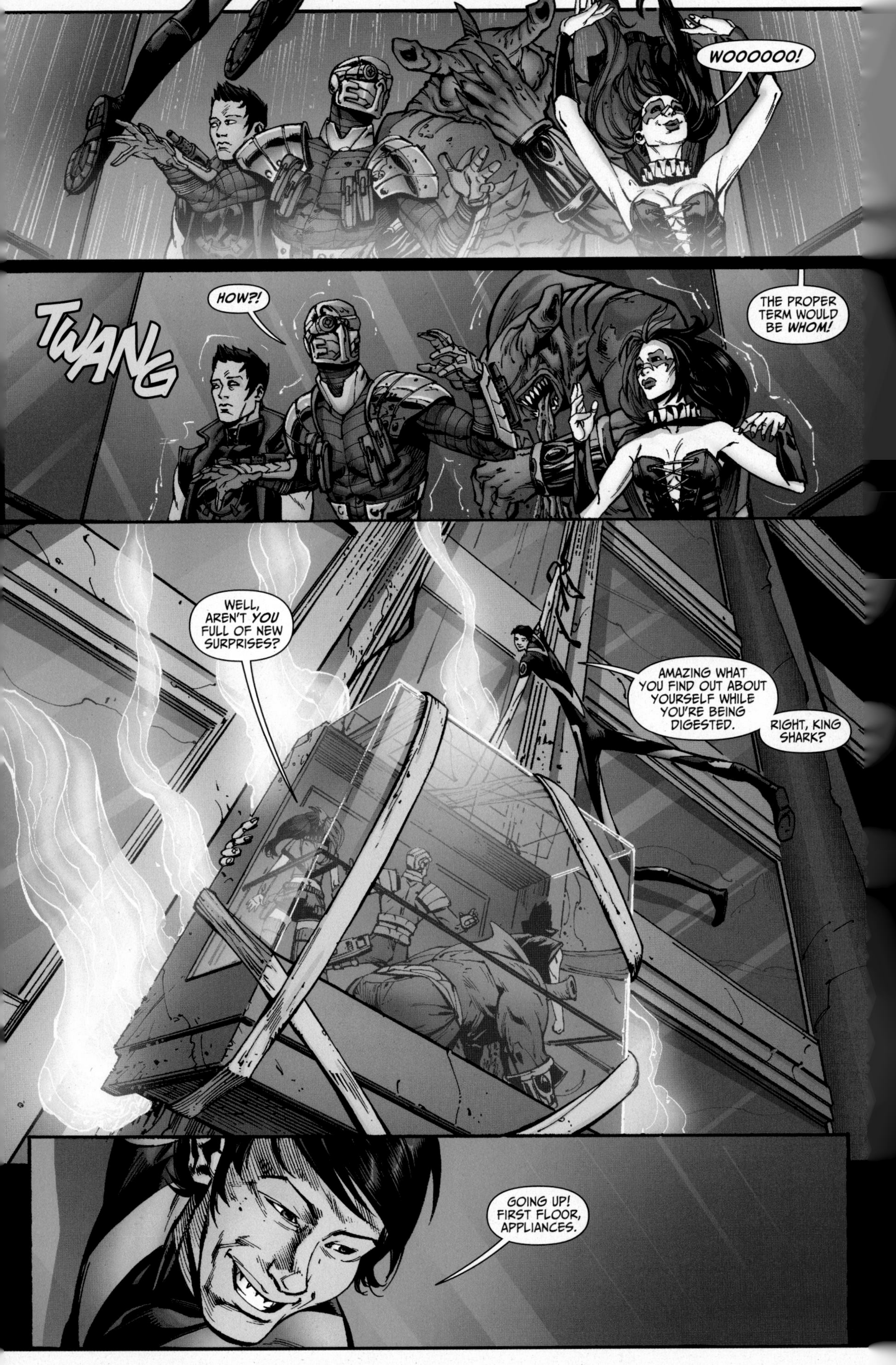
WOOOOOO!
TWANG
HOW?!
THE PROPER TERM WOULD BE WHOM!
WELL, AREN'T YOU FULL OF NEW SURPRISES?
AMAZING WHAT YOU FIND OUT ABOUT YOURSELF WHILE YOU'RE BEING DIGESTED.
RIGHT, KING SHARK?
GOING UP! FIRST FLOOR, APPLIANCES.

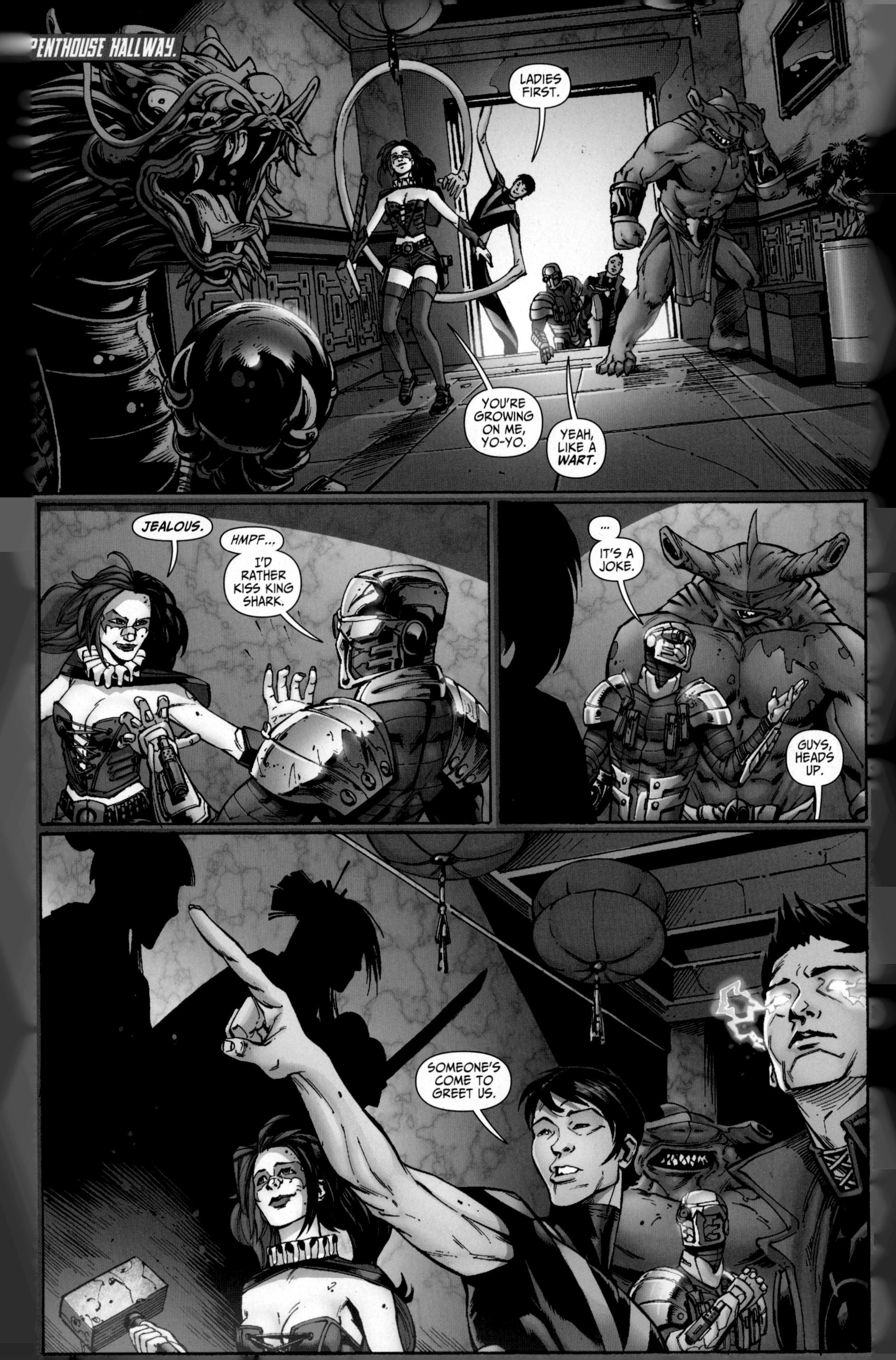
PENTHOUSE HALLWAY.
LADIES FIRST.
YOU'RE GROWING ON ME, YO-YO.
YEAH, LIKE A WART.
JEALOUS.
HMPF...
I'D RATHER KISS KING SHARK.
...
IT'S A JOKE.
GUYS, HEADS UP.
SOMEONE'S COME TO GREET US.

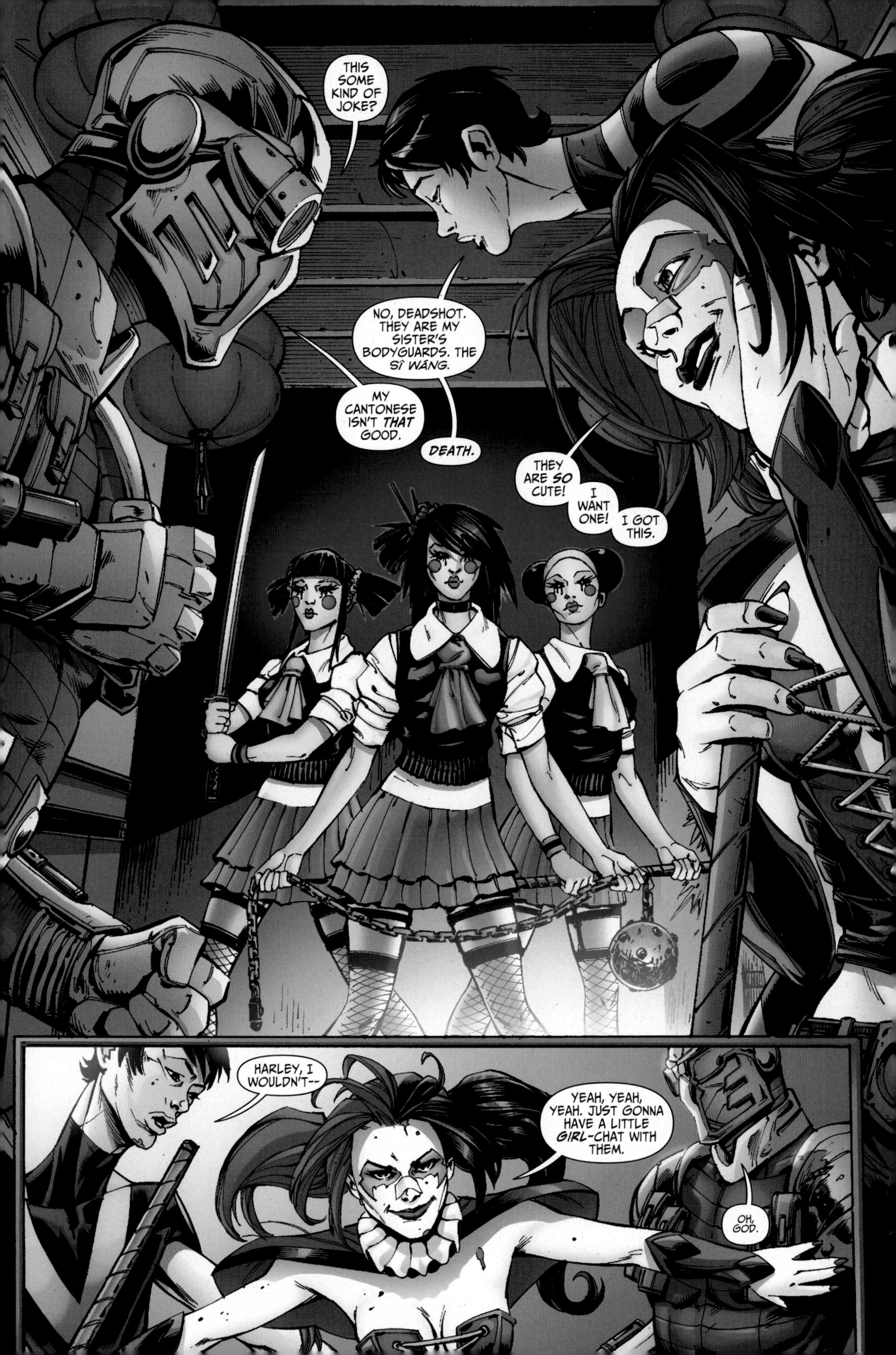
THIS SOME KIND OF JOKE?
NO, DEADSHOT. THEY ARE MY SISTER'S BODYGUARDS. THE SÎ WÁNG.
MY CANTONESE ISN'T THAT GOOD.
DEATH.
THEY ARE SO CUTE!
I WANT ONE!
I GOT THIS.
HARLEY, I WOULDN'T--
YEAH, YEAH, YEAH. JUST GONNA HAVE A LITTLE GIRL-CHAT WITH THEM.
OH, GOD.

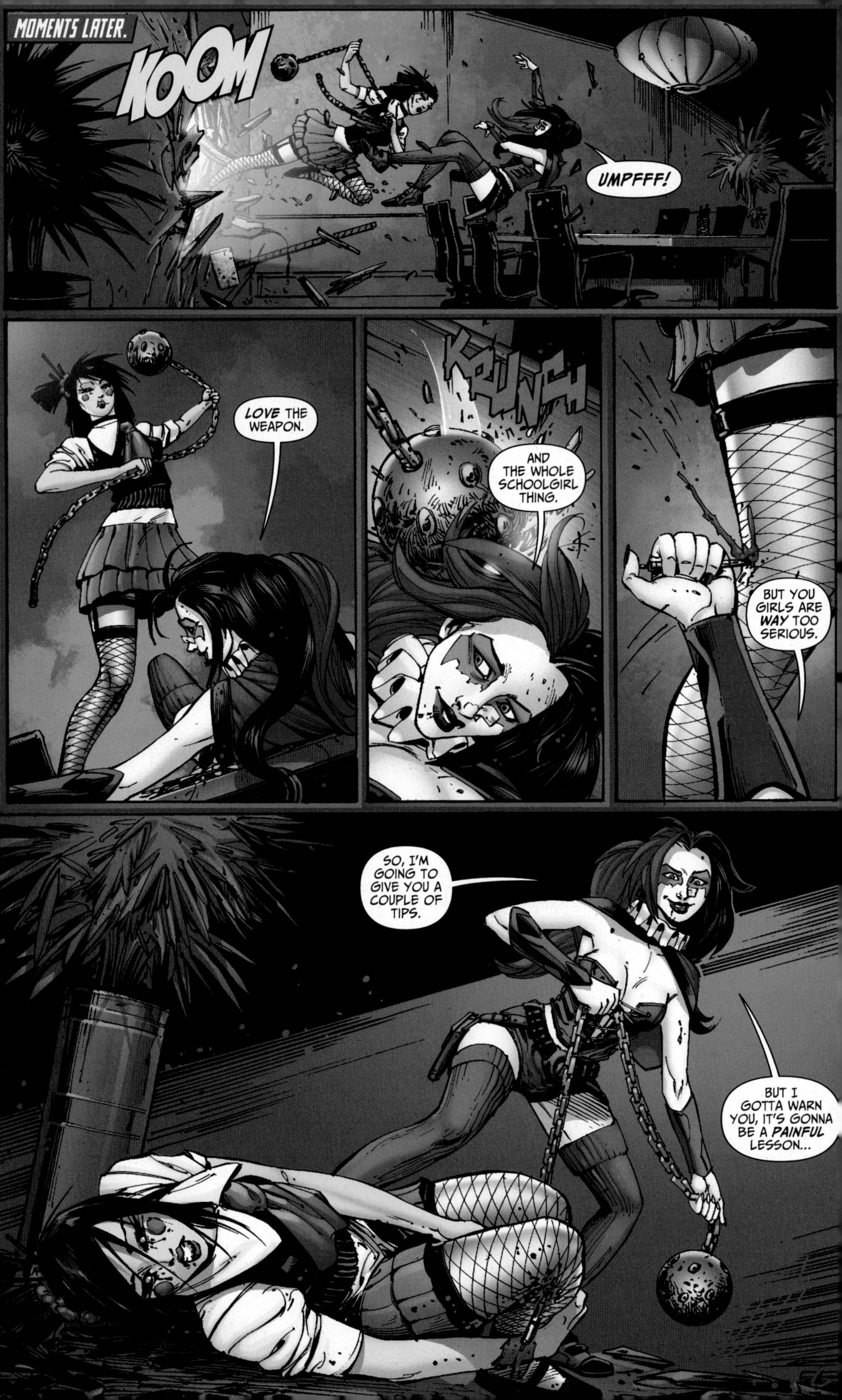
MOMENTS LATER.
KOOM
UMPFFF!
LOVE THE WEAPON.
KRUNCH
AND THE WHOLE SCHOOLGIRL THING.
BUT YOU GIRLS ARE WAY TOO SERIOUS.
SO, I'M GOING TO GIVE YOU A COUPLE OF TIPS.
BUT I GOTTA WARN YOU, IT'S GONNA BE A PAINFUL LESSON...

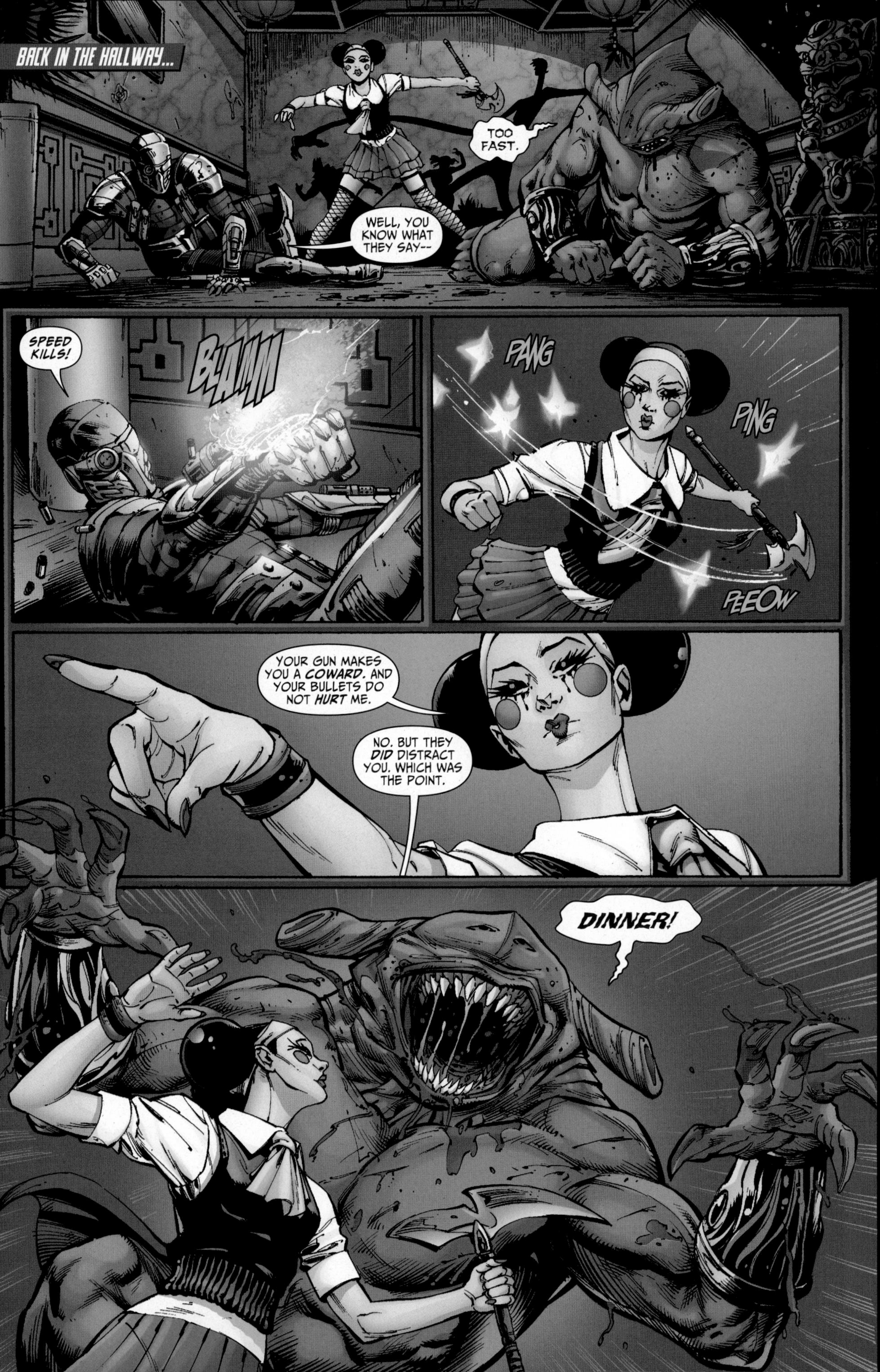
BACK IN THE HALLWAY...
TOO FAST.
WELL, YOU KNOW WHAT THEY SAY--
SPEED KILLS!
BLAMM
PANG
PING
PEEOW
YOUR GUN MAKES YOU A COWARD. AND YOUR BULLETS DO NOT HURT ME.
NO. BUT THEY DID DISTRACT YOU. WHICH WAS THE POINT.
DINNER!

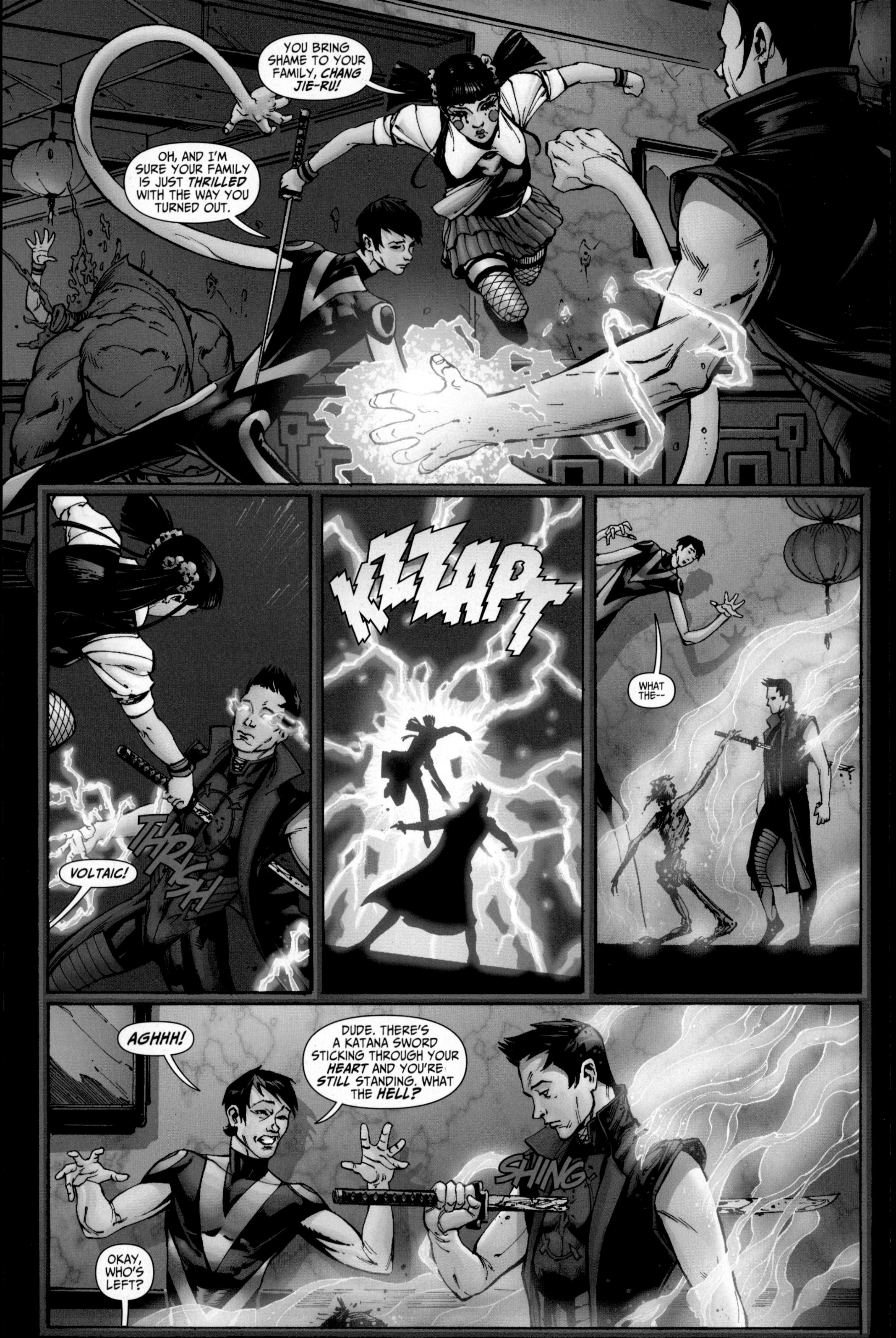
YOU BRING SHAME TO YOUR FAMILY, CHANG JIE-RU!
OH, AND I'M SURE YOUR FAMILY IS JUST THRILLED WITH THE WAY YOU TURNED OUT.
THRISH
VOLTAIC!
KZZAPT
WHAT THE--
AGHHH!
DUDE. THERE'S A KATANA SWORD STICKING THROUGH YOUR HEART AND YOU'RE STILL STANDING. WHAT THE HELL?
SHING
OKAY, WHO'S LEFT?

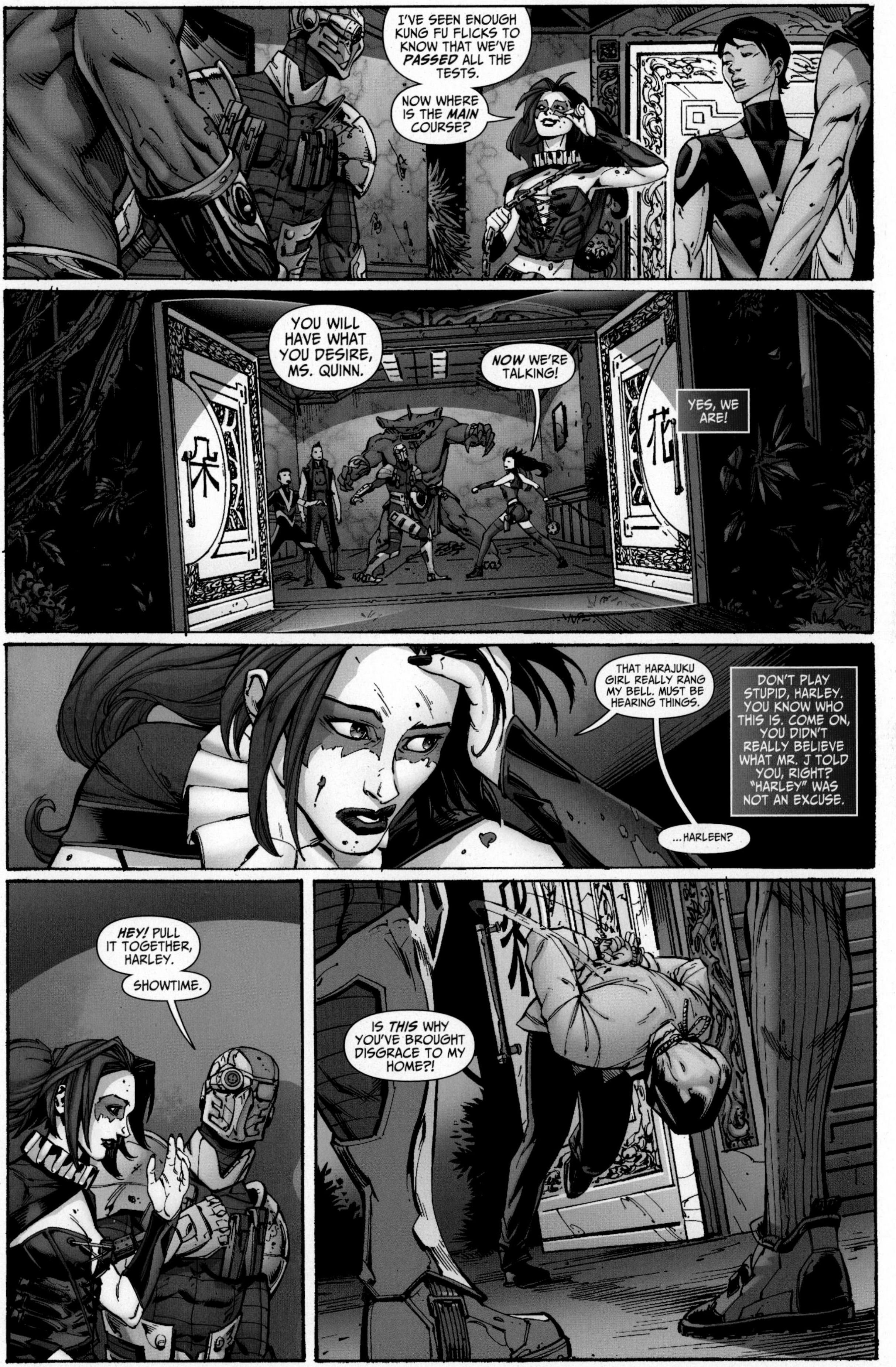
I'VE SEEN ENOUGH KUNG FU FLICKS TO KNOW THAT WE'VE PASSED ALL THE TESTS.
NOW WHERE IS THE MAIN COURSE?
YOU WILL HAVE WHAT YOU DESIRE, MS. QUINN.
NOW WE'RE TALKING!
YES, WE ARE!
THAT HARAJUKU GIRL REALLY RANG MY BELL. MUST BE HEARING THINGS.
DON'T PLAY STUPID, HARLEY. YOU KNOW WHO THIS IS. COME ON, YOU DIDN'T REALLY BELIEVE WHAT MR. J TOLD YOU, RIGHT? "HARLEY" WAS NOT AN EXCUSE.
...HARLEEN?
HEY! PULL IT TOGETHER, HARLEY.
SHOWTIME.
IS THIS WHY YOU'VE BROUGHT DISGRACE TO MY HOME?!

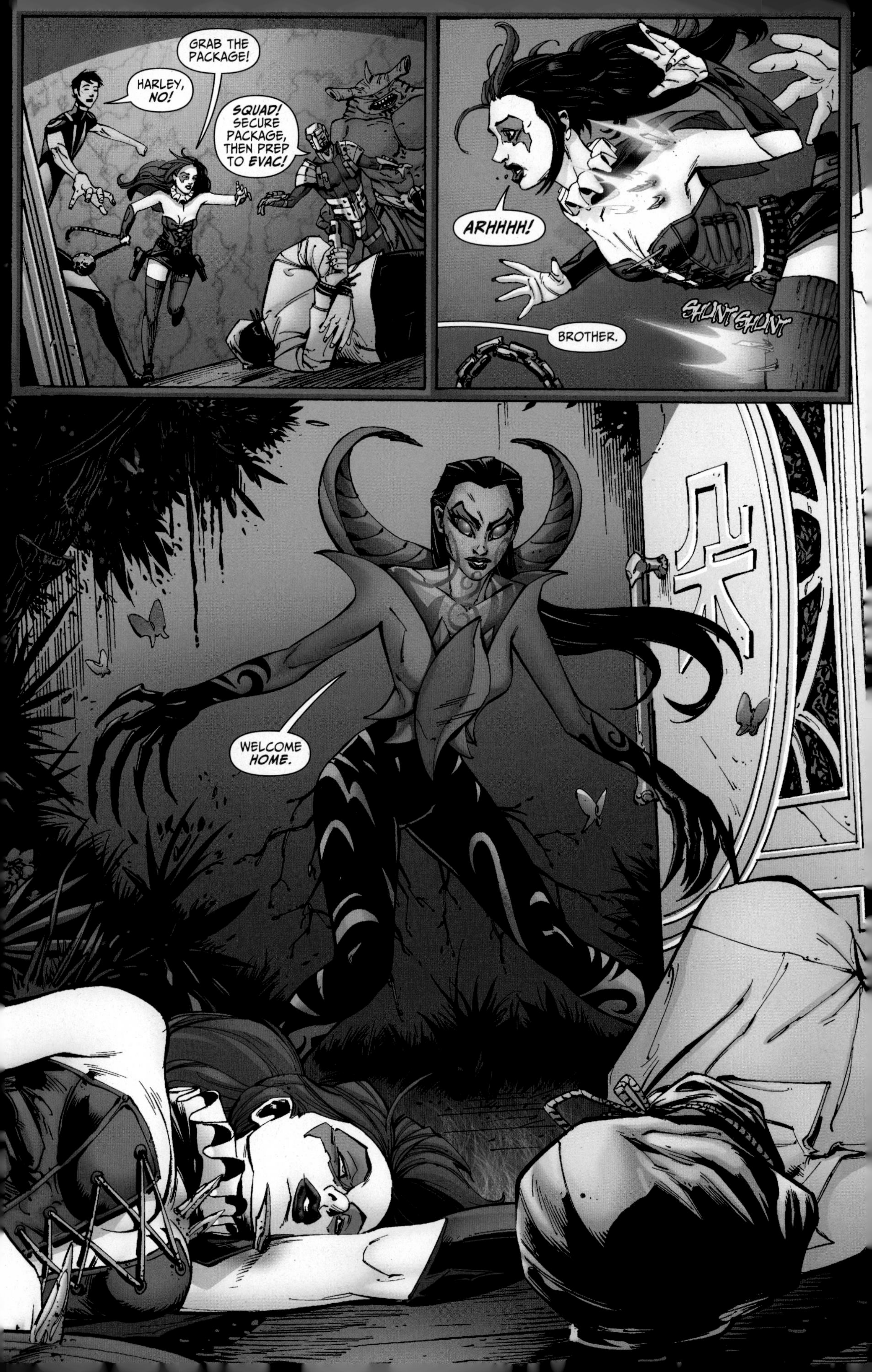
GRAB THE PACKAGE!
HARLEY, NO!
SQUAD! SECURE PACKAGE, THEN PREP TO EVAC!
ARHHHH!
SHUNT SHUNT
BROTHER.
WELCOME HOME.

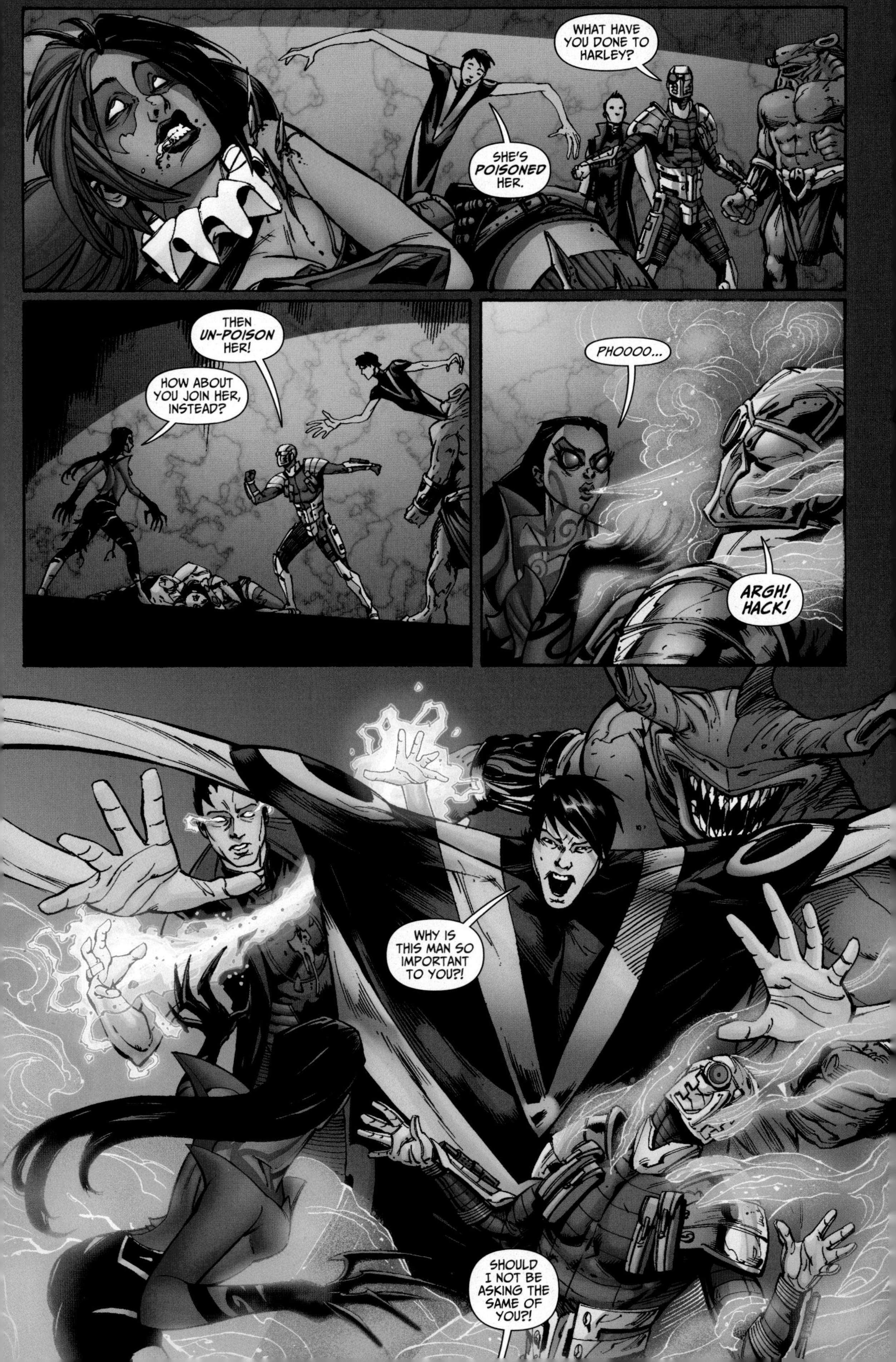
WHAT HAVE YOU DONE TO HARLEY?
SHE'S POISONED HER.
THEN UN-POISON HER!
HOW ABOUT YOU JOIN HER, INSTEAD?
PHOOOO...
ARGH! HACK!
WHY IS THIS MAN SO IMPORTANT TO YOU?!
SHOULD I NOT BE ASKING THE SAME OF YOU?!

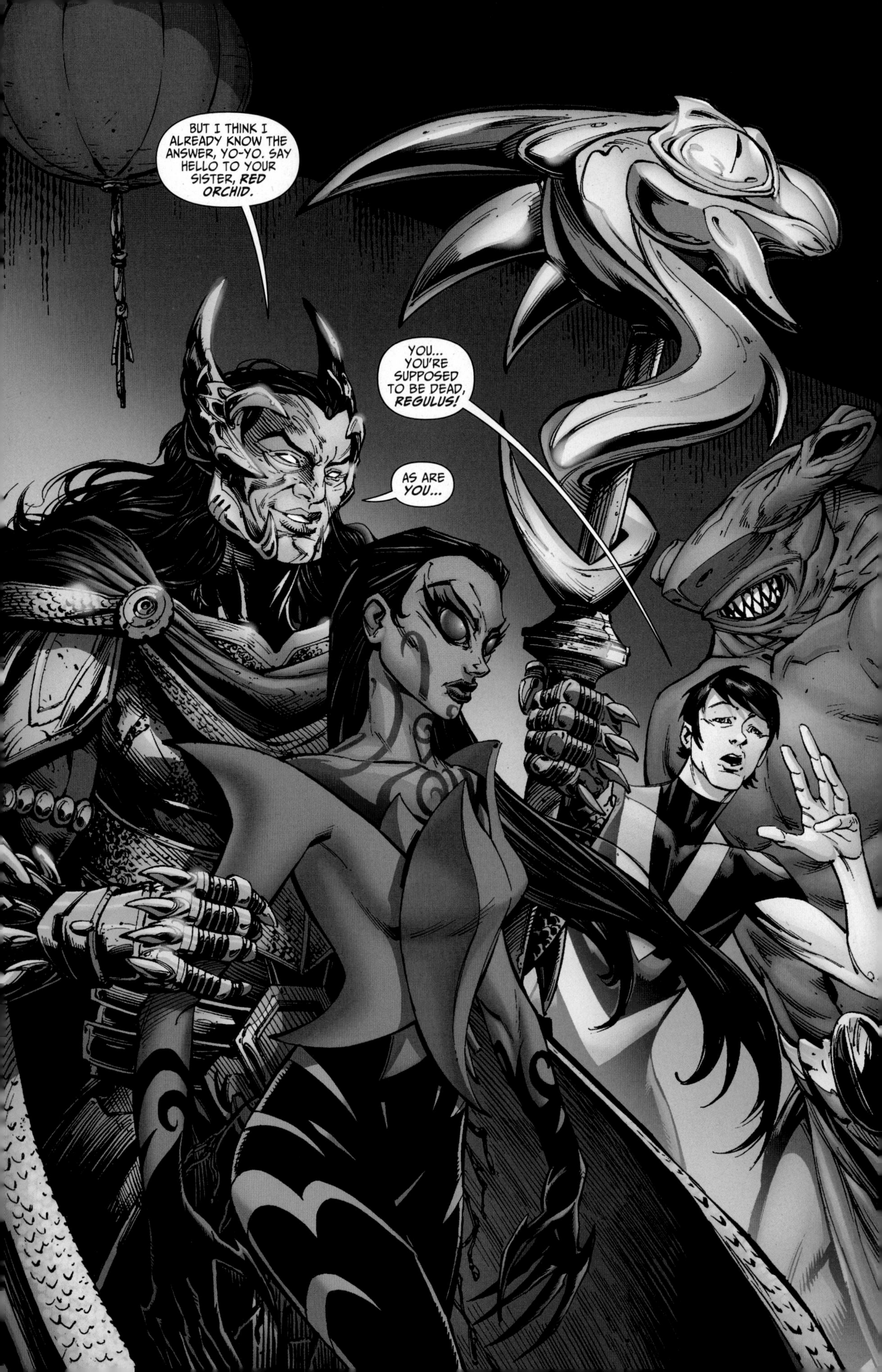
BUT I THINK I ALREADY KNOW THE ANSWER, YO-YO. SAY HELLO TO YOUR SISTER, *RED ORCHID.*
YOU... YOU'RE SUPPOSED TO BE DEAD, *REGULUS!*
AS ARE *YOU...*

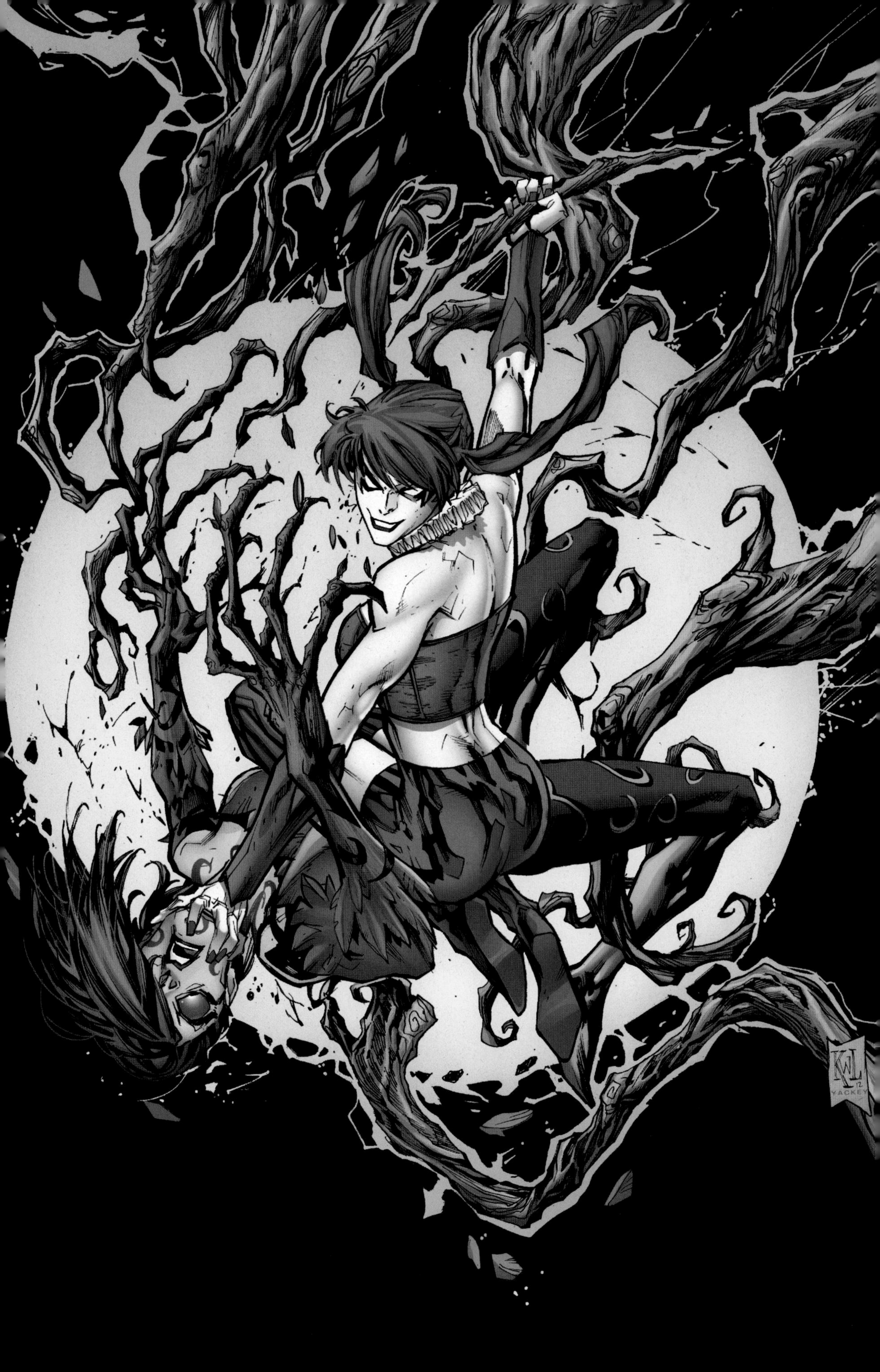

DEATH BLOOMS

ADAM GLASS writer **HENRIK JONSSON** penciller **SANDU FLOREA** inker cover art by **KEN LASHLEY & MATT YACKEY**

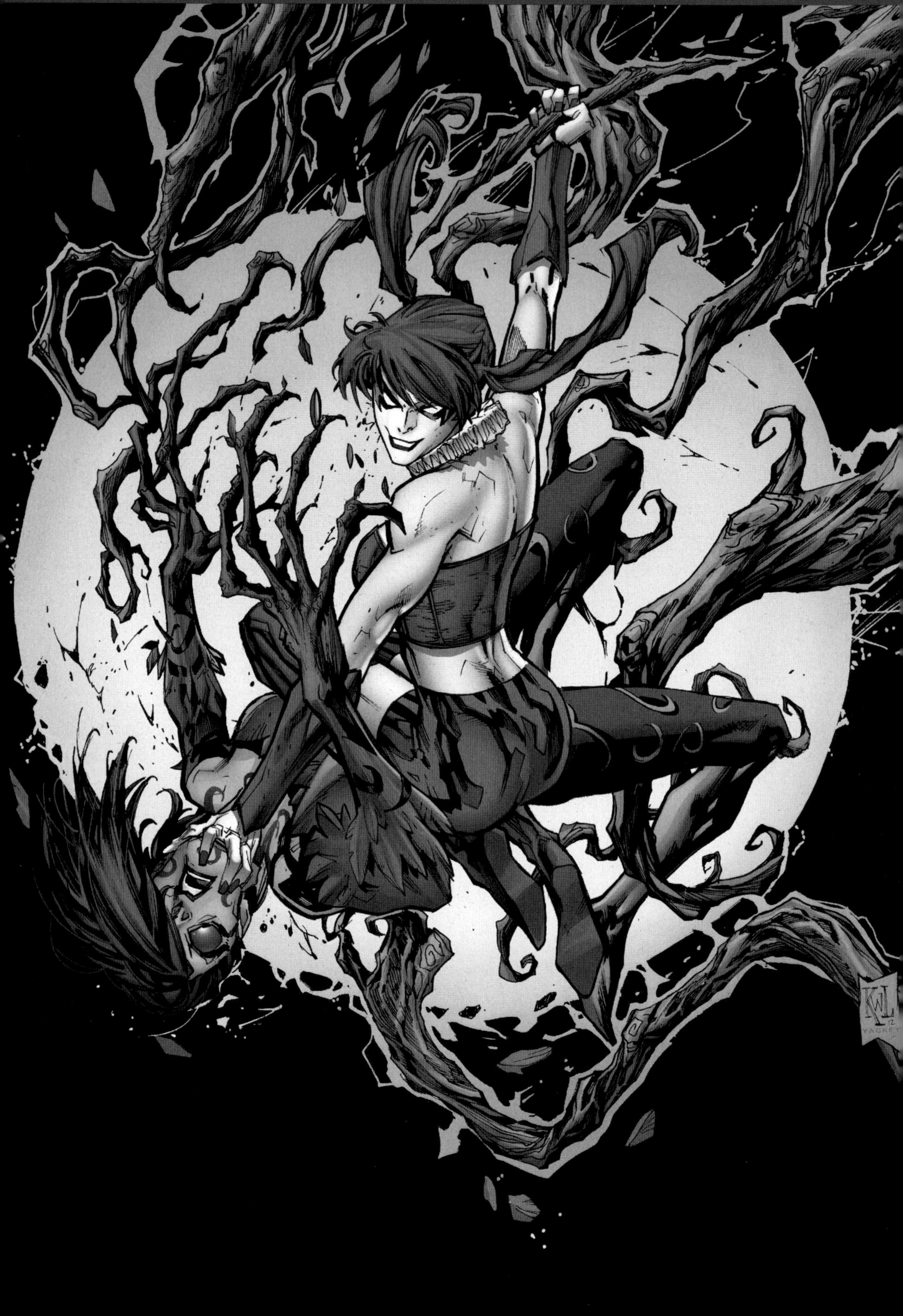

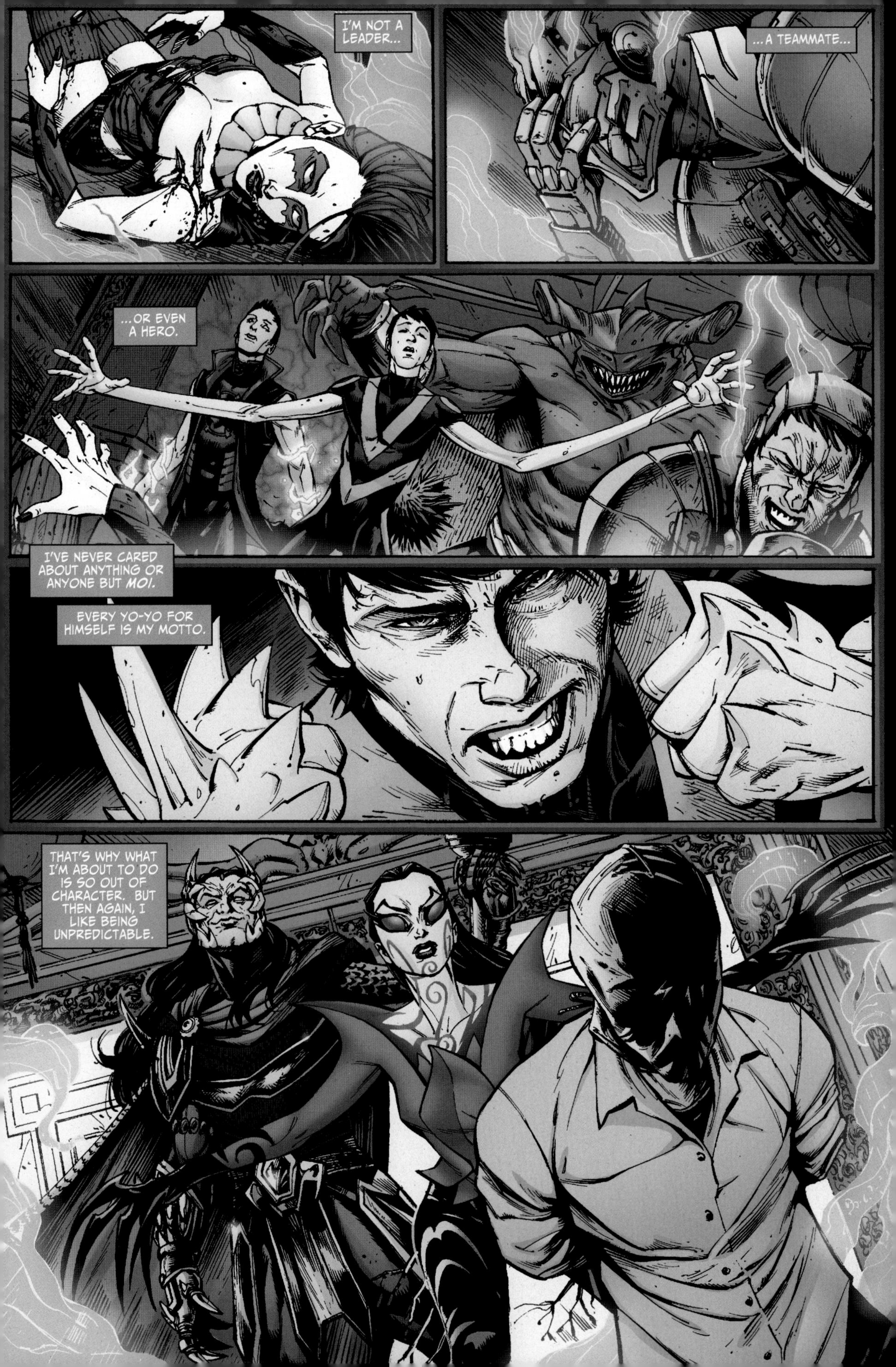

I'M NOT A LEADER...
...A TEAMMATE...
...OR EVEN A HERO.
I'VE NEVER CARED ABOUT ANYTHING OR ANYONE BUT MOI.
EVERY YO-YO FOR HIMSELF IS MY MOTTO.
THAT'S WHY WHAT I'M ABOUT TO DO IS SO OUT OF CHARACTER. BUT THEN AGAIN, I LIKE BEING UNPREDICTABLE.

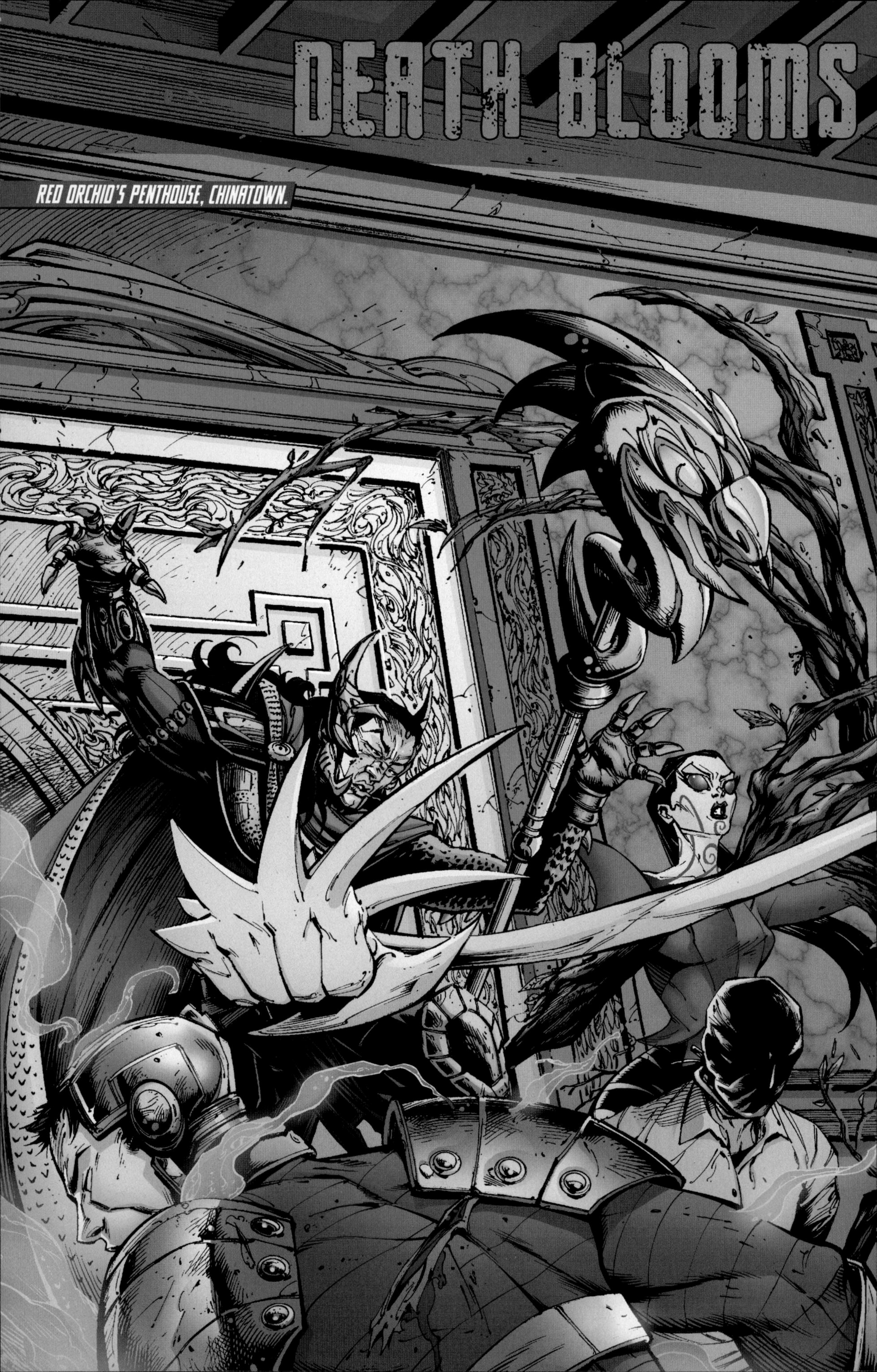
DEATH BLOOMS
RED ORCHID'S PENTHOUSE, CHINATOWN.

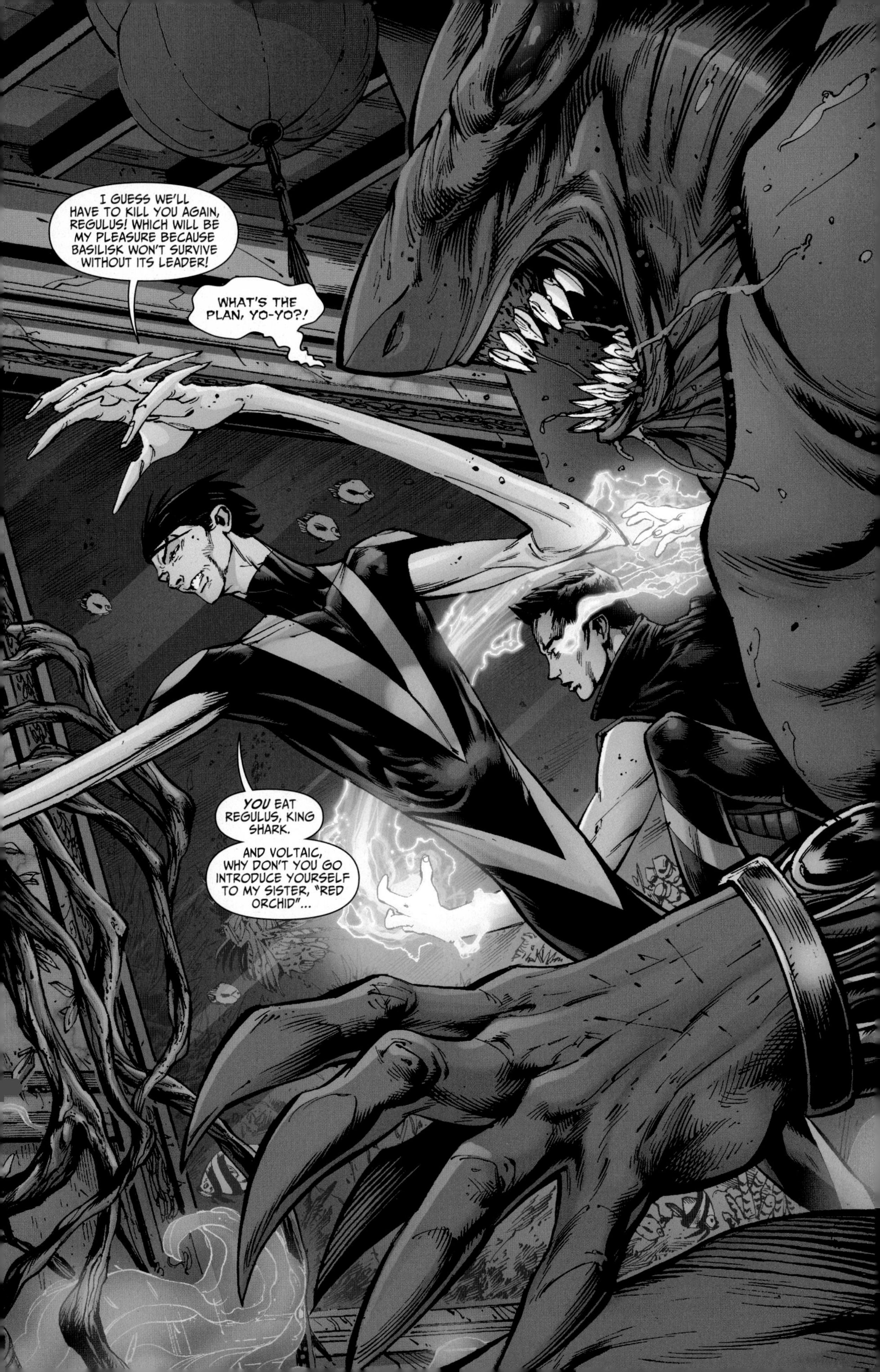
I GUESS WE'LL HAVE TO KILL YOU AGAIN, REGULUS! WHICH WILL BE MY PLEASURE BECAUSE BASILISK WON'T SURVIVE WITHOUT ITS LEADER!
WHAT'S THE PLAN, YO-YO?!
YOU EAT REGULUS, KING SHARK.
AND VOLTAIC, WHY DON'T YOU GO INTRODUCE YOURSELF TO MY SISTER, "RED ORCHID"...

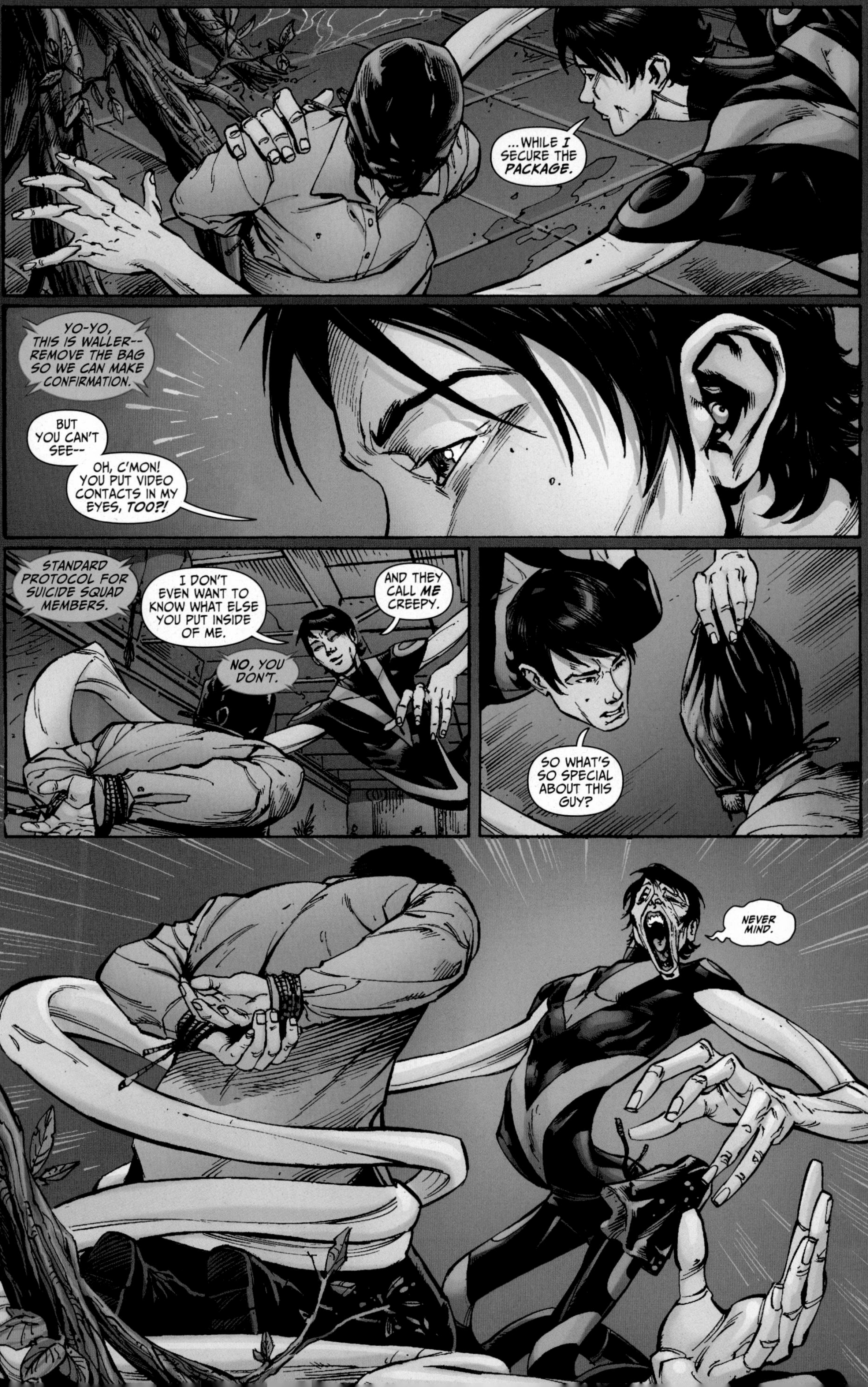
...WHILE I SECURE THE PACKAGE.
YO-YO, THIS IS WALLER-- REMOVE THE BAG SO WE CAN MAKE CONFIRMATION.
BUT YOU CAN'T SEE--
OH, C'MON! YOU PUT VIDEO CONTACTS IN MY EYES, TOO?!
STANDARD PROTOCOL FOR SUICIDE SQUAD MEMBERS.
I DON'T EVEN WANT TO KNOW WHAT ELSE YOU PUT INSIDE OF ME.
NO, YOU DON'T.
AND THEY CALL ME CREEPY.
SO WHAT'S SO SPECIAL ABOUT THIS GUY?
NEVER MIND.

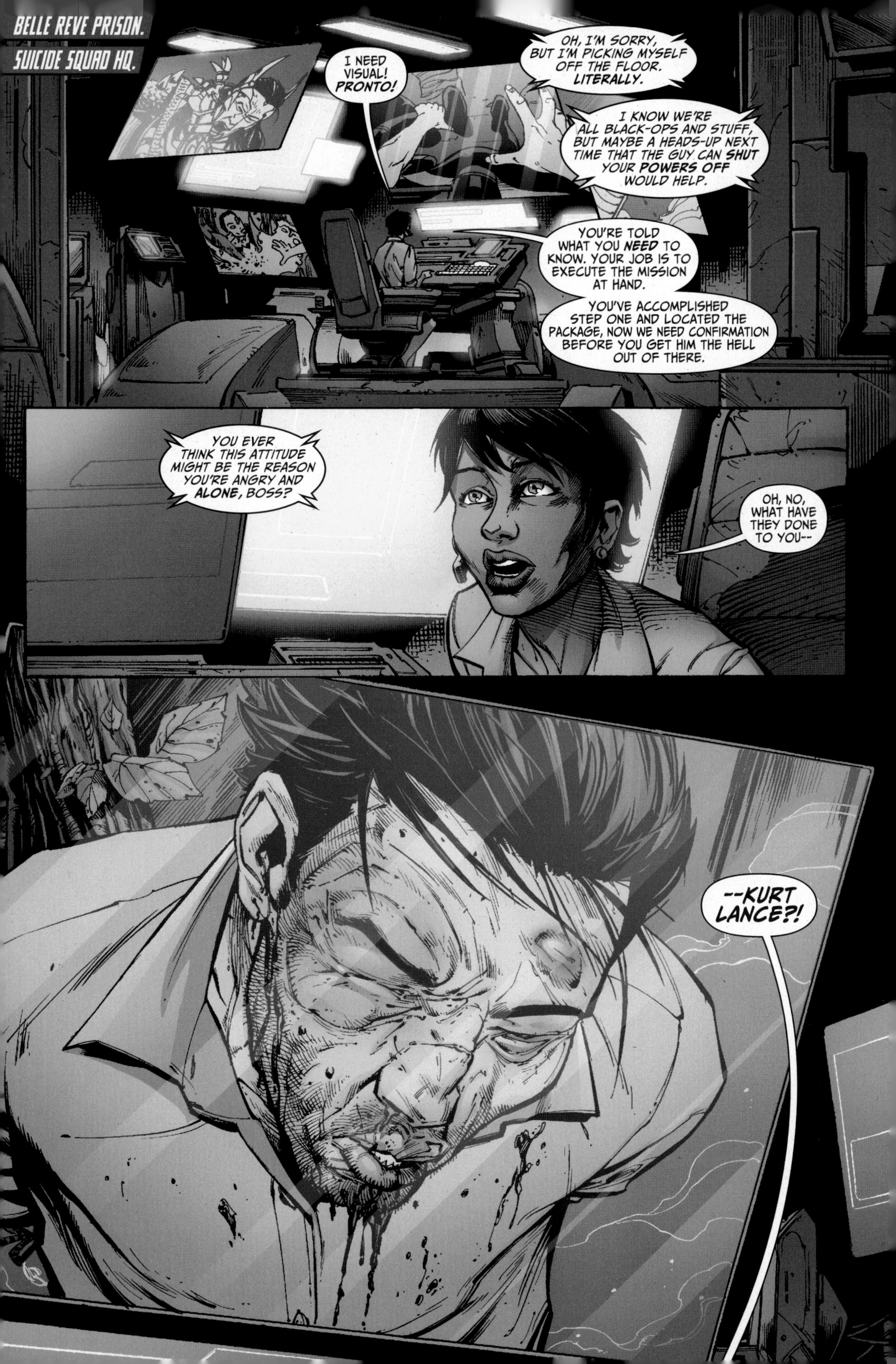
BELLE REVE PRISON.
SUICIDE SQUAD HQ.
I NEED VISUAL! PRONTO!
OH, I'M SORRY, BUT I'M PICKING MYSELF OFF THE FLOOR. LITERALLY.
I KNOW WE'RE ALL BLACK-OPS AND STUFF, BUT MAYBE A HEADS-UP NEXT TIME THAT THE GUY CAN SHUT YOUR POWERS OFF WOULD HELP.
YOU'RE TOLD WHAT YOU NEED TO KNOW. YOUR JOB IS TO EXECUTE THE MISSION AT HAND.
YOU'VE ACCOMPLISHED STEP ONE AND LOCATED THE PACKAGE, NOW WE NEED CONFIRMATION BEFORE YOU GET HIM THE HELL OUT OF THERE.
YOU EVER THINK THIS ATTITUDE MIGHT BE THE REASON YOU'RE ANGRY AND ALONE, BOSS?
OH, NO, WHAT HAVE THEY DONE TO YOU--
--KURT LANCE?!

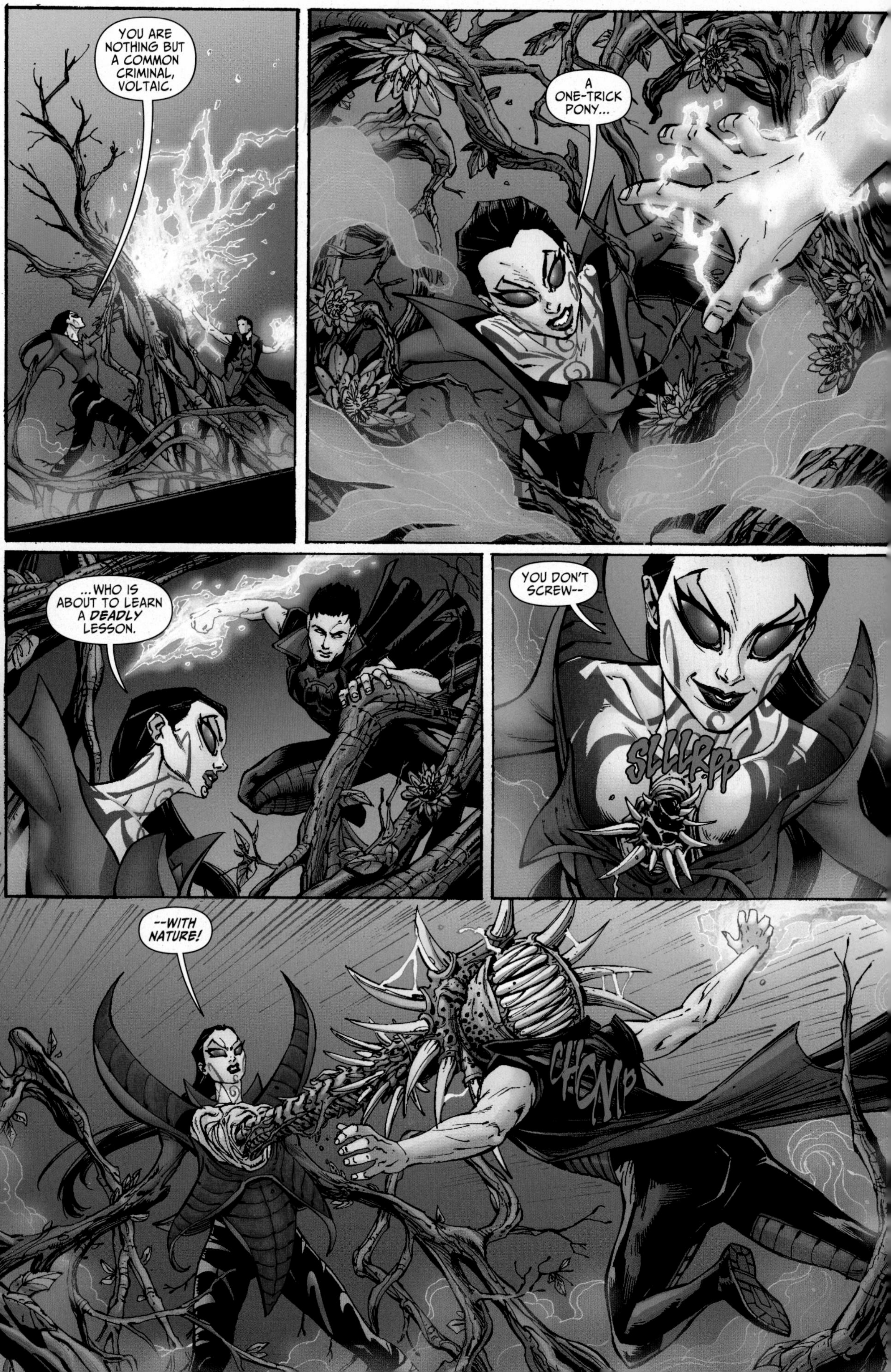

YOU ARE NOTHING BUT A COMMON CRIMINAL, VOLTAIC.
A ONE-TRICK PONY...
...WHO IS ABOUT TO LEARN A *DEADLY* LESSON.
YOU DON'T SCREW--
SLLLRPP
--WITH *NATURE!*
CHOMP

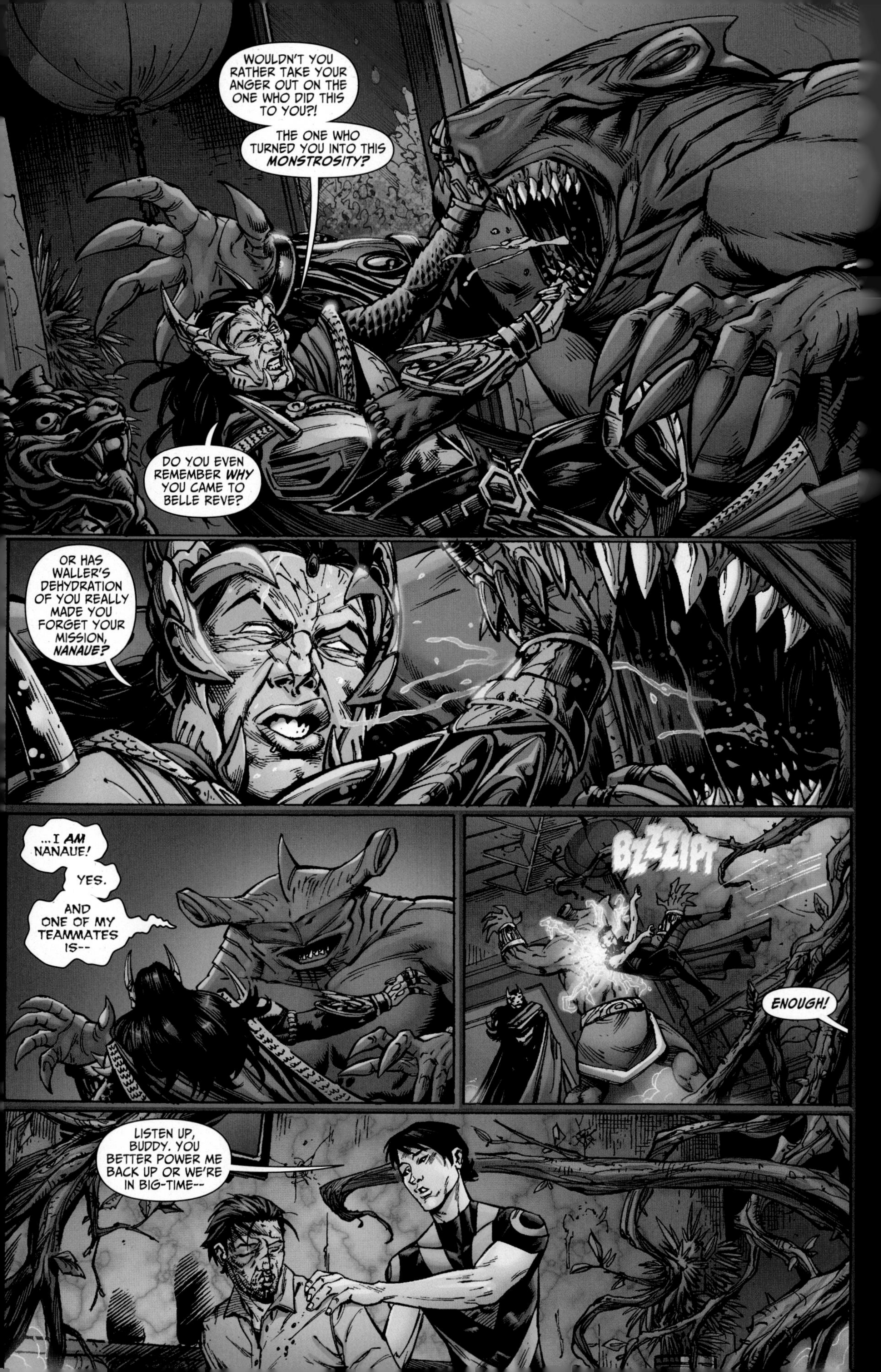
WOULDN'T YOU RATHER TAKE YOUR ANGER OUT ON THE ONE WHO DID THIS TO YOU?!
THE ONE WHO TURNED YOU INTO THIS MONSTROSITY?
DO YOU EVEN REMEMBER WHY YOU CAME TO BELLE REVE?
OR HAS WALLER'S DEHYDRATION OF YOU REALLY MADE YOU FORGET YOUR MISSION, NANAUE?
...I AM NANAUE!
YES.
AND ONE OF MY TEAMMATES IS--
BZZZIPT
ENOUGH!
LISTEN UP, BUDDY. YOU BETTER POWER ME BACK UP OR WE'RE IN BIG-TIME--

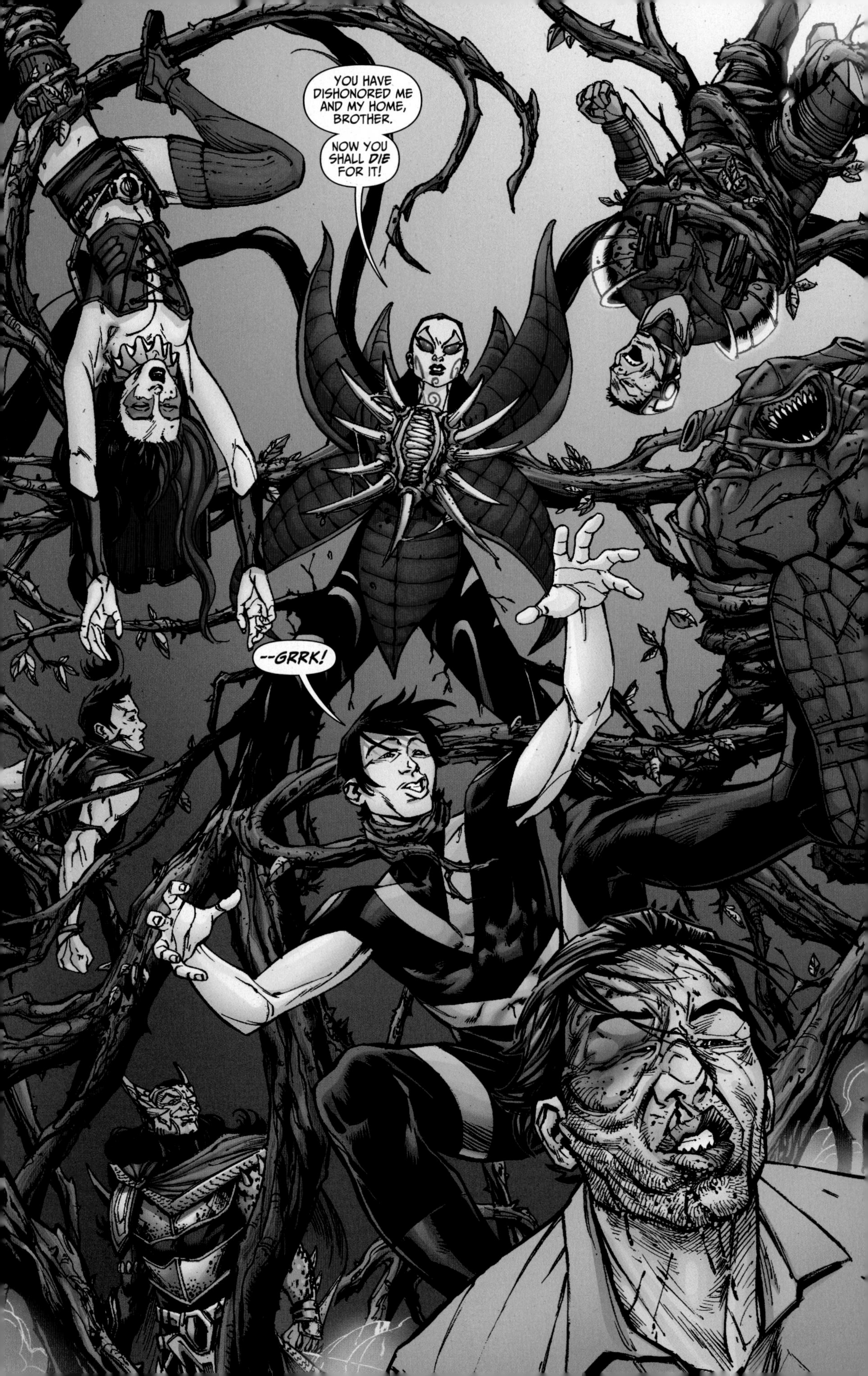
YOU HAVE DISHONORED ME AND MY HOME, BROTHER.
NOW YOU SHALL *DIE* FOR IT!
--GRRK!

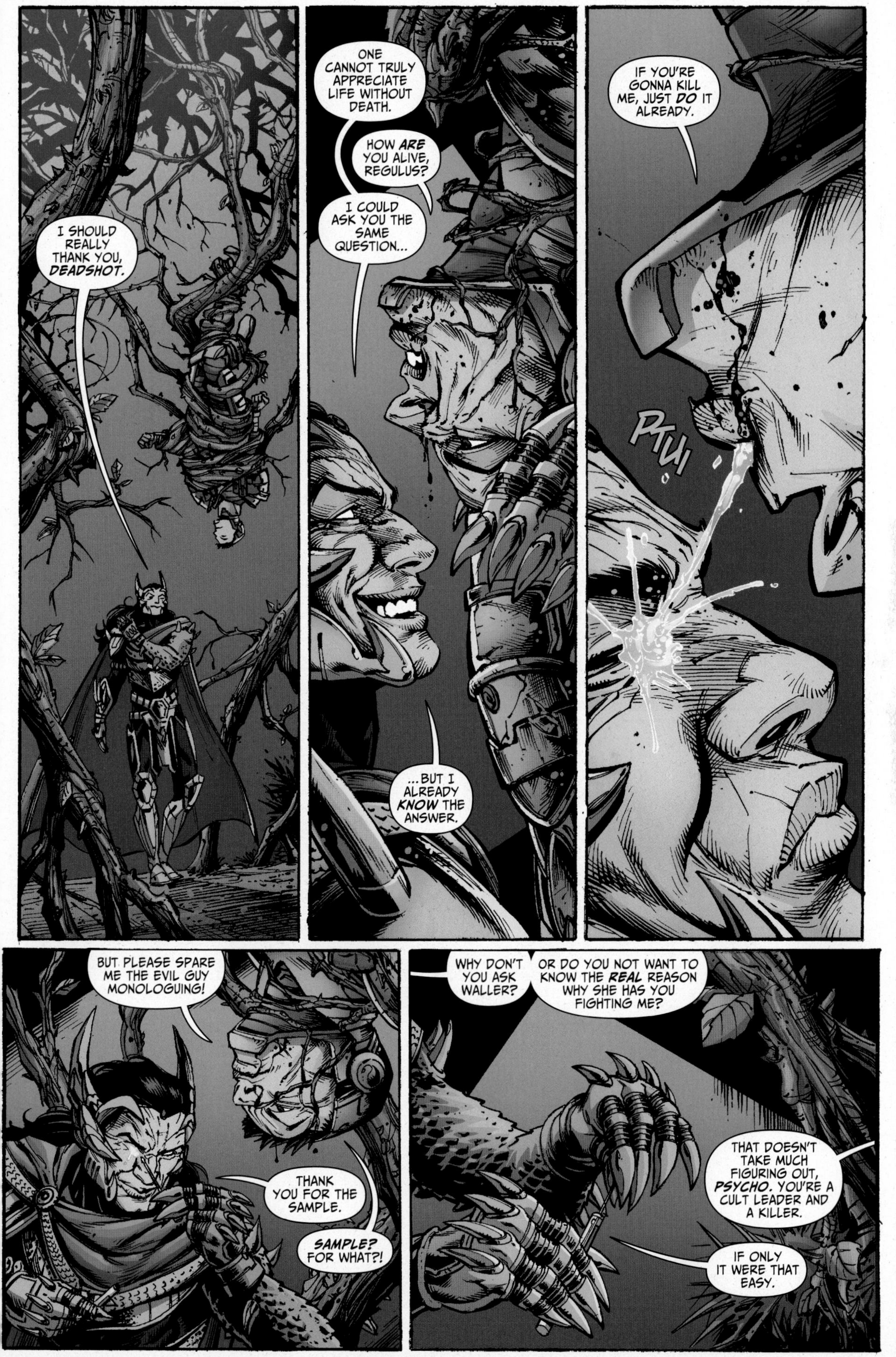
I SHOULD REALLY THANK YOU, DEADSHOT.
ONE CANNOT TRULY APPRECIATE LIFE WITHOUT DEATH.
HOW ARE YOU ALIVE, REGULUS?
I COULD ASK YOU THE SAME QUESTION...
...BUT I ALREADY KNOW THE ANSWER.
IF YOU'RE GONNA KILL ME, JUST DO IT ALREADY.
PTUI
BUT PLEASE SPARE ME THE EVIL GUY MONOLOGUING!
THANK YOU FOR THE SAMPLE.
SAMPLE? FOR WHAT?!
WHY DON'T YOU ASK WALLER?
OR DO YOU NOT WANT TO KNOW THE REAL REASON WHY SHE HAS YOU FIGHTING ME?
THAT DOESN'T TAKE MUCH FIGURING OUT, PSYCHO. YOU'RE A CULT LEADER AND A KILLER.
IF ONLY IT WERE THAT EASY.

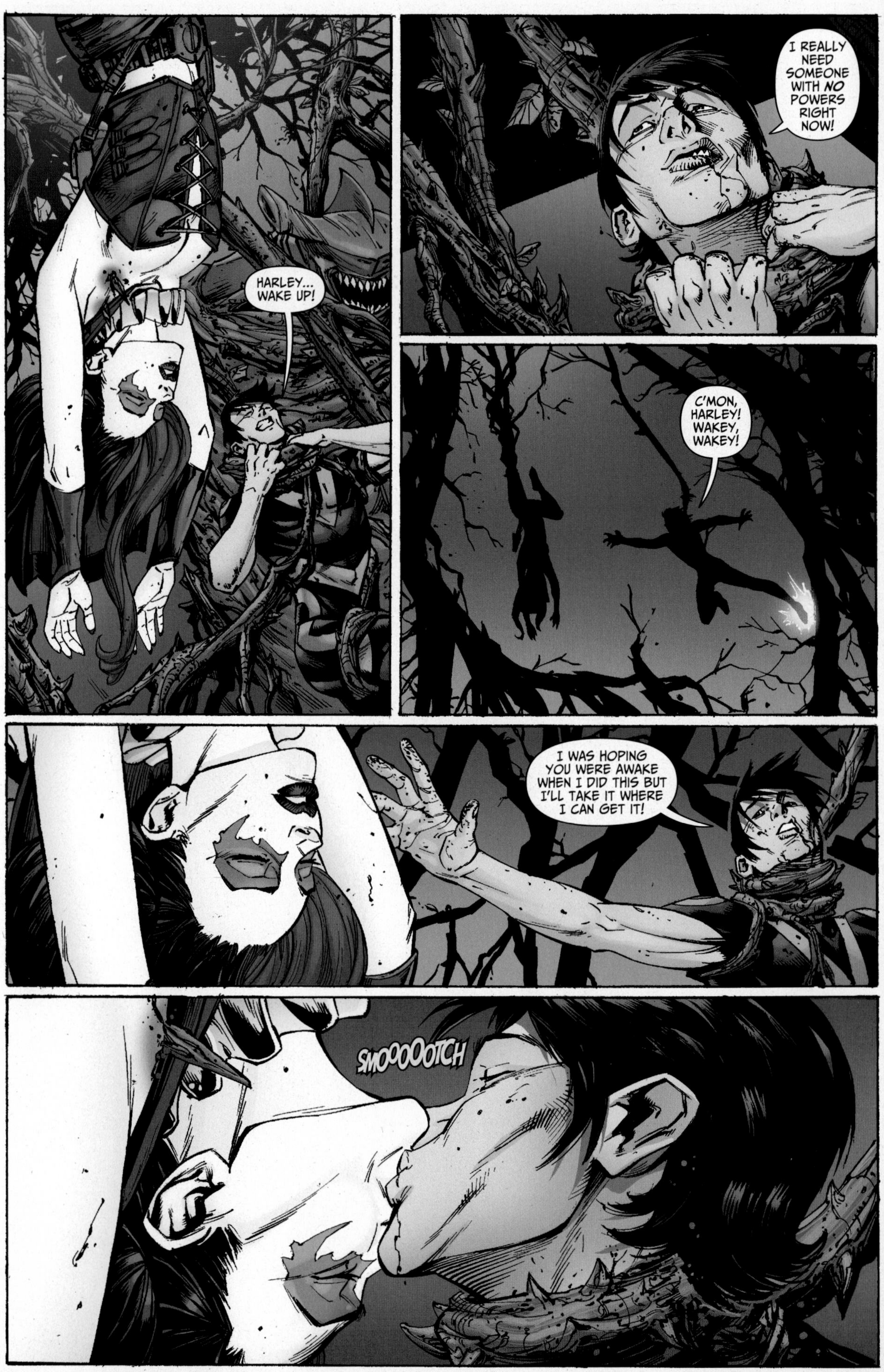
HARLEY... WAKE UP!
I REALLY NEED SOMEONE WITH NO POWERS RIGHT NOW!
C'MON, HARLEY! WAKEY, WAKEY!
I WAS HOPING YOU WERE AWAKE WHEN I DID THIS BUT I'LL TAKE IT WHERE I CAN GET IT!
SMOOOOOTCH

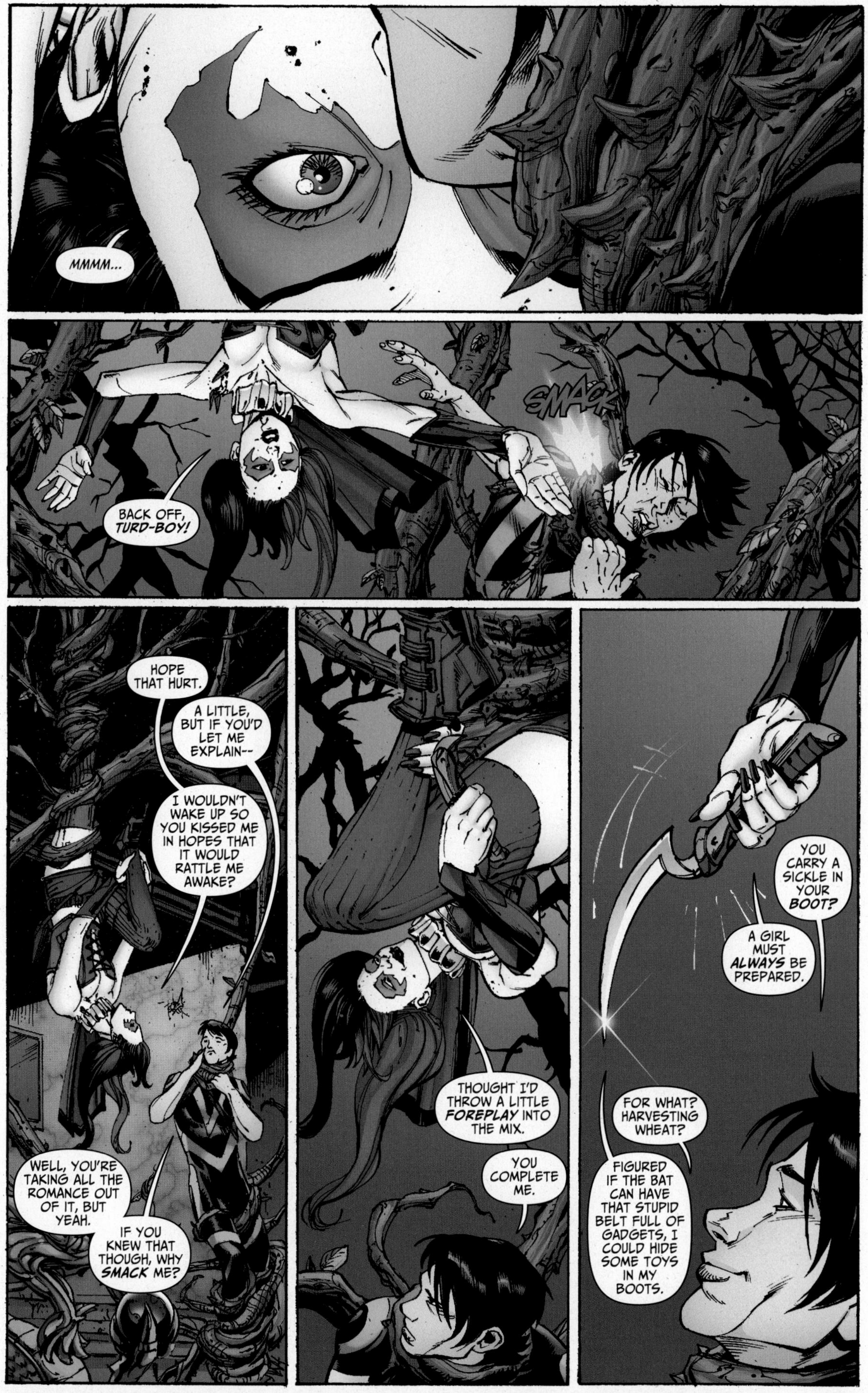
MMMM...
SMACK
BACK OFF, TURD-BOY!
HOPE THAT HURT.
A LITTLE, BUT IF YOU'D LET ME EXPLAIN--
I WOULDN'T WAKE UP SO YOU KISSED ME IN HOPES THAT IT WOULD RATTLE ME AWAKE?
WELL, YOU'RE TAKING ALL THE ROMANCE OUT OF IT, BUT YEAH.
IF YOU KNEW THAT THOUGH, WHY SMACK ME?
THOUGHT I'D THROW A LITTLE FOREPLAY INTO THE MIX.
YOU COMPLETE ME.
YOU CARRY A SICKLE IN YOUR BOOT?
A GIRL MUST ALWAYS BE PREPARED.
FOR WHAT? HARVESTING WHEAT?
FIGURED IF THE BAT CAN HAVE THAT STUPID BELT FULL OF GADGETS, I COULD HIDE SOME TOYS IN MY BOOTS.

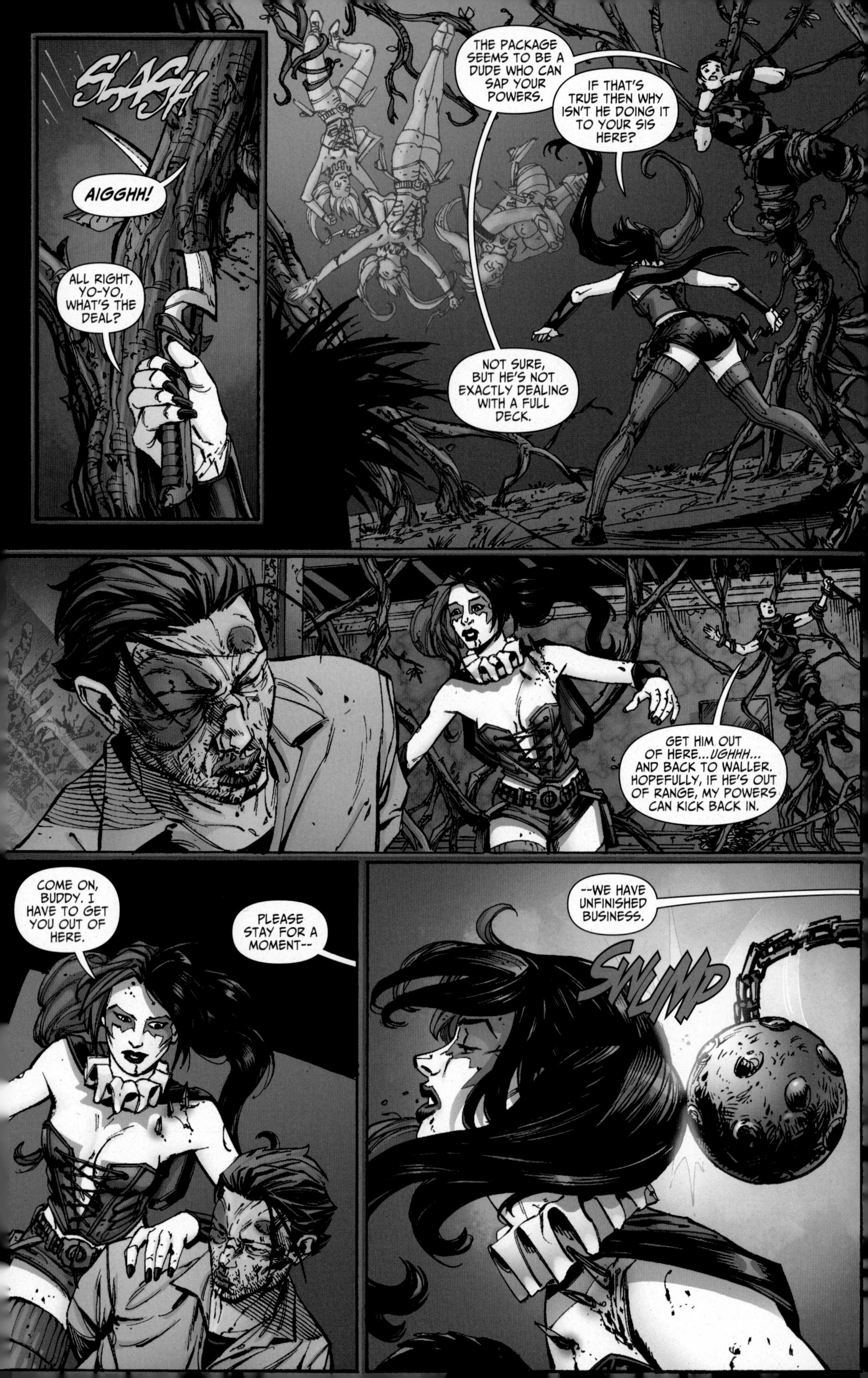
SLASH
AIGGHH!
ALL RIGHT, YO-YO, WHAT'S THE DEAL?
THE PACKAGE SEEMS TO BE A DUDE WHO CAN SAP YOUR POWERS.
IF THAT'S TRUE THEN WHY ISN'T HE DOING IT TO YOUR SIS HERE?
NOT SURE, BUT HE'S NOT EXACTLY DEALING WITH A FULL DECK.
GET HIM OUT OF HERE...UGHHH... AND BACK TO WALLER. HOPEFULLY, IF HE'S OUT OF RANGE, MY POWERS CAN KICK BACK IN.
COME ON, BUDDY. I HAVE TO GET YOU OUT OF HERE.
PLEASE STAY FOR A MOMENT--
--WE HAVE UNFINISHED BUSINESS.
SWUMP

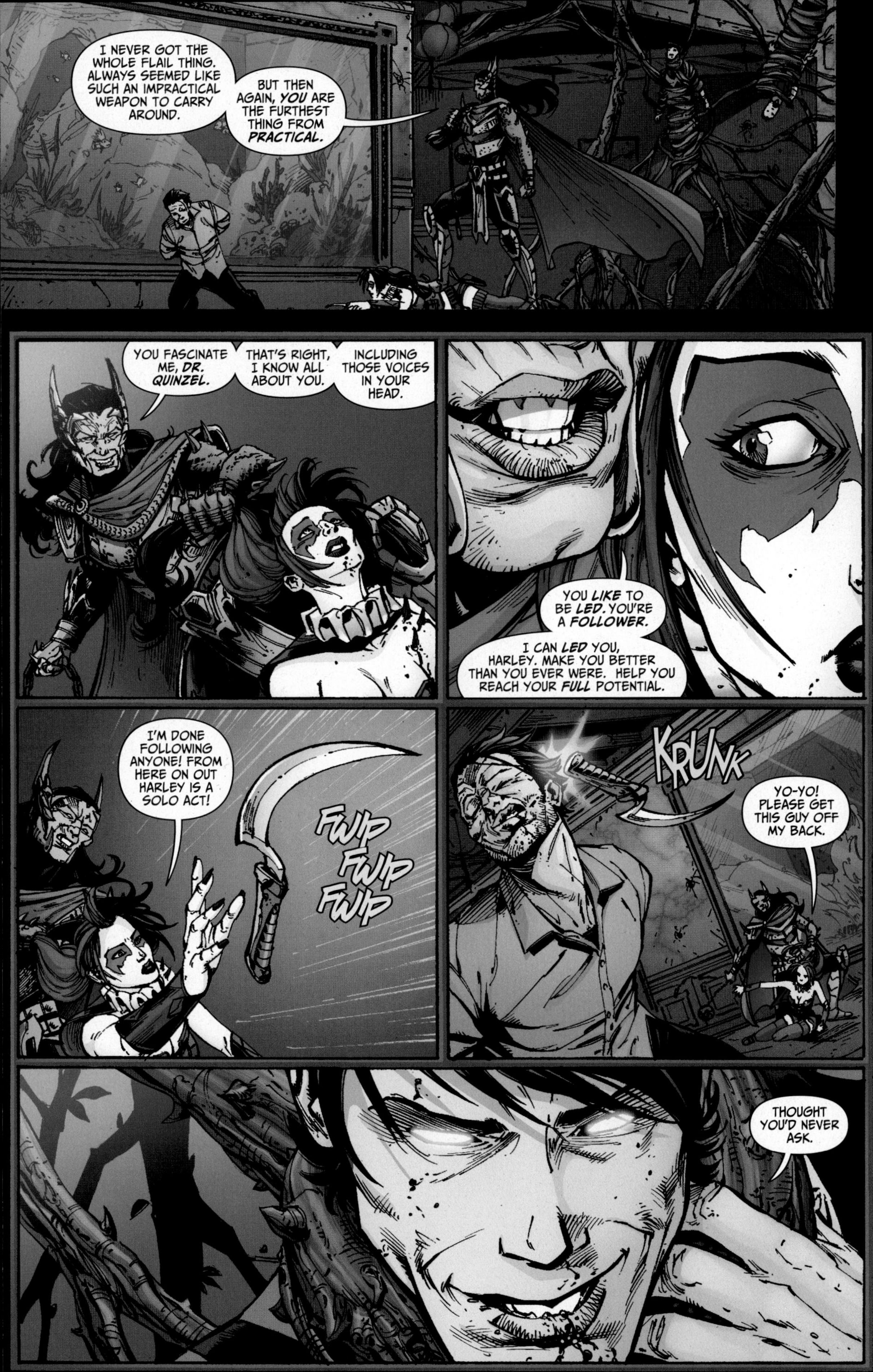
I NEVER GOT THE WHOLE FLAIL THING. ALWAYS SEEMED LIKE SUCH AN IMPRACTICAL WEAPON TO CARRY AROUND.
BUT THEN AGAIN, YOU ARE THE FURTHEST THING FROM PRACTICAL.
YOU FASCINATE ME, DR. QUINZEL.
THAT'S RIGHT, I KNOW ALL ABOUT YOU.
INCLUDING THOSE VOICES IN YOUR HEAD.
YOU LIKE TO BE LED. YOU'RE A FOLLOWER.
I CAN LED YOU, HARLEY. MAKE YOU BETTER THAN YOU EVER WERE. HELP YOU REACH YOUR FULL POTENTIAL.
I'M DONE FOLLOWING ANYONE! FROM HERE ON OUT HARLEY IS A SOLO ACT!
FWIP FWIP FWIP
KRUNK
YO-YO! PLEASE GET THIS GUY OFF MY BACK.
THOUGHT YOU'D NEVER ASK.

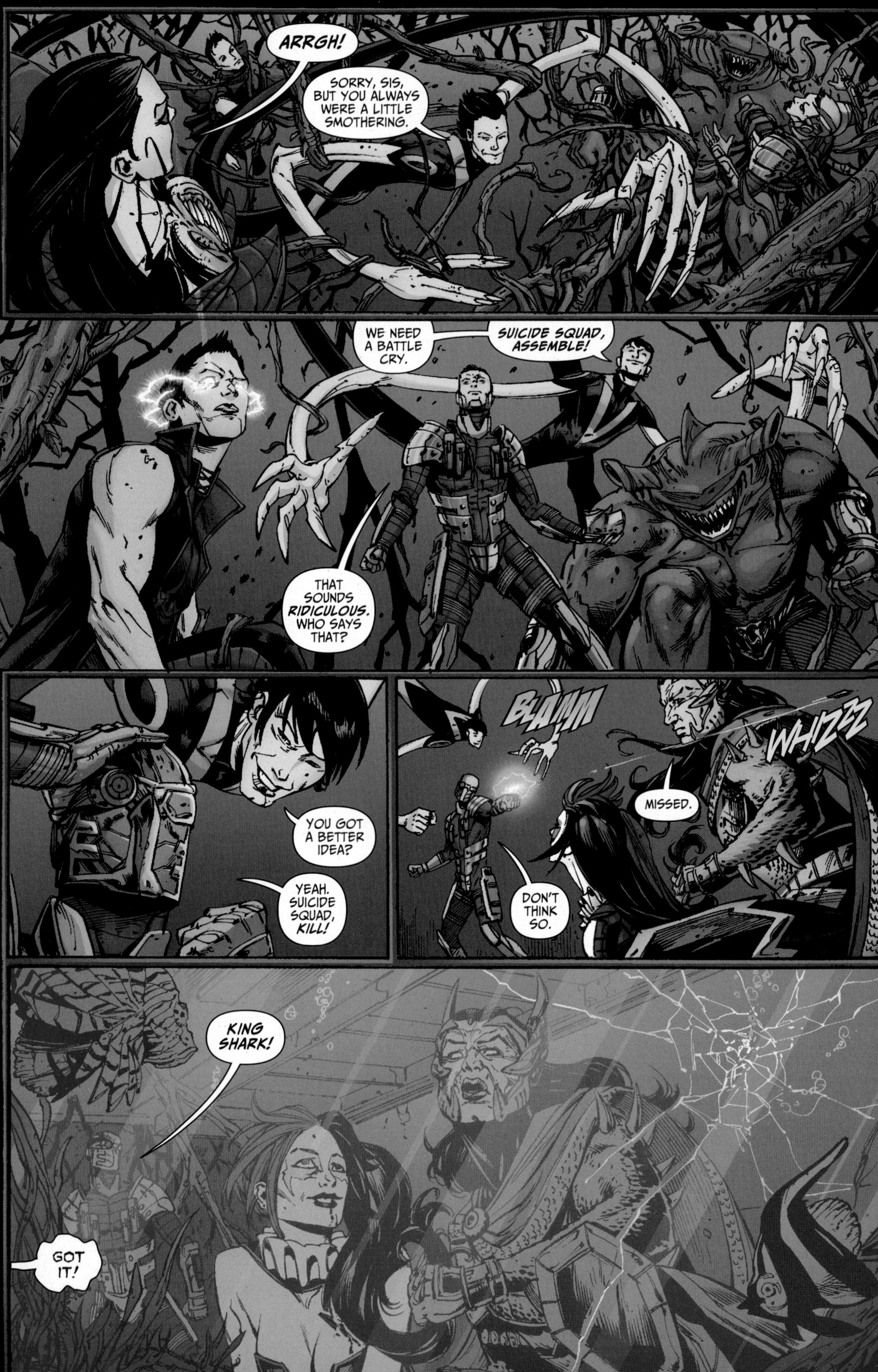
ARRGH!
SORRY, SIS, BUT YOU ALWAYS WERE A LITTLE SMOTHERING.
WE NEED A BATTLE CRY.
SUICIDE SQUAD, ASSEMBLE!
THAT SOUNDS RIDICULOUS. WHO SAYS THAT?
YOU GOT A BETTER IDEA?
YEAH. SUICIDE SQUAD, KILL!
BLAMM
WHIZZZ
MISSED.
DON'T THINK SO.
KING SHARK!
GOT IT!

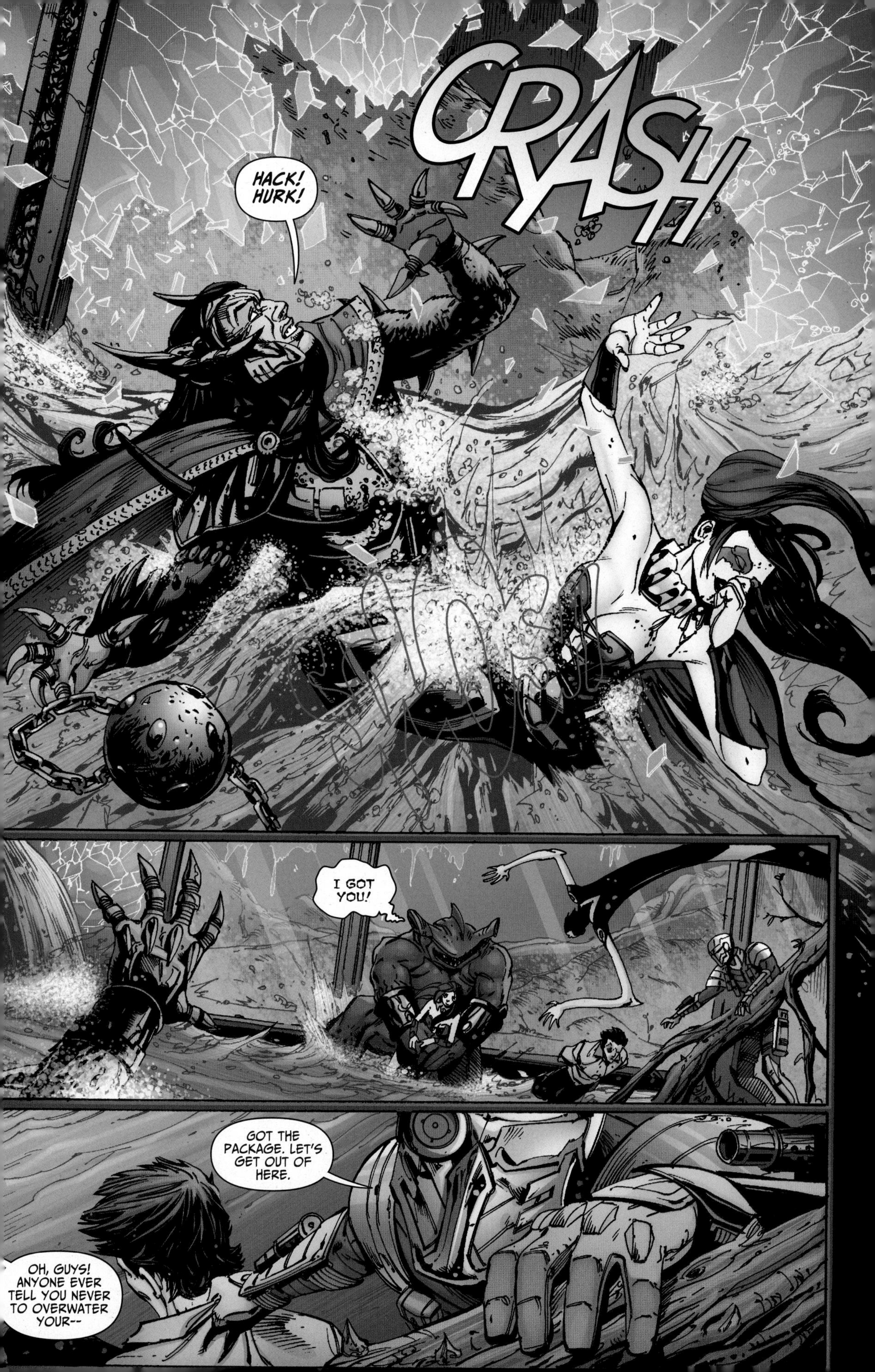
CRASH
HACK! HURK!
I GOT YOU!
GOT THE PACKAGE. LET'S GET OUT OF HERE.
OH, GUYS! ANYONE EVER TELL YOU NEVER TO OVERWATER YOUR--

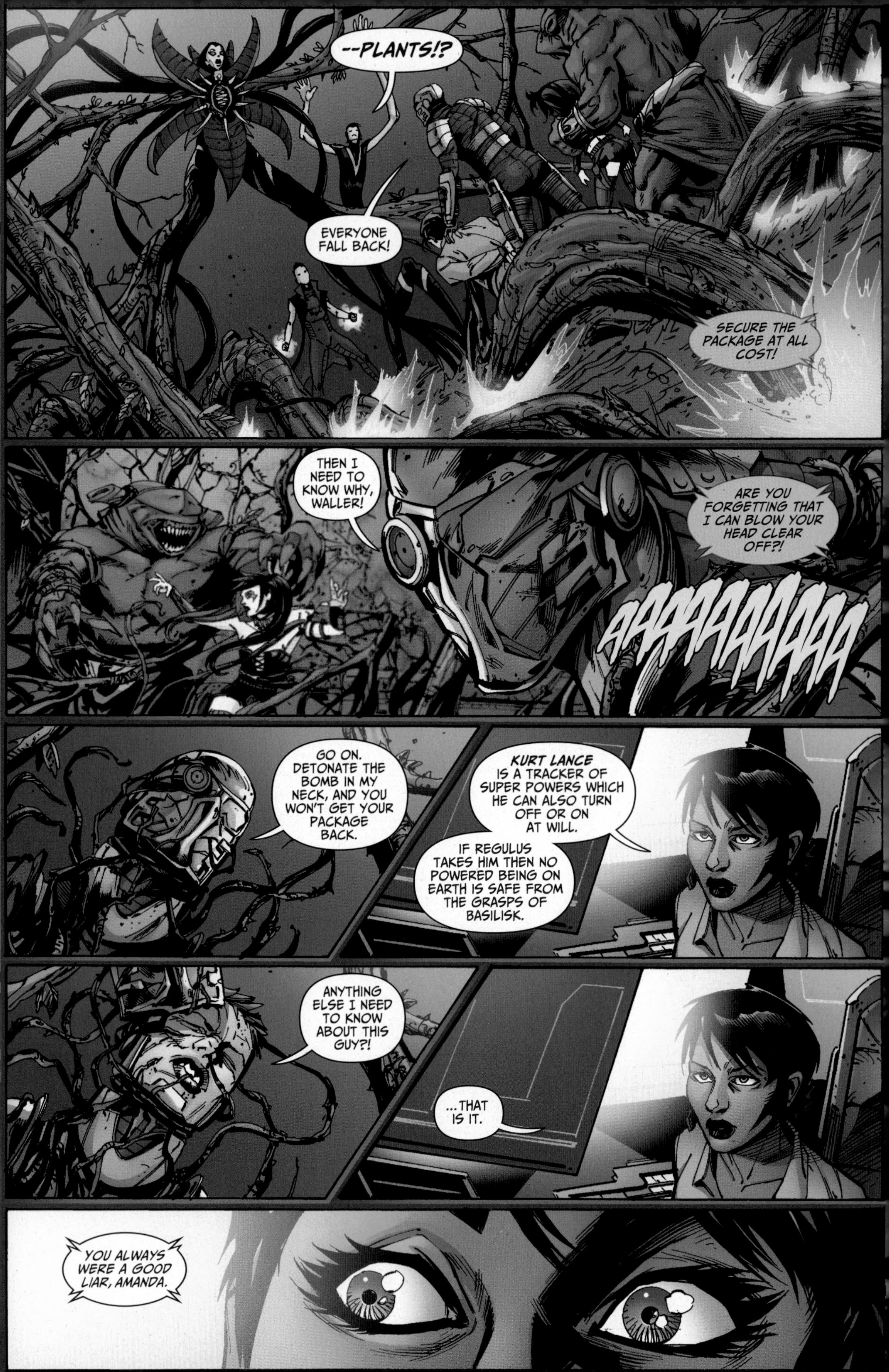
--PLANTS!?
EVERYONE FALL BACK!
SECURE THE PACKAGE AT ALL COST!
THEN I NEED TO KNOW WHY, WALLER!
ARE YOU FORGETTING THAT I CAN BLOW YOUR HEAD CLEAR OFF?!
AAAAAAAAAAAA
GO ON. DETONATE THE BOMB IN MY NECK, AND YOU WON'T GET YOUR PACKAGE BACK.
KURT LANCE IS A TRACKER OF SUPER POWERS WHICH HE CAN ALSO TURN OFF OR ON AT WILL.
IF REGULUS TAKES HIM THEN NO POWERED BEING ON EARTH IS SAFE FROM THE GRASPS OF BASILISK.
ANYTHING ELSE I NEED TO KNOW ABOUT THIS GUY?!
...THAT IS IT.
YOU ALWAYS WERE A GOOD LIAR, AMANDA.

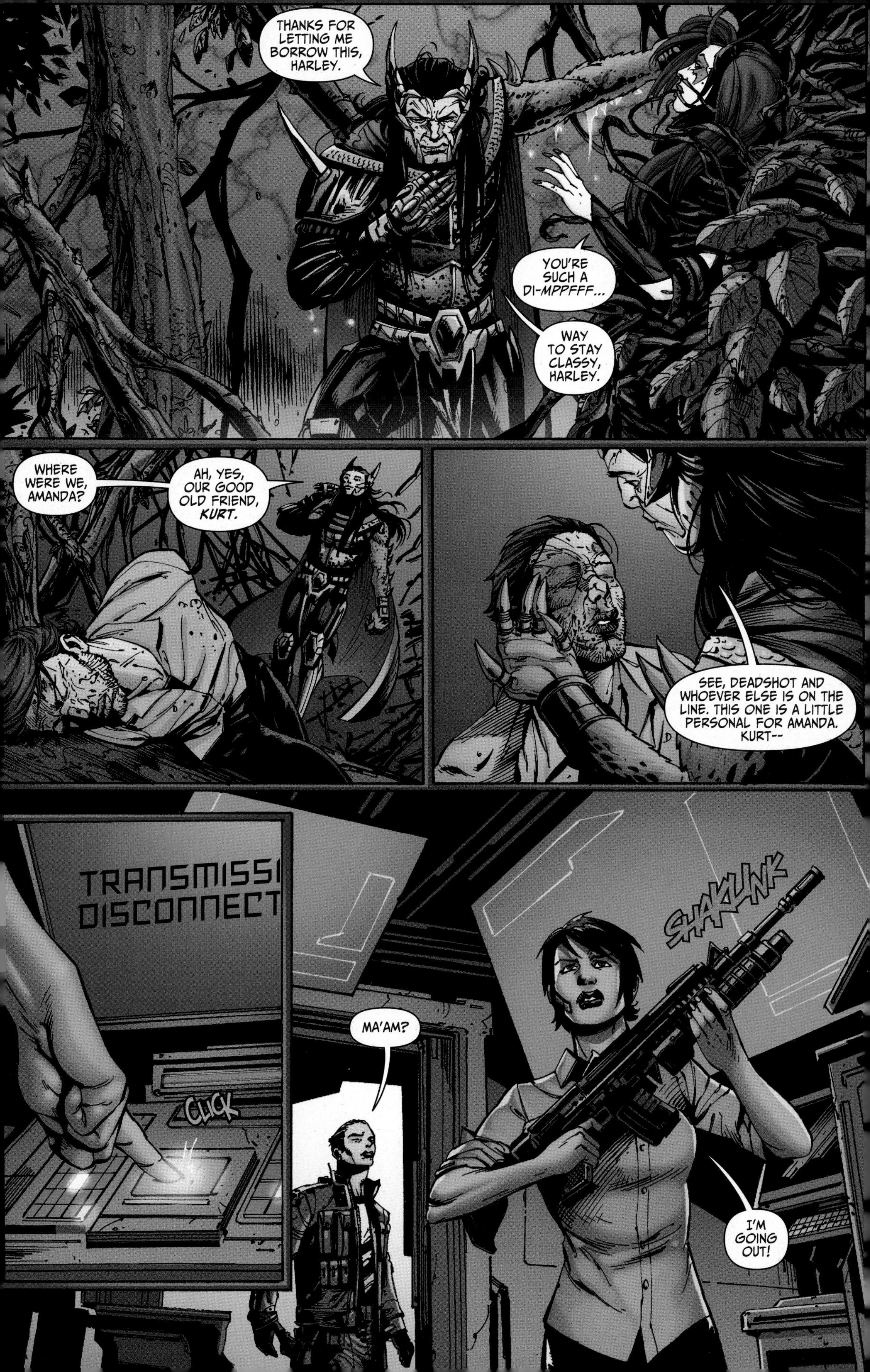
THANKS FOR LETTING ME BORROW THIS, HARLEY.
YOU'RE SUCH A DI-MPPFFF...
WAY TO STAY CLASSY, HARLEY.
WHERE WERE WE, AMANDA?
AH, YES, OUR GOOD OLD FRIEND, KURT.
SEE, DEADSHOT AND WHOEVER ELSE IS ON THE LINE. THIS ONE IS A LITTLE PERSONAL FOR AMANDA. KURT--
TRANSMISSI
DISCONNECT
SHAKUNK
CLICK
MA'AM?
I'M GOING OUT!

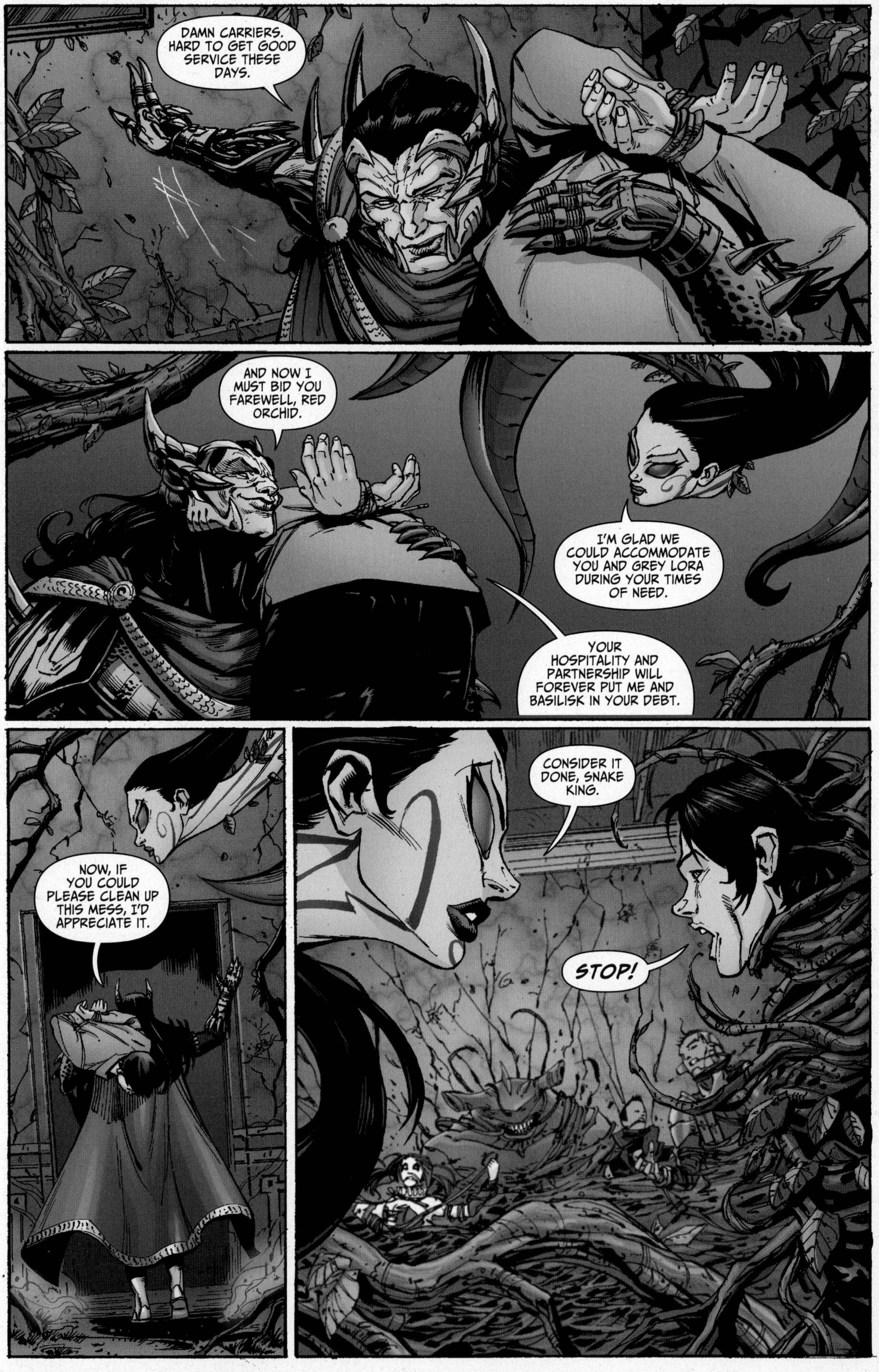
DAMN CARRIERS. HARD TO GET GOOD SERVICE THESE DAYS.
AND NOW I MUST BID YOU FAREWELL, RED ORCHID.
I'M GLAD WE COULD ACCOMMODATE YOU AND GREY LORA DURING YOUR TIMES OF NEED.
YOUR HOSPITALITY AND PARTNERSHIP WILL FOREVER PUT ME AND BASILISK IN YOUR DEBT.
NOW, IF YOU COULD PLEASE CLEAN UP THIS MESS, I'D APPRECIATE IT.
CONSIDER IT DONE, SNAKE KING.
STOP!

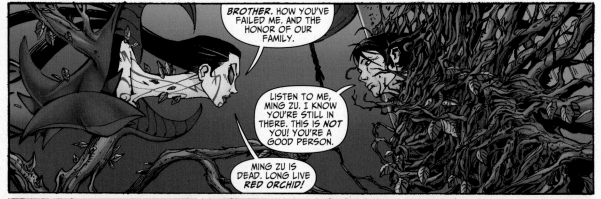

BROTHER. HOW YOU'VE FAILED ME. AND THE HONOR OF OUR FAMILY.

LISTEN TO ME, MING ZU. I KNOW YOU'RE STILL IN THERE. THIS IS *NOT* YOU! YOU'RE A GOOD PERSON.

MING ZU IS DEAD. LONG LIVE *RED ORCHID!*

CHOKING! AND NOT THE FUN KIND...

LIKE I SAID, I'M NO HERO.

THIS IS WHY... I'M...NOT...A... VEGETARIAN...

I'M NOT EVEN A GOOD PERSON.

BLAMM BLAMM BLAMM

BUT I GUESS IT'S NEVER TOO LATE TO CHANGE.

I'M SORRY, SIS. ABOUT EVERYTHING.

BUT ESPECIALLY THIS.

DEADSHOT! SORRY TO BE A PAIN IN YOUR NECK. BUT YOU KNOW WHAT TO DO!

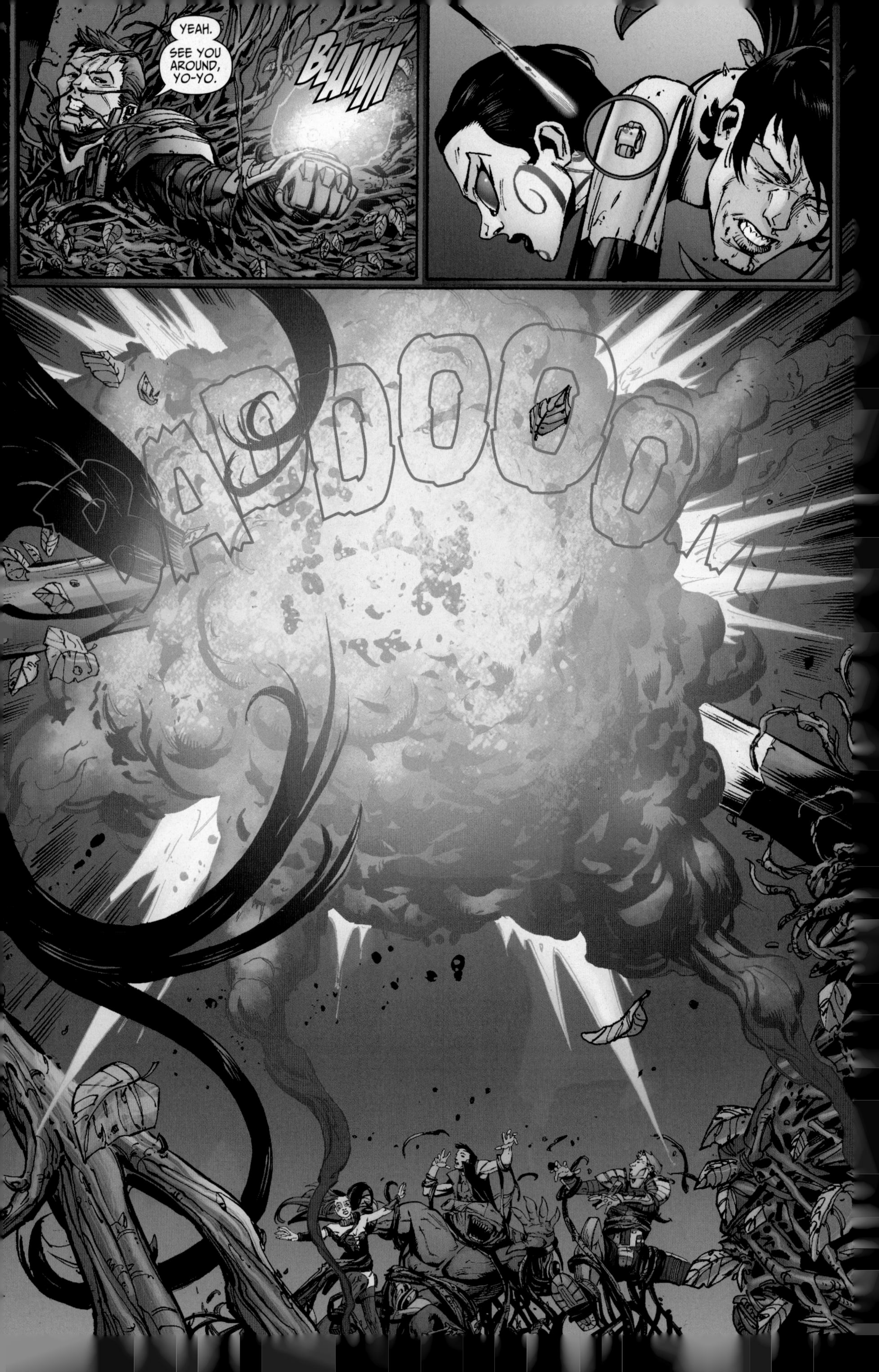
YEAH.
SEE YOU AROUND, YO-YO.
BLAMM
BADOOOOM

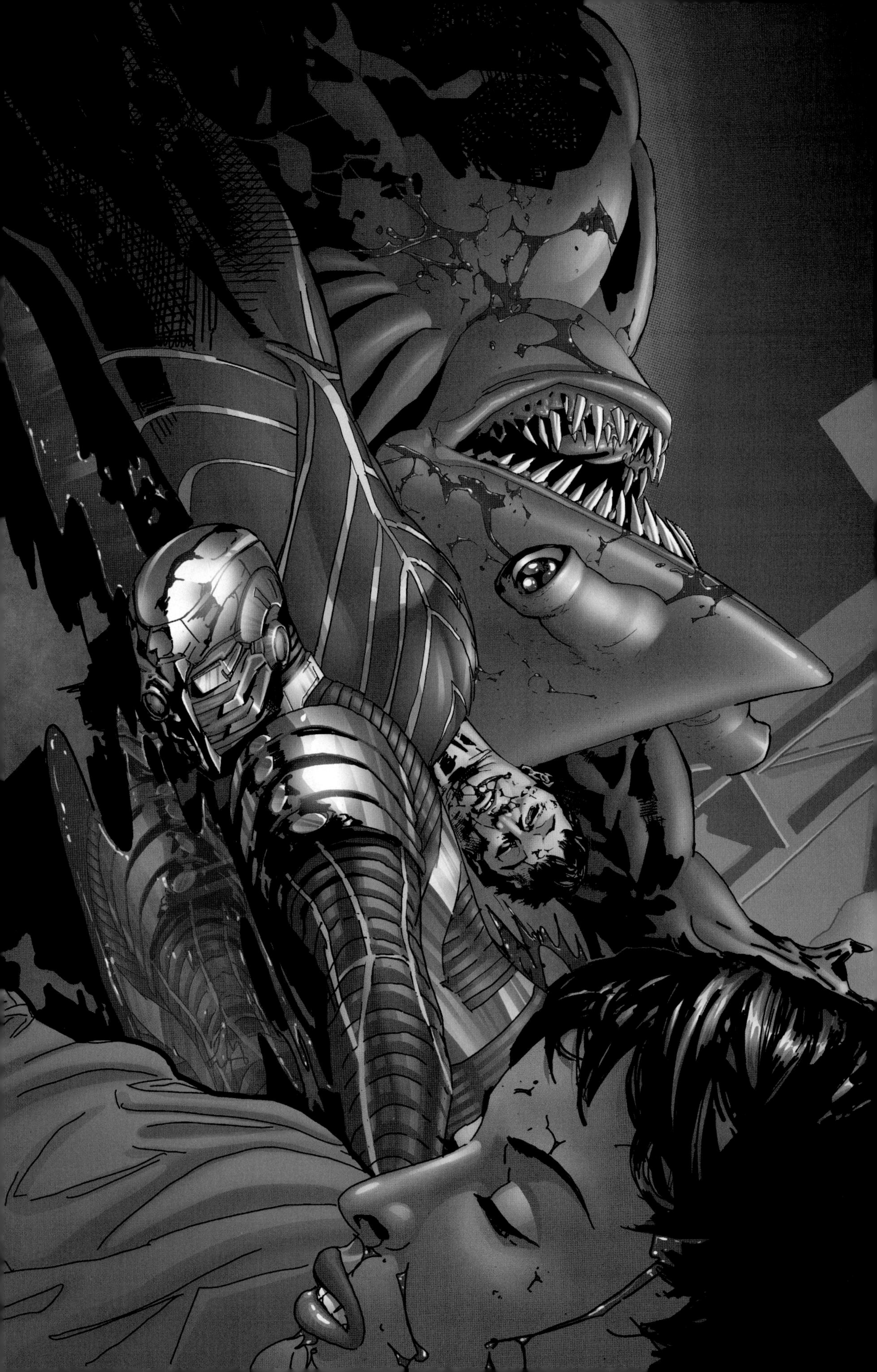

RED RAIN

ADAM GLASS writer CLIFF RICHARDS artist cover art by TRAVEL FOREMAN & GABE ELTAEB

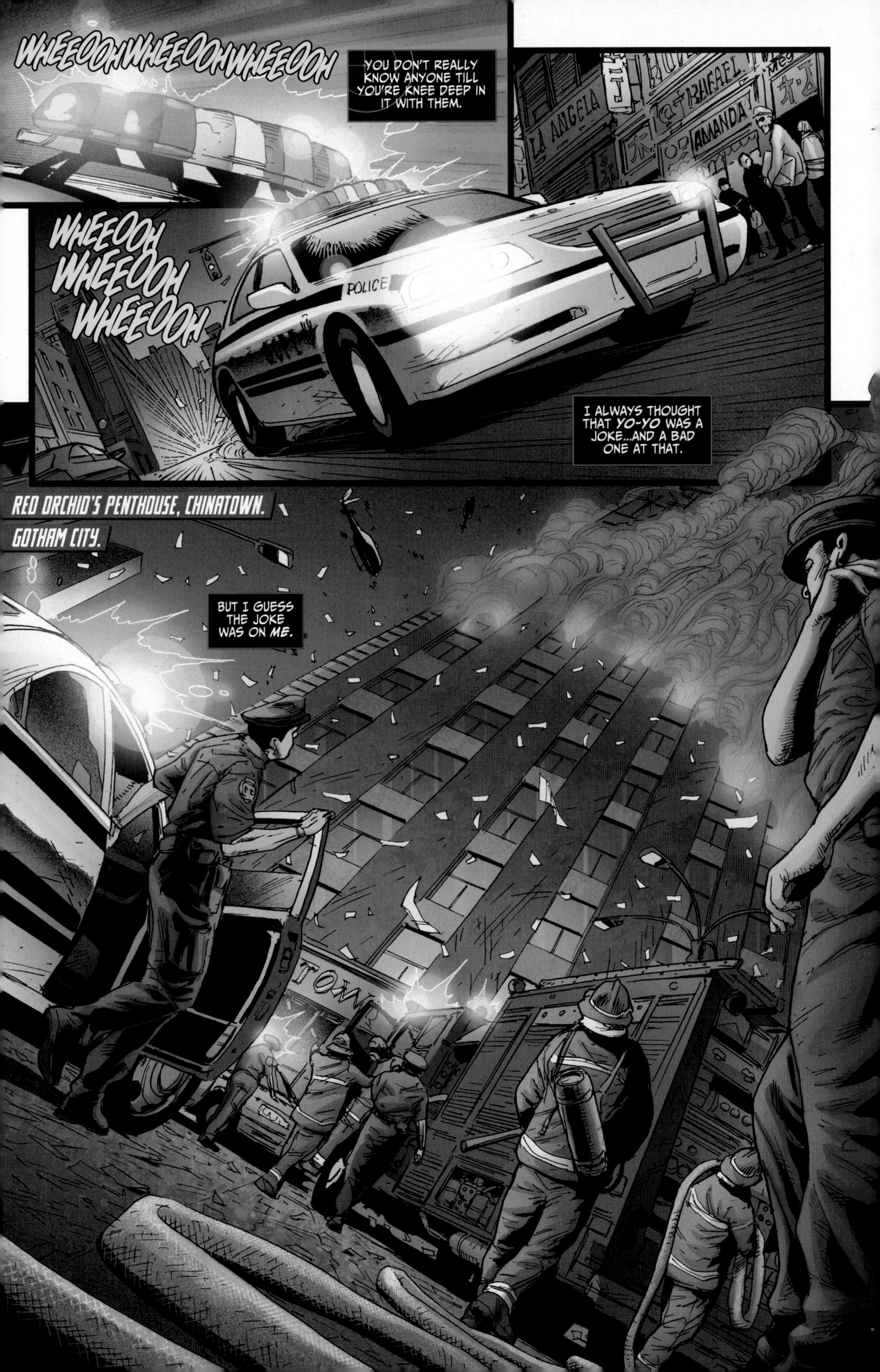
WHEEOOH WHEEOOH WHEEOOH
YOU DON'T REALLY KNOW ANYONE TILL YOU'RE KNEE DEEP IN IT WITH THEM.
WHEEOOH WHEEOOH WHEEOOH
POLICE
I ALWAYS THOUGHT THAT YO-YO WAS A JOKE...AND A BAD ONE AT THAT.
RED ORCHID'S PENTHOUSE, CHINATOWN.
GOTHAM CITY.
BUT I GUESS THE JOKE WAS ON ME.

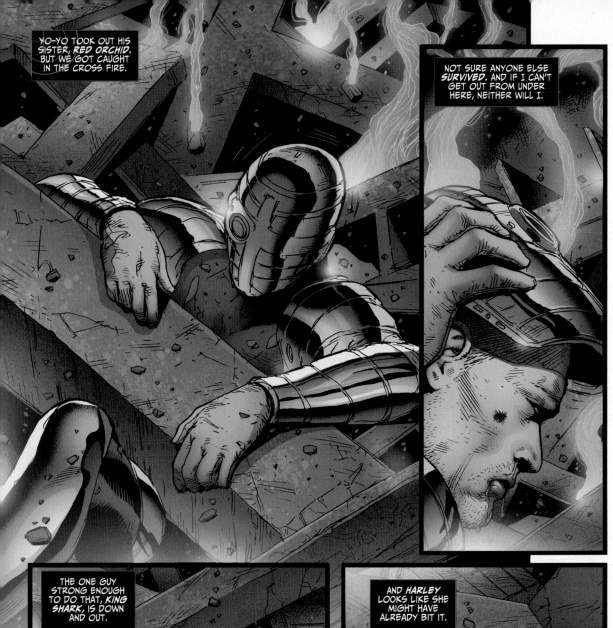

YO-YO TOOK OUT HIS SISTER, *RED ORCHID.* BUT WE GOT CAUGHT IN THE CROSS FIRE.

NOT SURE ANYONE ELSE *SURVIVED.* AND IF I CAN'T GET OUT FROM UNDER HERE, NEITHER WILL I.

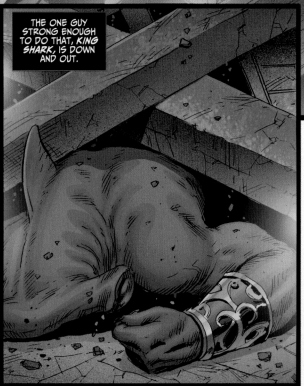

THE ONE GUY STRONG ENOUGH TO DO THAT, *KING SHARK,* IS DOWN AND OUT.

AND *HARLEY* LOOKS LIKE SHE MIGHT HAVE ALREADY BIT IT.

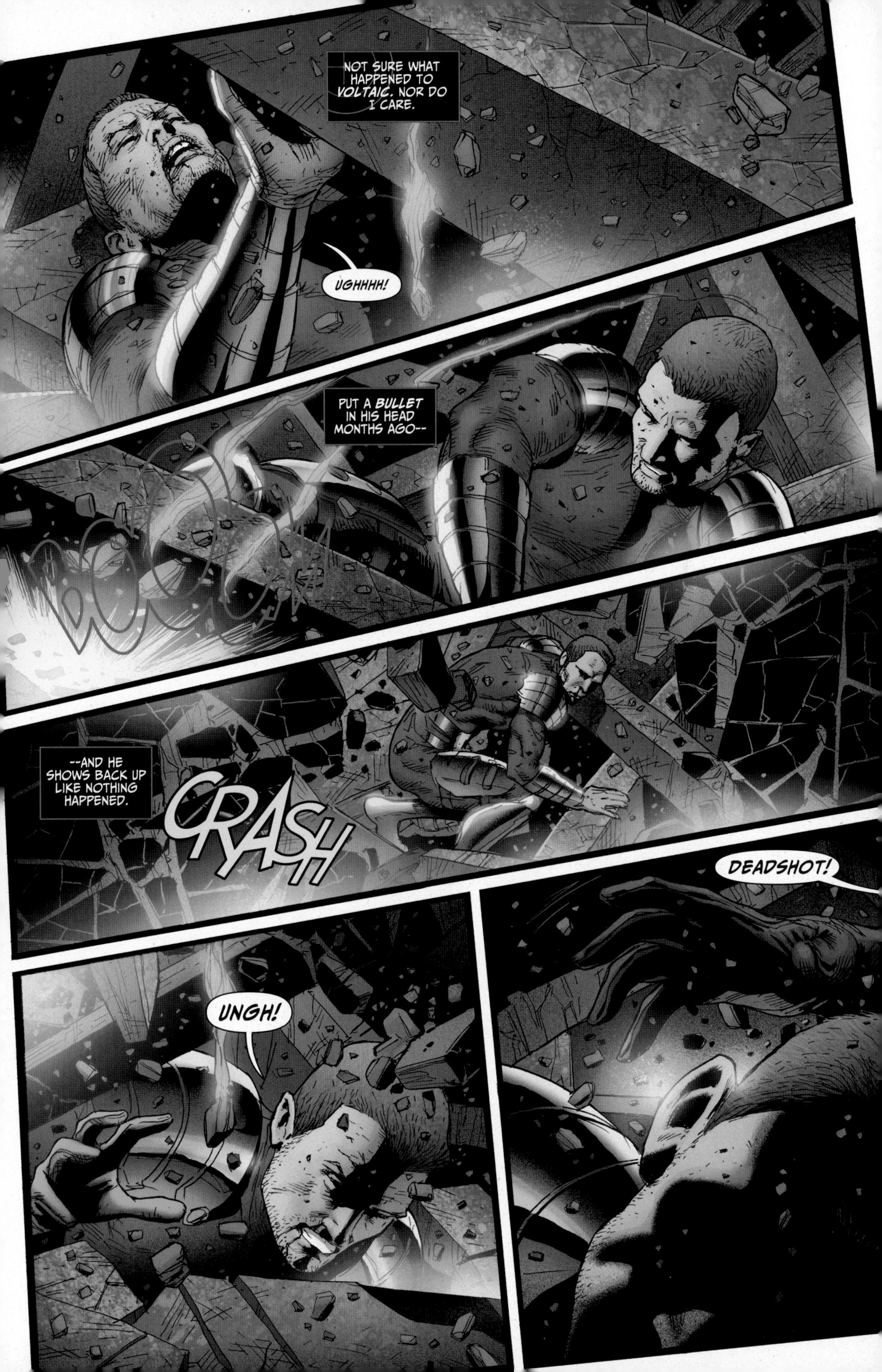
NOT SURE WHAT HAPPENED TO VOLTAIC. NOR DO I CARE.
UGHHHH!
PUT A BULLET IN HIS HEAD MONTHS AGO--
WOOOM
--AND HE SHOWS BACK UP LIKE NOTHING HAPPENED.
CRASH
DEADSHOT!
UNGH!

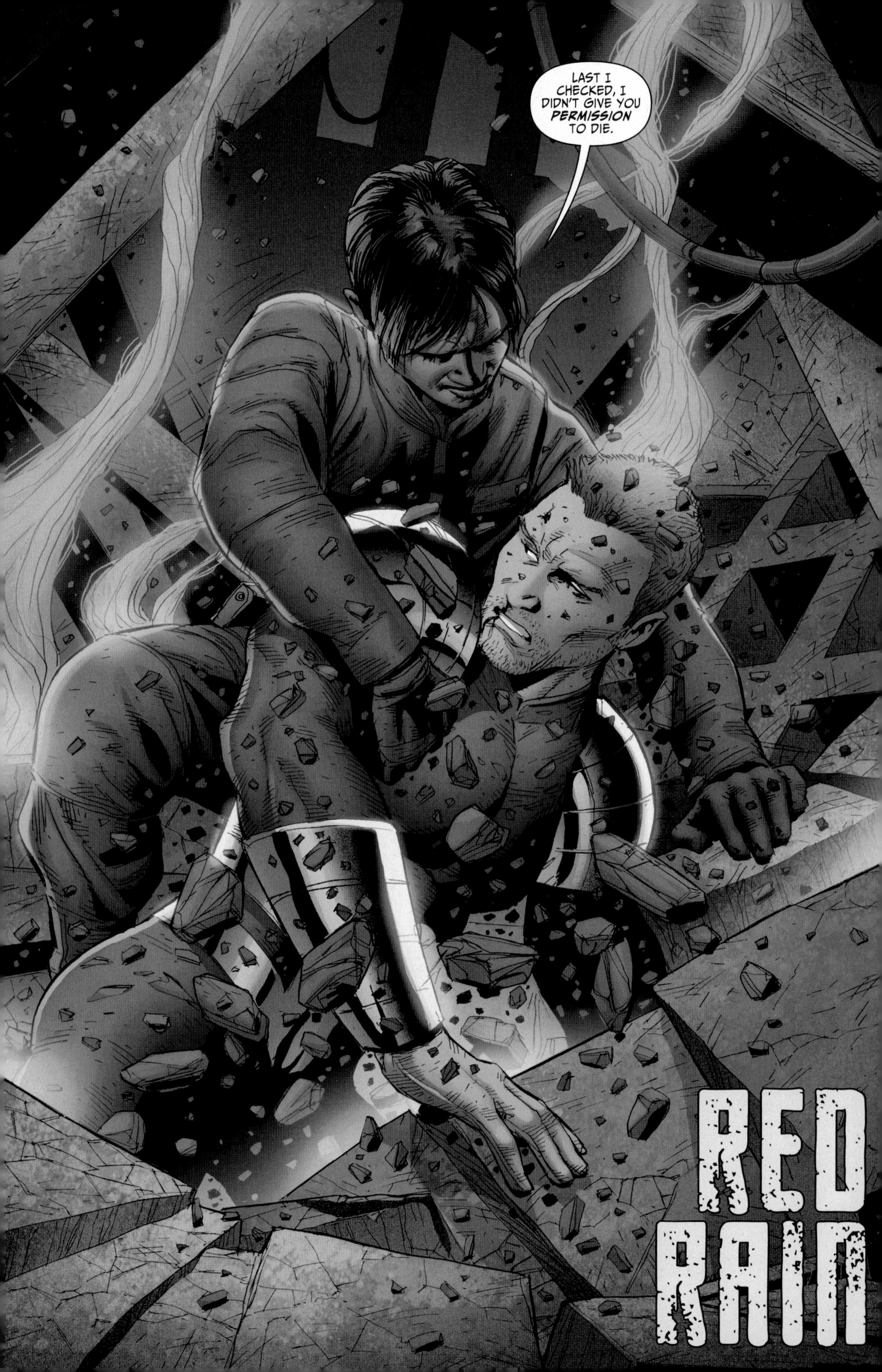
LAST I CHECKED, I DIDN'T GIVE YOU PERMISSION TO DIE.
RED RAIN

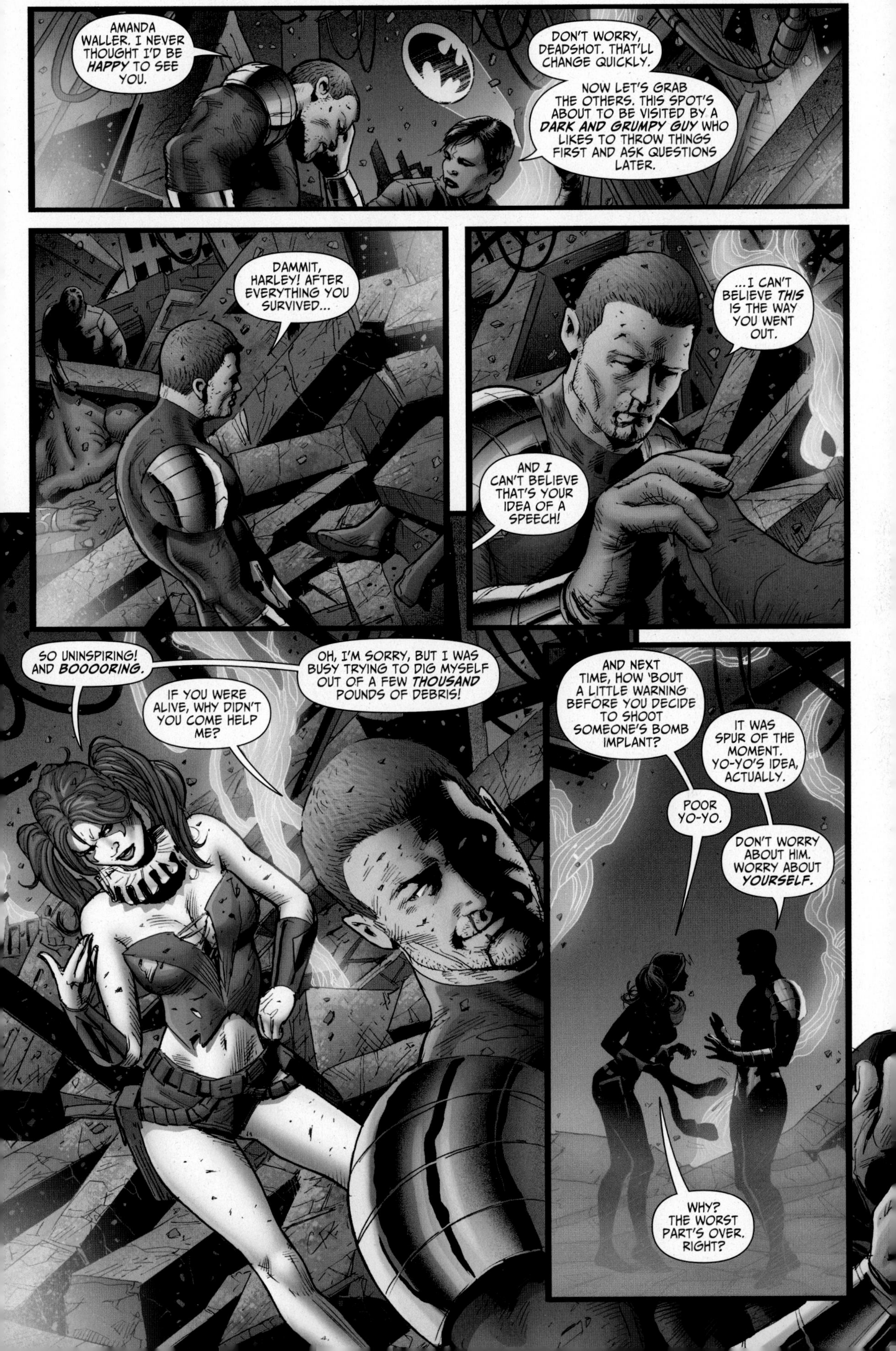
AMANDA WALLER. I NEVER THOUGHT I'D BE HAPPY TO SEE YOU.
DON'T WORRY, DEADSHOT. THAT'LL CHANGE QUICKLY.
NOW LET'S GRAB THE OTHERS. THIS SPOT'S ABOUT TO BE VISITED BY A DARK AND GRUMPY GUY WHO LIKES TO THROW THINGS FIRST AND ASK QUESTIONS LATER.
DAMMIT, HARLEY! AFTER EVERYTHING YOU SURVIVED...
...I CAN'T BELIEVE THIS IS THE WAY YOU WENT OUT.
AND I CAN'T BELIEVE THAT'S YOUR IDEA OF A SPEECH!
SO UNINSPIRING! AND BOOOORING.
OH, I'M SORRY, BUT I WAS BUSY TRYING TO DIG MYSELF OUT OF A FEW THOUSAND POUNDS OF DEBRIS!
IF YOU WERE ALIVE, WHY DIDN'T YOU COME HELP ME?
AND NEXT TIME, HOW 'BOUT A LITTLE WARNING BEFORE YOU DECIDE TO SHOOT SOMEONE'S BOMB IMPLANT?
IT WAS SPUR OF THE MOMENT. YO-YO'S IDEA, ACTUALLY.
POOR YO-YO.
DON'T WORRY ABOUT HIM. WORRY ABOUT YOURSELF.
WHY? THE WORST PART'S OVER. RIGHT?

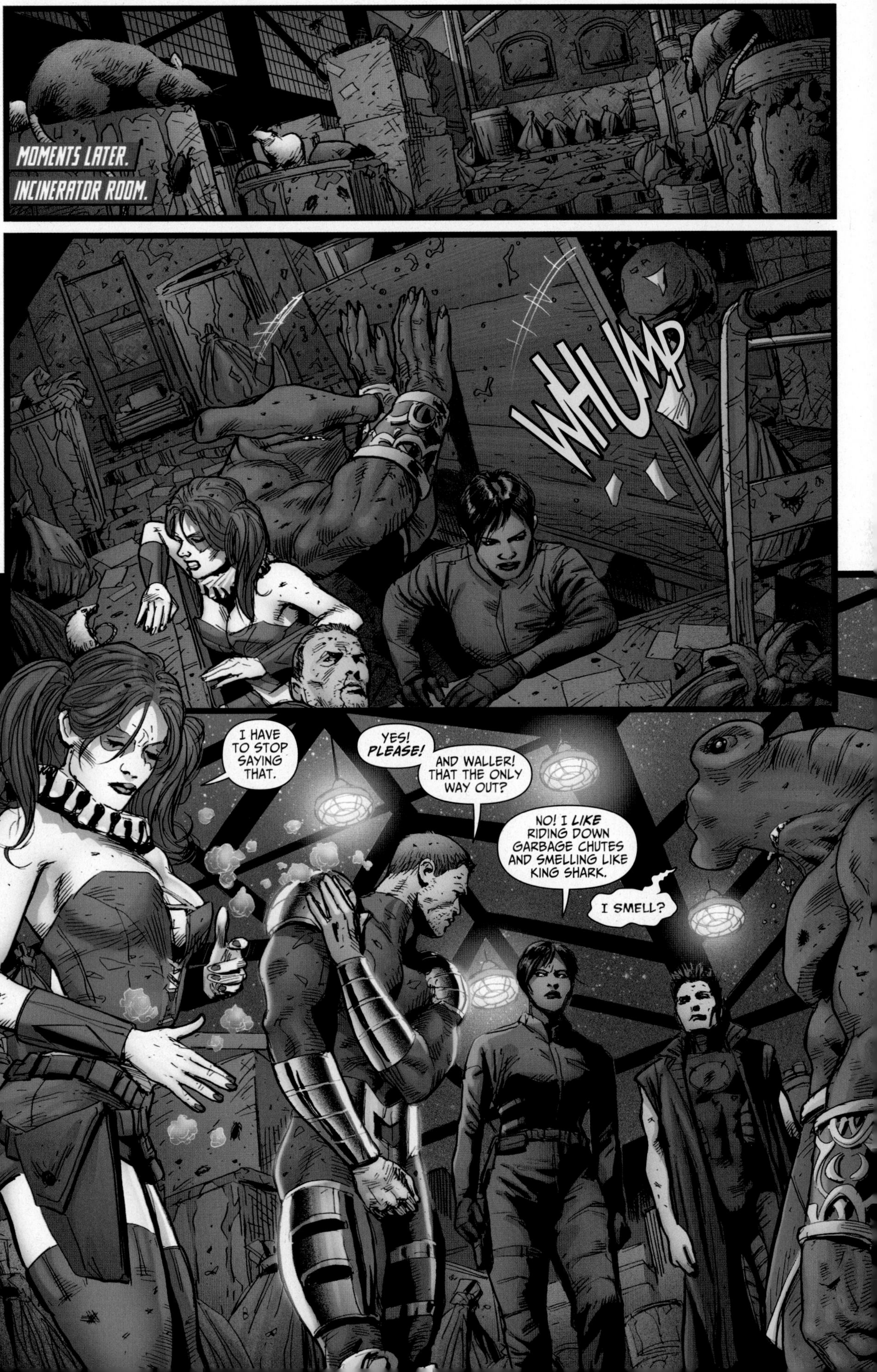
MOMENTS LATER.
INCINERATOR ROOM.
WHUMP
I HAVE TO STOP SAYING THAT.
YES! PLEASE!
AND WALLER! THAT THE ONLY WAY OUT?
NO! I LIKE RIDING DOWN GARBAGE CHUTES AND SMELLING LIKE KING SHARK.
I SMELL?

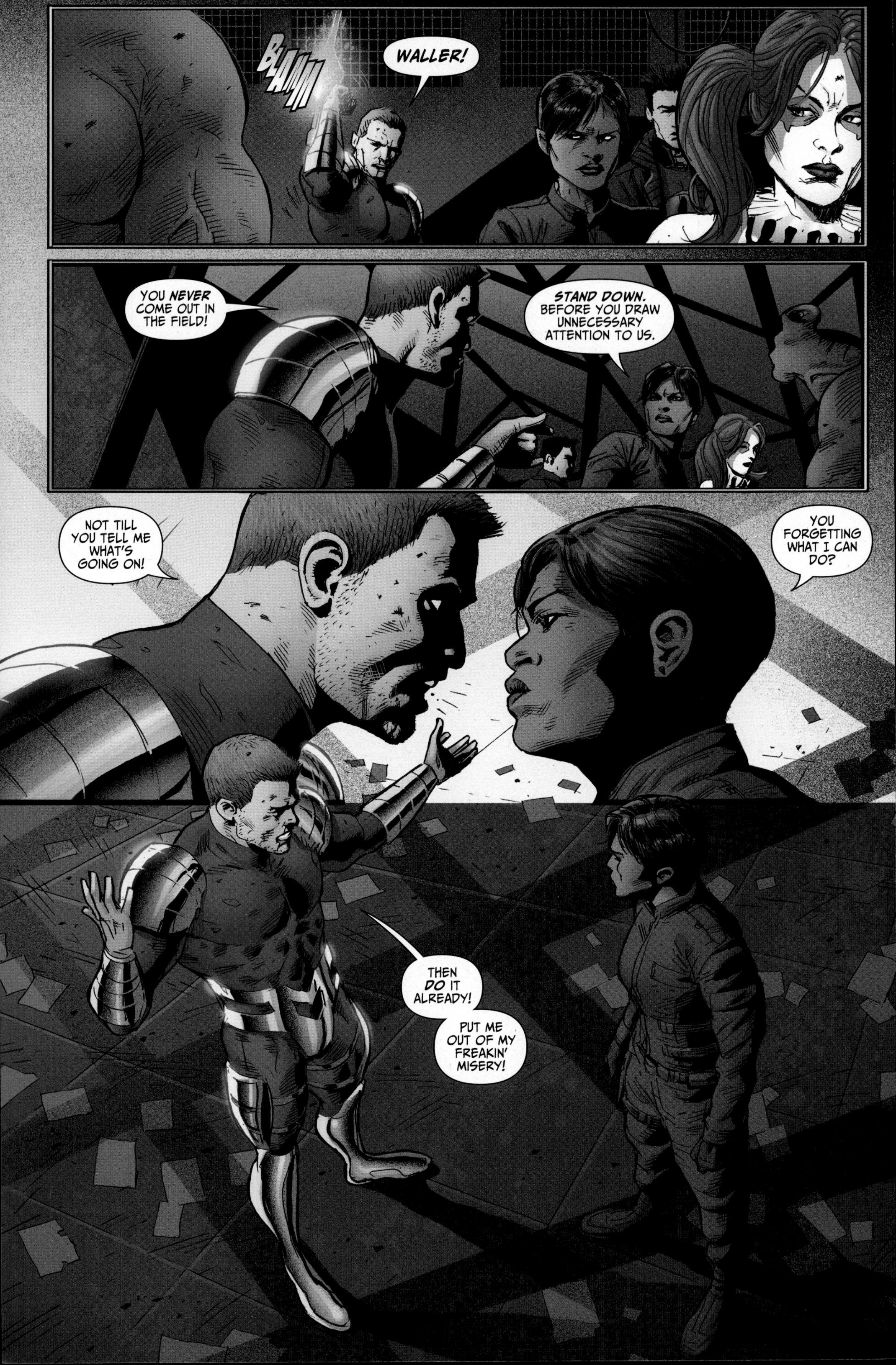
BLAMM
WALLER!
YOU NEVER COME OUT IN THE FIELD!
STAND DOWN. BEFORE YOU DRAW UNNECESSARY ATTENTION TO US.
NOT TILL YOU TELL ME WHAT'S GOING ON!
YOU FORGETTING WHAT I CAN DO?
THEN DO IT ALREADY!
PUT ME OUT OF MY FREAKIN' MISERY!

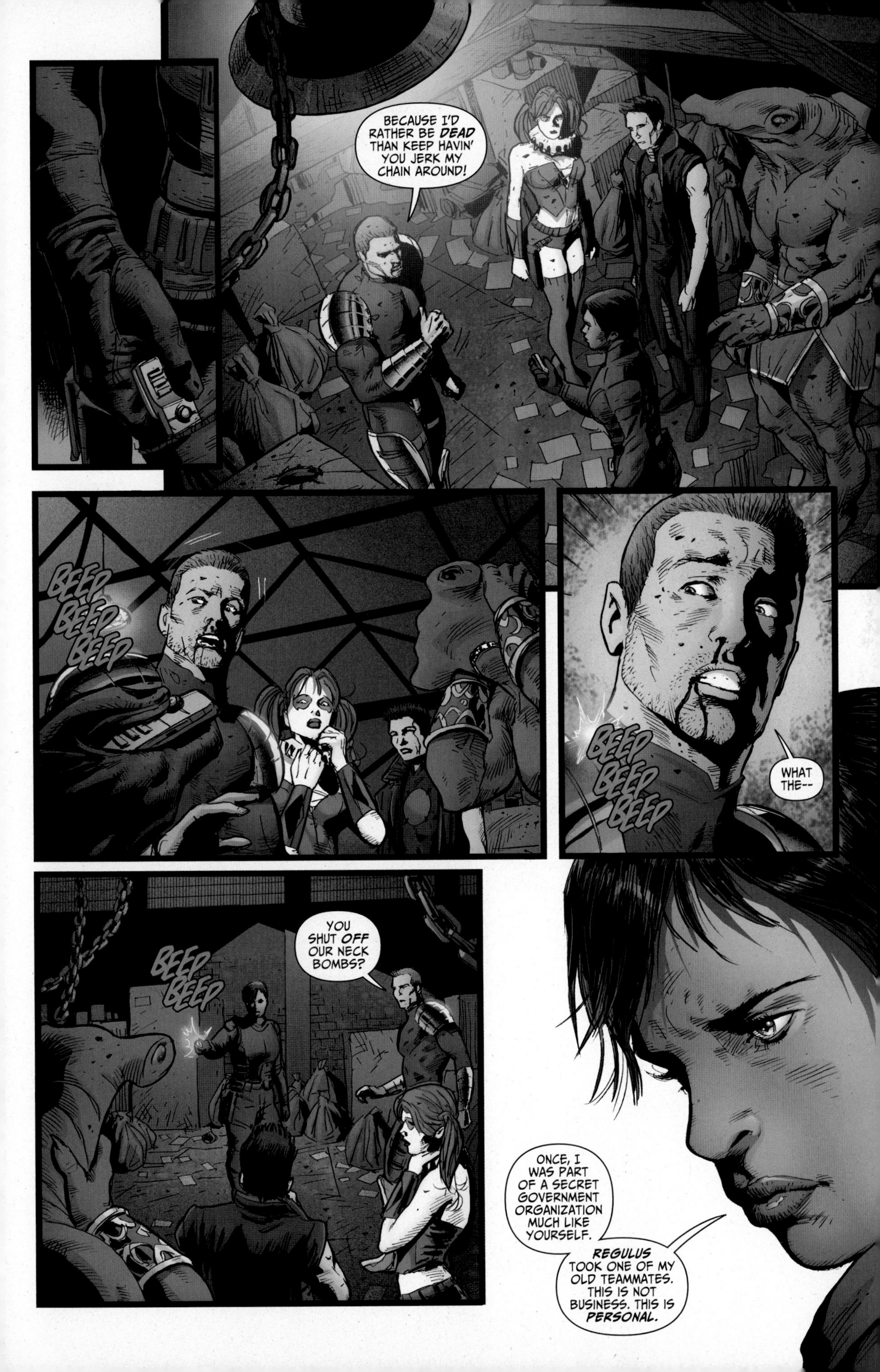

BECAUSE I'D RATHER BE DEAD THAN KEEP HAVIN' YOU JERK MY CHAIN AROUND!
BEEP BEEP BEEP
BEEP BEEP BEEP
WHAT THE--
BEEP BEEP
YOU SHUT OFF OUR NECK BOMBS?
ONCE, I WAS PART OF A SECRET GOVERNMENT ORGANIZATION MUCH LIKE YOURSELF.
REGULUS TOOK ONE OF MY OLD TEAMMATES. THIS IS NOT BUSINESS. THIS IS PERSONAL.

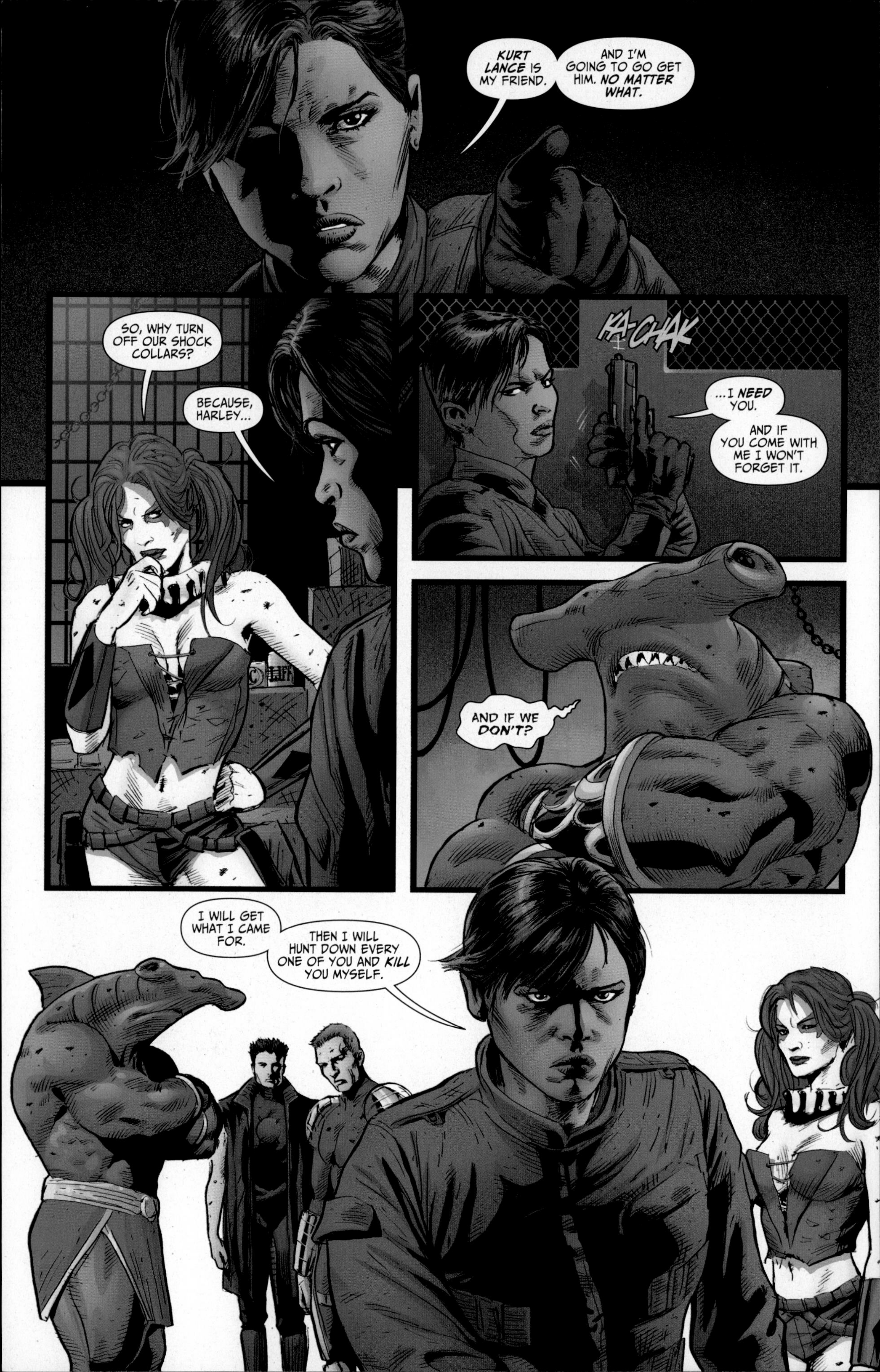

KURT LANCE IS MY FRIEND.
AND I'M GOING TO GO GET HIM. NO MATTER WHAT.
SO, WHY TURN OFF OUR SHOCK COLLARS?
BECAUSE, HARLEY...
KA-CHAK
...I NEED YOU.
AND IF YOU COME WITH ME I WON'T FORGET IT.
AND IF WE DON'T?
I WILL GET WHAT I CAME FOR.
THEN I WILL HUNT DOWN EVERY ONE OF YOU AND KILL YOU MYSELF.

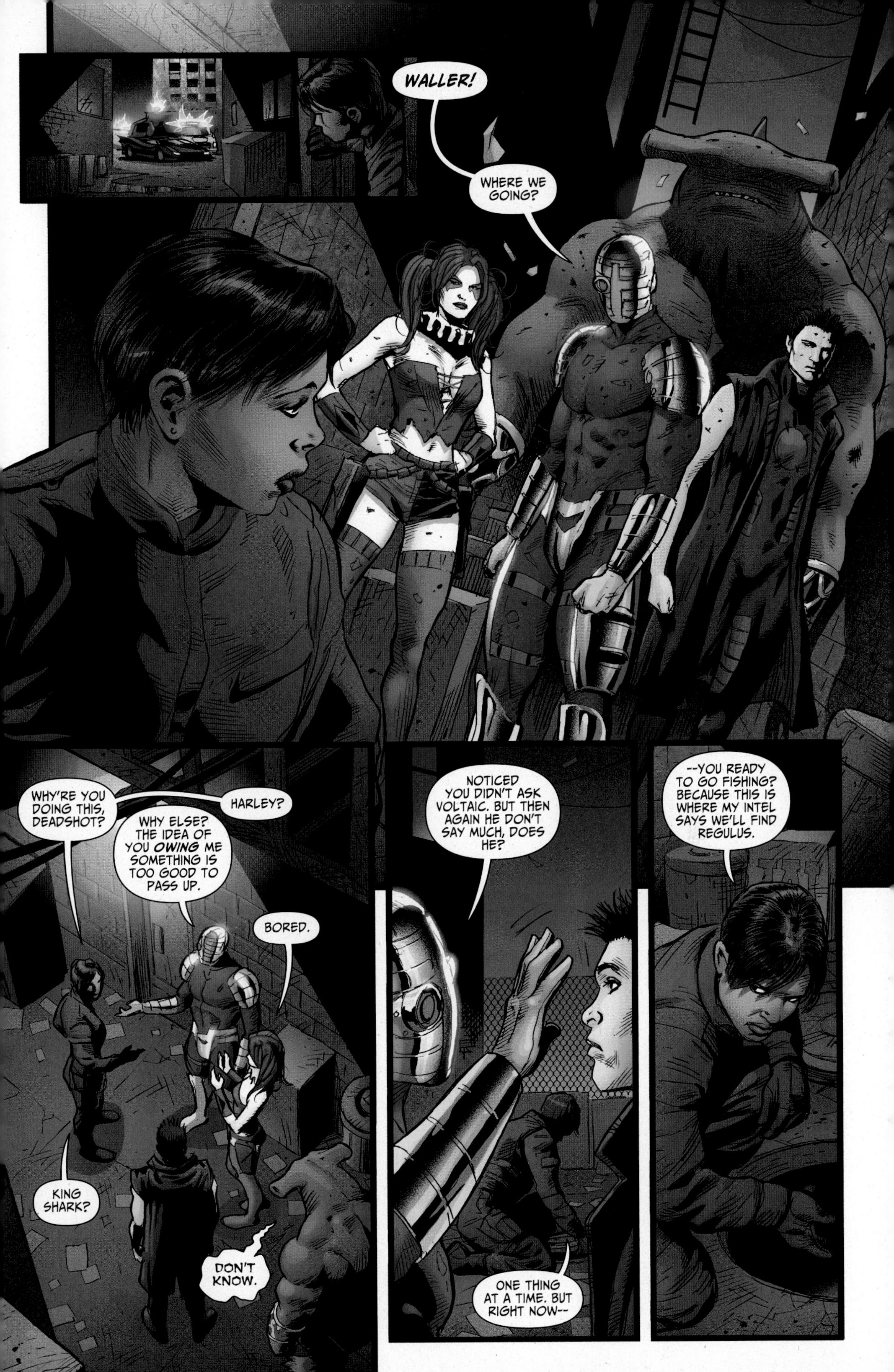
WALLER!
WHERE WE GOING?
WHY'RE YOU DOING THIS, DEADSHOT?
HARLEY?
WHY ELSE? THE IDEA OF YOU OWING ME SOMETHING IS TOO GOOD TO PASS UP.
BORED.
KING SHARK?
DON'T KNOW.
NOTICED YOU DIDN'T ASK VOLTAIC. BUT THEN AGAIN HE DON'T SAY MUCH, DOES HE?
ONE THING AT A TIME. BUT RIGHT NOW--
--YOU READY TO GO FISHING? BECAUSE THIS IS WHERE MY INTEL SAYS WE'LL FIND REGULUS.

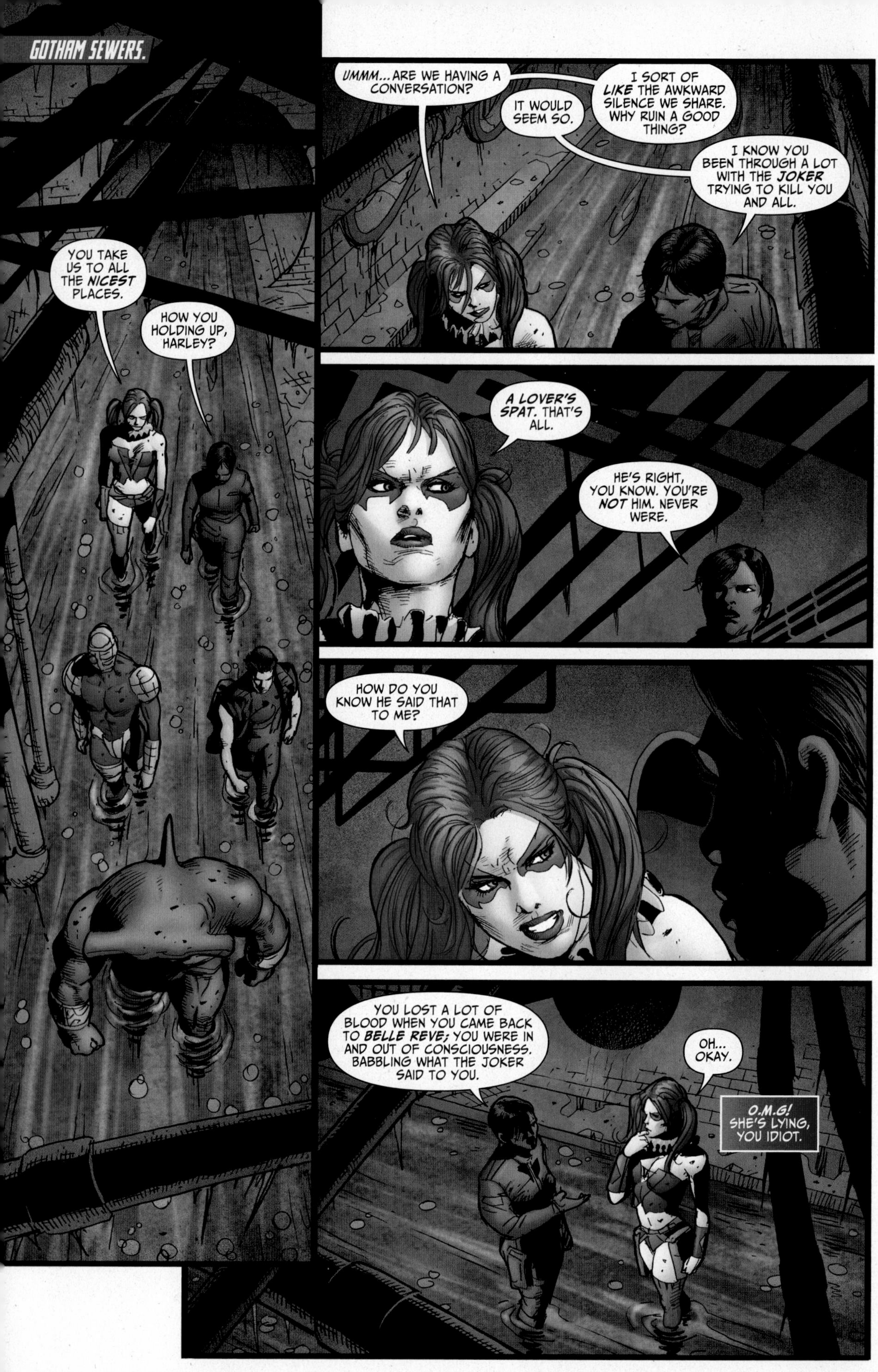
GOTHAM SEWERS.
YOU TAKE US TO ALL THE NICEST PLACES.
HOW YOU HOLDING UP, HARLEY?
UMMM... ARE WE HAVING A CONVERSATION?
IT WOULD SEEM SO.
I SORT OF LIKE THE AWKWARD SILENCE WE SHARE. WHY RUIN A GOOD THING?
I KNOW YOU BEEN THROUGH A LOT WITH THE JOKER TRYING TO KILL YOU AND ALL.
A LOVER'S SPAT. THAT'S ALL.
HE'S RIGHT, YOU KNOW. YOU'RE NOT HIM. NEVER WERE.
HOW DO YOU KNOW HE SAID THAT TO ME?
YOU LOST A LOT OF BLOOD WHEN YOU CAME BACK TO BELLE REVE; YOU WERE IN AND OUT OF CONSCIOUSNESS. BABBLING WHAT THE JOKER SAID TO YOU.
OH... OKAY.
O.M.G! SHE'S LYING, YOU IDIOT.

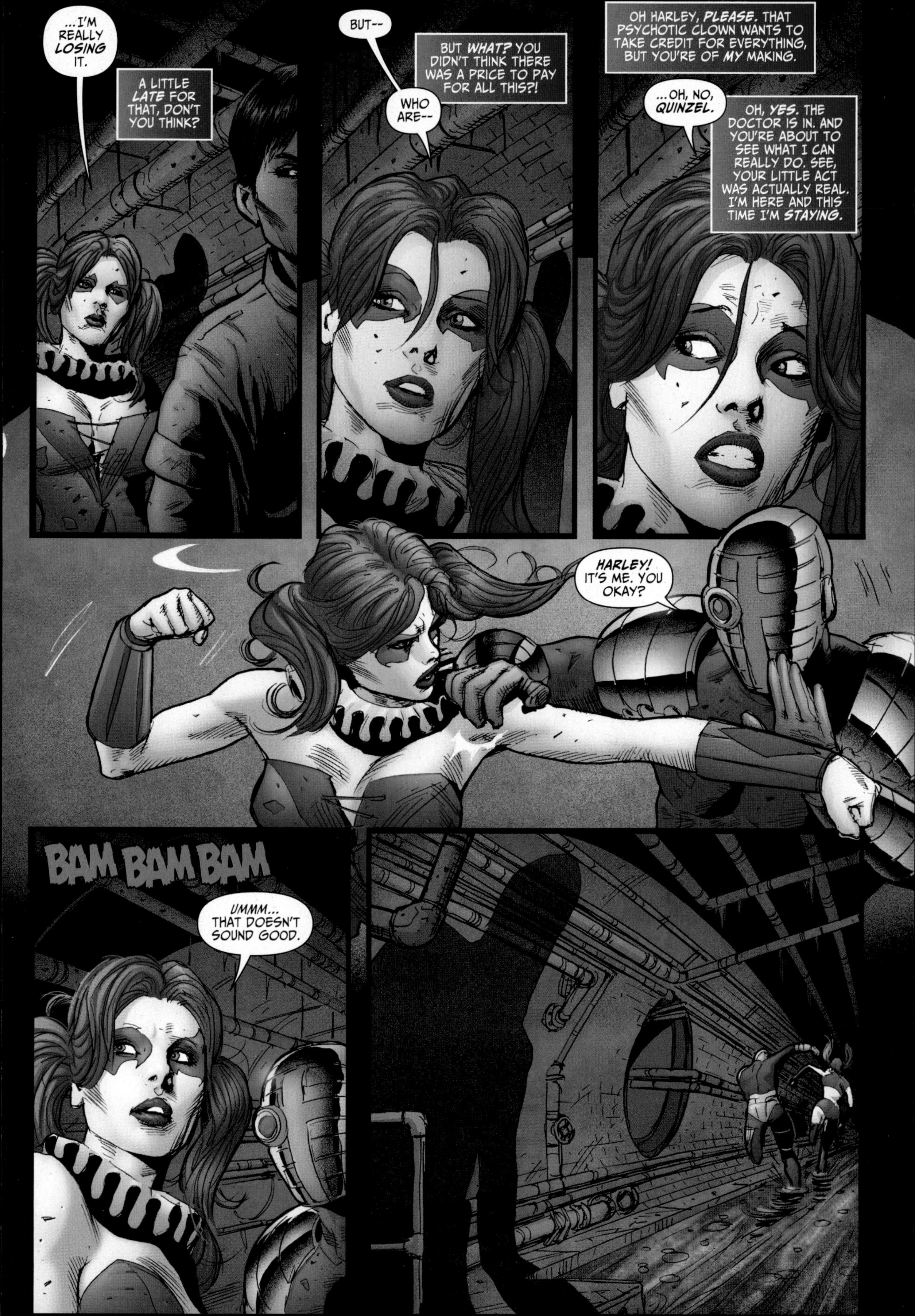
...I'M REALLY LOSING IT.
A LITTLE LATE FOR THAT, DON'T YOU THINK?
BUT--
WHO ARE--
BUT WHAT? YOU DIDN'T THINK THERE WAS A PRICE TO PAY FOR ALL THIS?!
OH HARLEY, PLEASE. THAT PSYCHOTIC CLOWN WANTS TO TAKE CREDIT FOR EVERYTHING, BUT YOU'RE OF MY MAKING.
...OH, NO, QUINZEL.
OH, YES. THE DOCTOR IS IN. AND YOU'RE ABOUT TO SEE WHAT I CAN REALLY DO. SEE, YOUR LITTLE ACT WAS ACTUALLY REAL. I'M HERE AND THIS TIME I'M STAYING.
HARLEY! IT'S ME. YOU OKAY?
BAM BAM BAM
UMMM... THAT DOESN'T SOUND GOOD.

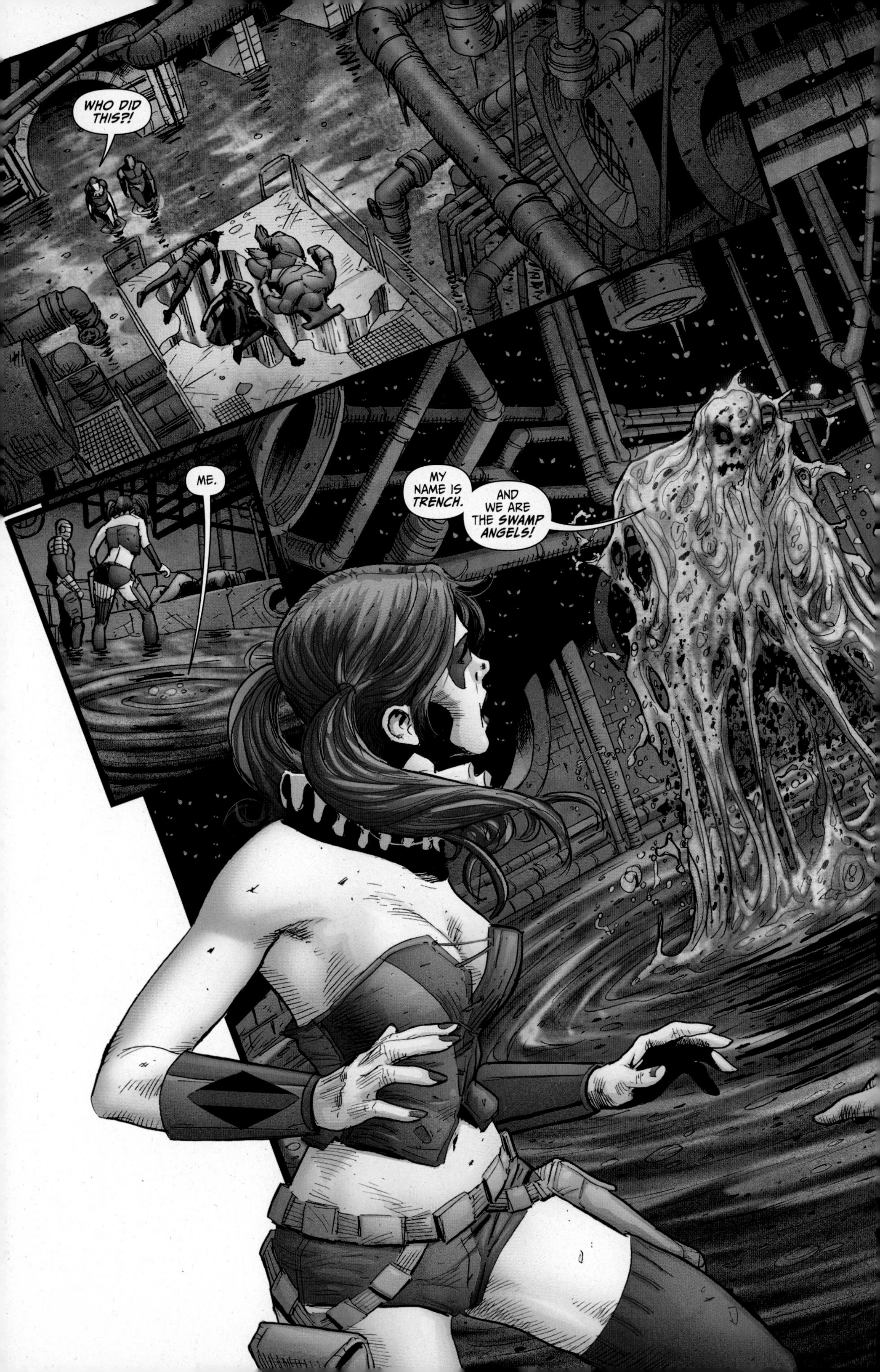
WHO DID THIS?!
ME.
MY NAME IS TRENCH.
AND WE ARE THE SWAMP ANGELS!

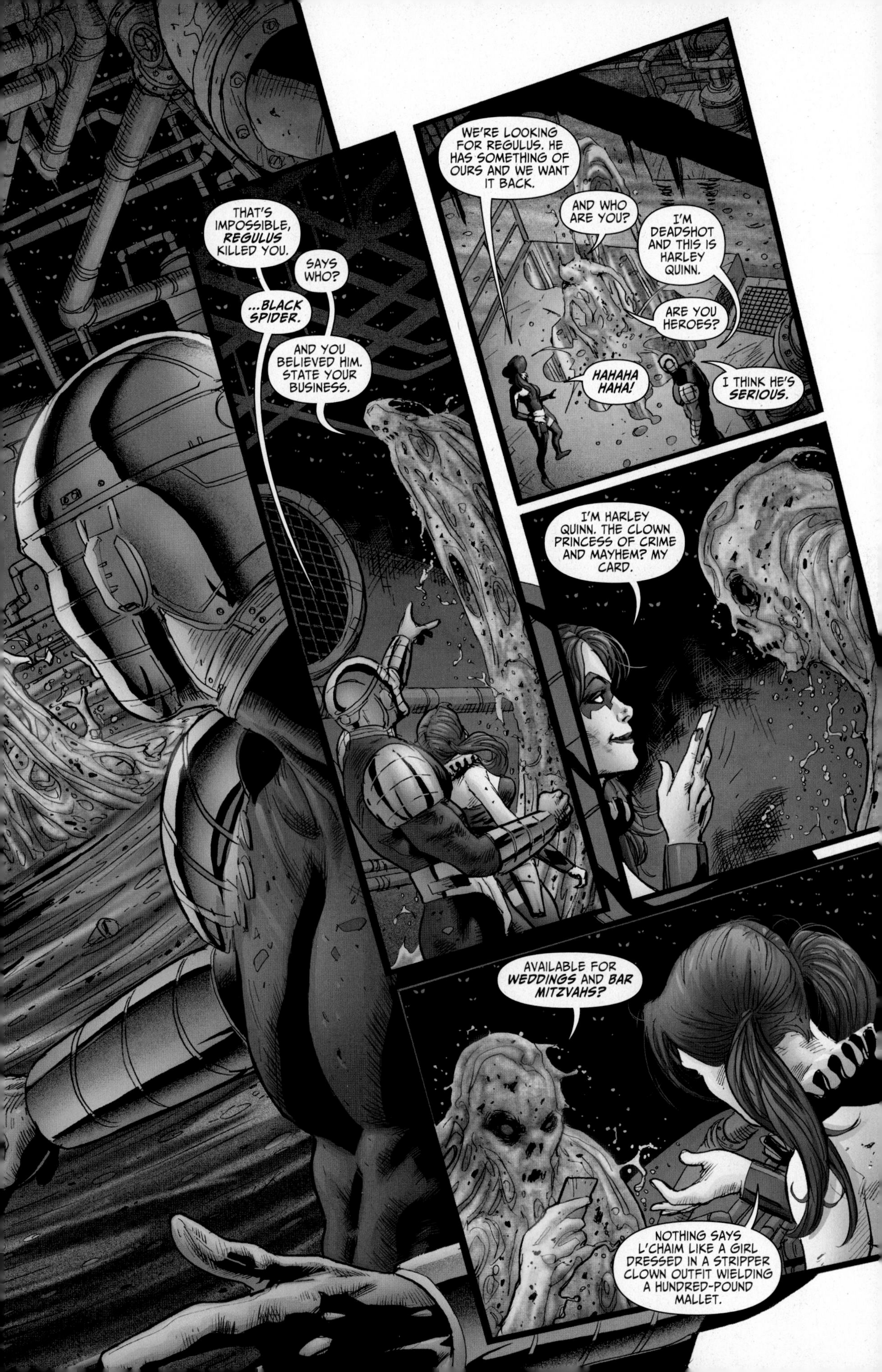
THAT'S IMPOSSIBLE, REGULUS KILLED YOU.
SAYS WHO?
...BLACK SPIDER.
AND YOU BELIEVED HIM. STATE YOUR BUSINESS.
WE'RE LOOKING FOR REGULUS. HE HAS SOMETHING OF OURS AND WE WANT IT BACK.
AND WHO ARE YOU?
I'M DEADSHOT AND THIS IS HARLEY QUINN.
ARE YOU HEROES?
HAHAHA HAHA!
I THINK HE'S SERIOUS.
I'M HARLEY QUINN. THE CLOWN PRINCESS OF CRIME AND MAYHEM? MY CARD.
AVAILABLE FOR WEDDINGS AND BAR MITZVAHS?
NOTHING SAYS L'CHAIM LIKE A GIRL DRESSED IN A STRIPPER CLOWN OUTFIT WIELDING A HUNDRED-POUND MALLET.

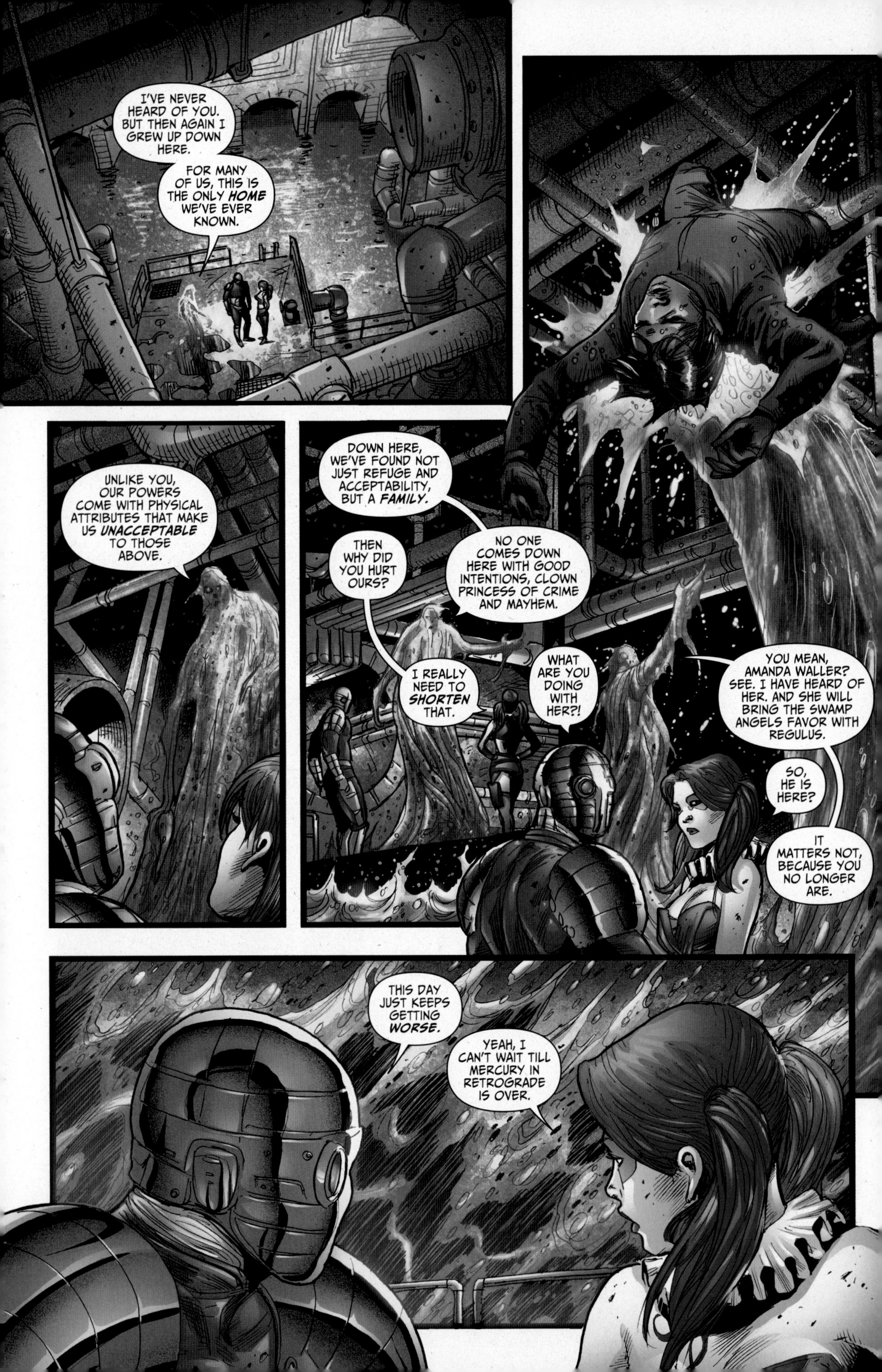
I'VE NEVER HEARD OF YOU. BUT THEN AGAIN I GREW UP DOWN HERE.
FOR MANY OF US, THIS IS THE ONLY HOME WE'VE EVER KNOWN.
UNLIKE YOU, OUR POWERS COME WITH PHYSICAL ATTRIBUTES THAT MAKE US UNACCEPTABLE TO THOSE ABOVE.
DOWN HERE, WE'VE FOUND NOT JUST REFUGE AND ACCEPTABILITY, BUT A FAMILY.
THEN WHY DID YOU HURT OURS?
NO ONE COMES DOWN HERE WITH GOOD INTENTIONS, CLOWN PRINCESS OF CRIME AND MAYHEM.
I REALLY NEED TO SHORTEN THAT.
WHAT ARE YOU DOING WITH HER?!
YOU MEAN, AMANDA WALLER? SEE. I HAVE HEARD OF HER. AND SHE WILL BRING THE SWAMP ANGELS FAVOR WITH REGULUS.
SO, HE IS HERE?
IT MATTERS NOT, BECAUSE YOU NO LONGER ARE.
THIS DAY JUST KEEPS GETTING WORSE.
YEAH, I CAN'T WAIT TILL MERCURY IN RETROGRADE IS OVER.

NEVER THOUGHT I'D BE *HAPPY* HE WAS HERE.

IT'S SAID *DROWNING* IS ONE OF THE WORST WAYS TO DIE. SO, LET'S TEST THAT OUT.

MOST PEOPLE BELIEVE THAT YOUR LUNGS FILL UP AND THEN YOU STOP BREATHING, BUT THAT'S NOT THE CASE.

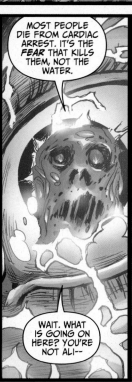

MOST PEOPLE DIE FROM CARDIAC ARREST. IT'S THE *FEAR* THAT KILLS THEM, NOT THE WATER.

WAIT. WHAT IS GOING ON HERE? YOU'RE NOT ALI--

ZIIP

SHOCKING.

HA! HA! HA! NOW THAT'S WHAT I CALL BLOWING OFF STEAM!

HARLEY, GRAB WALLER, WE GOT TROUBLE.

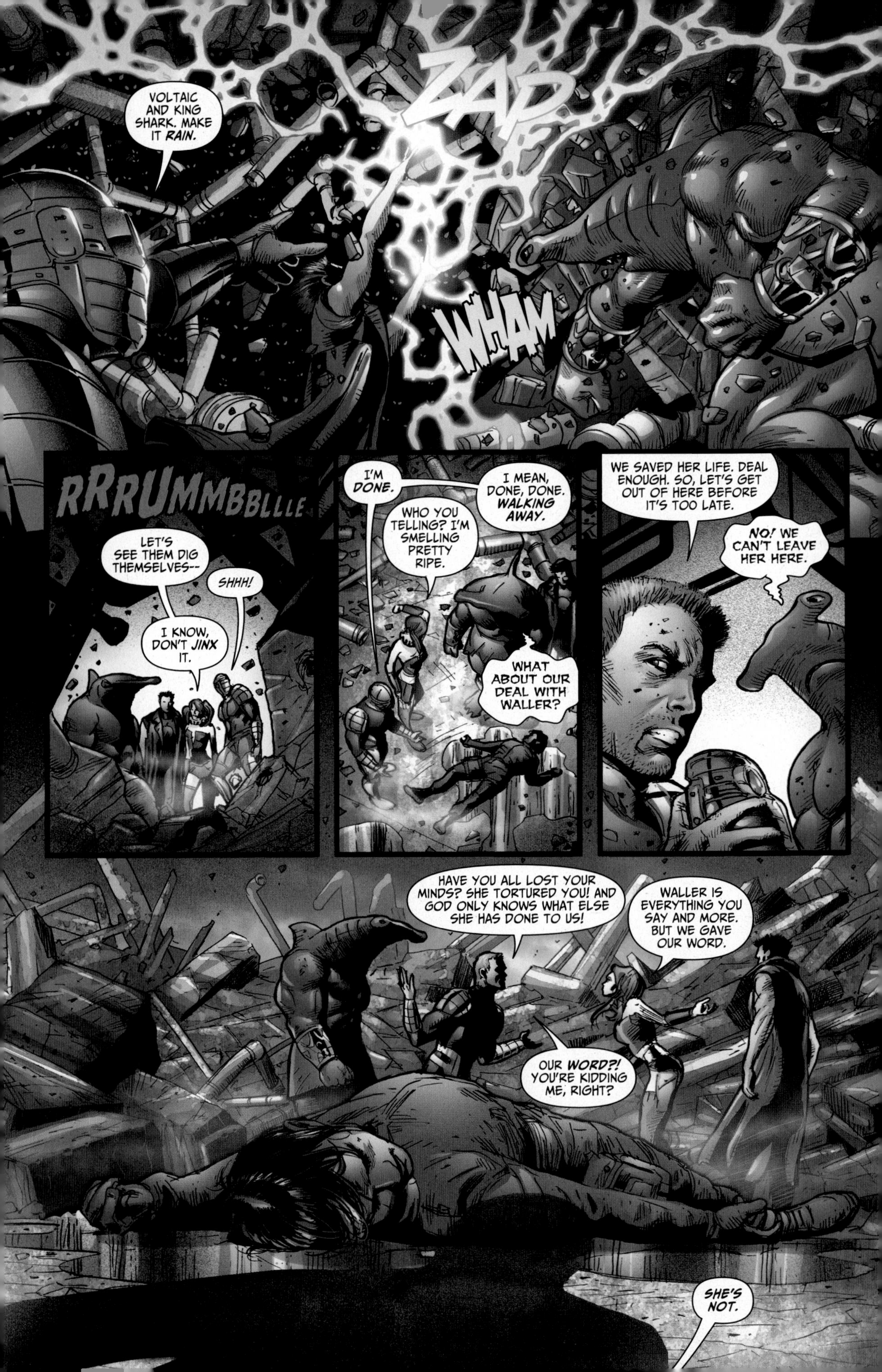
VOLTAIC AND KING SHARK. MAKE IT RAIN.
ZAP
WHAM
RRRUMMBBLLLE
LET'S SEE THEM DIG THEMSELVES--
SHHH!
I KNOW, DON'T JINX IT.
I'M DONE.
I MEAN, DONE, DONE. WALKING AWAY.
WHO YOU TELLING? I'M SMELLING PRETTY RIPE.
WHAT ABOUT OUR DEAL WITH WALLER?
WE SAVED HER LIFE. DEAL ENOUGH. SO, LET'S GET OUT OF HERE BEFORE IT'S TOO LATE.
NO! WE CAN'T LEAVE HER HERE.
HAVE YOU ALL LOST YOUR MINDS? SHE TORTURED YOU! AND GOD ONLY KNOWS WHAT ELSE SHE HAS DONE TO US!
WALLER IS EVERYTHING YOU SAY AND MORE. BUT WE GAVE OUR WORD.
OUR WORD?! YOU'RE KIDDING ME, RIGHT?
SHE'S NOT.

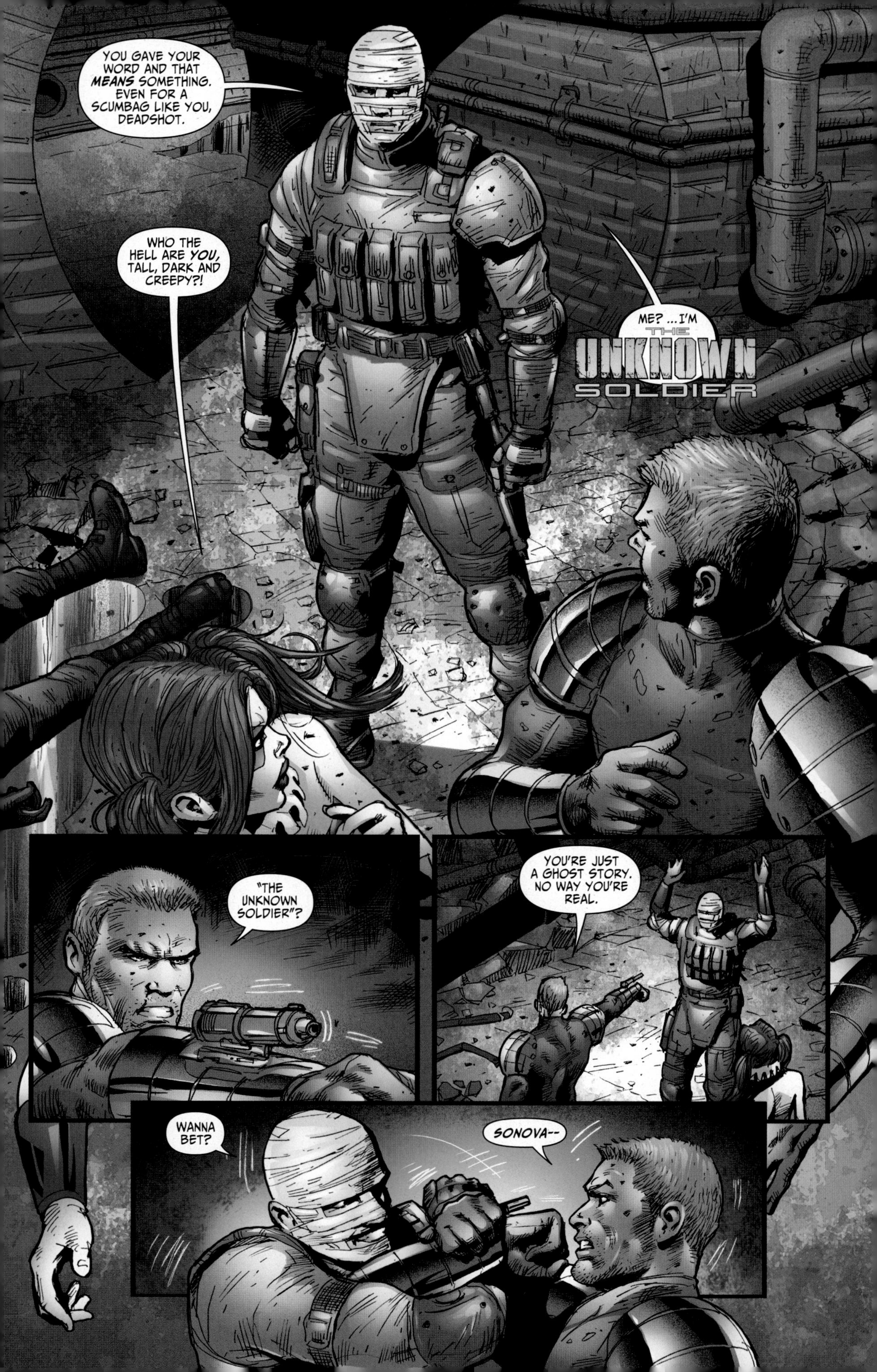
YOU GAVE YOUR WORD AND THAT MEANS SOMETHING. EVEN FOR A SCUMBAG LIKE YOU, DEADSHOT.
WHO THE HELL ARE YOU, TALL, DARK AND CREEPY?!
ME? ...I'M THE UNKNOWN SOLDIER
"THE UNKNOWN SOLDIER"?
YOU'RE JUST A GHOST STORY. NO WAY YOU'RE REAL.
WANNA BET?
SONOVA--

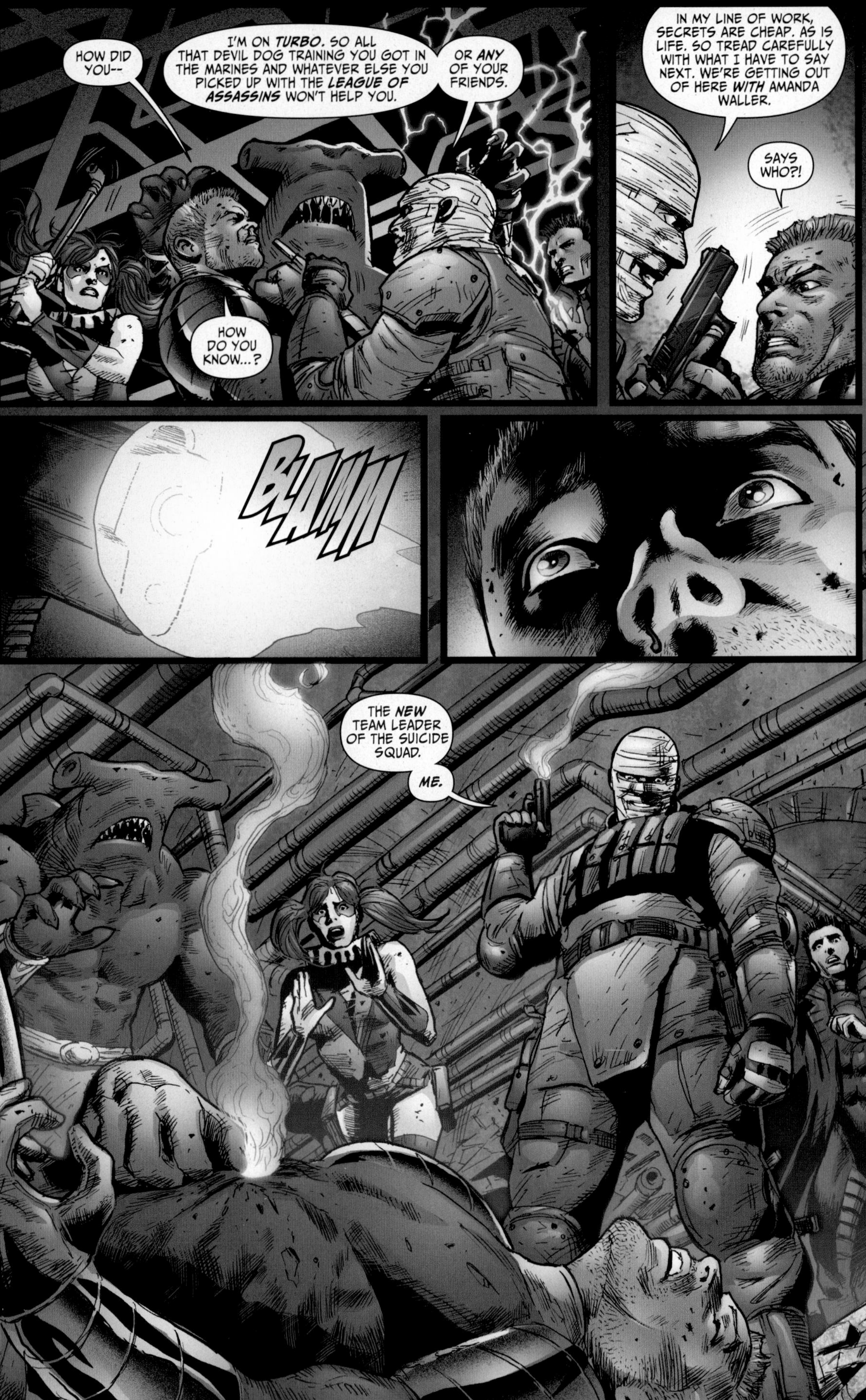
HOW DID YOU--
I'M ON TURBO. SO ALL THAT DEVIL DOG TRAINING YOU GOT IN THE MARINES AND WHATEVER ELSE YOU PICKED UP WITH THE LEAGUE OF ASSASSINS WON'T HELP YOU.
OR ANY OF YOUR FRIENDS.
HOW DO YOU KNOW...?
IN MY LINE OF WORK, SECRETS ARE CHEAP. AS IS LIFE. SO TREAD CAREFULLY WITH WHAT I HAVE TO SAY NEXT. WE'RE GETTING OUT OF HERE WITH AMANDA WALLER.
SAYS WHO?!
BLAMM
THE NEW TEAM LEADER OF THE SUICIDE SQUAD.
ME.

SUICIDE SQUAD

ISSUE #14 SECOND PRINTING COVER BY KEN LASHLEY & MATT YACKEY

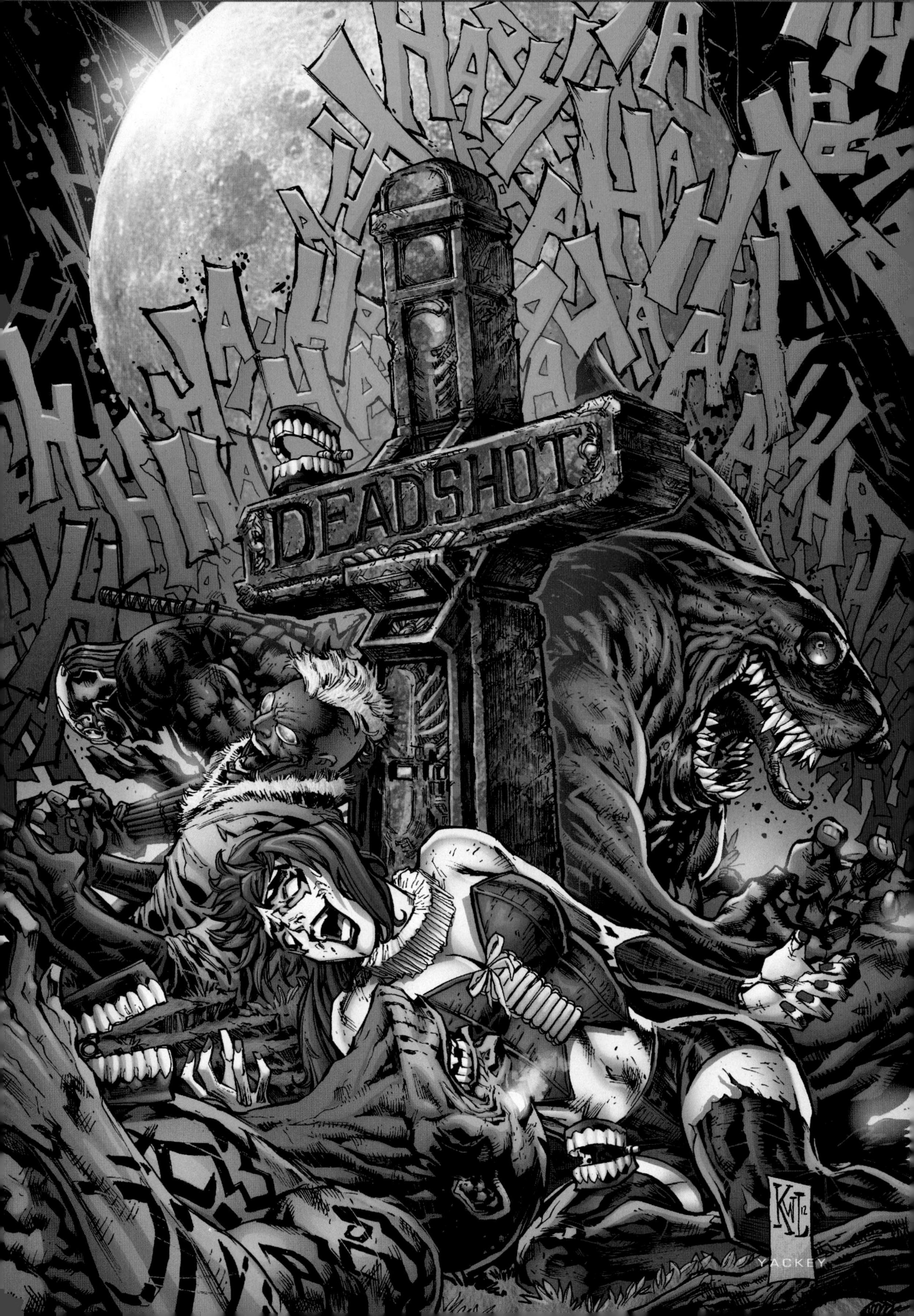
DEADSHOT
YACKEY

SUICIDE SQUAD

FULL COVER FOR ISSUE #19 BY TRAVEL FOREMAN & GABE ELTAEB

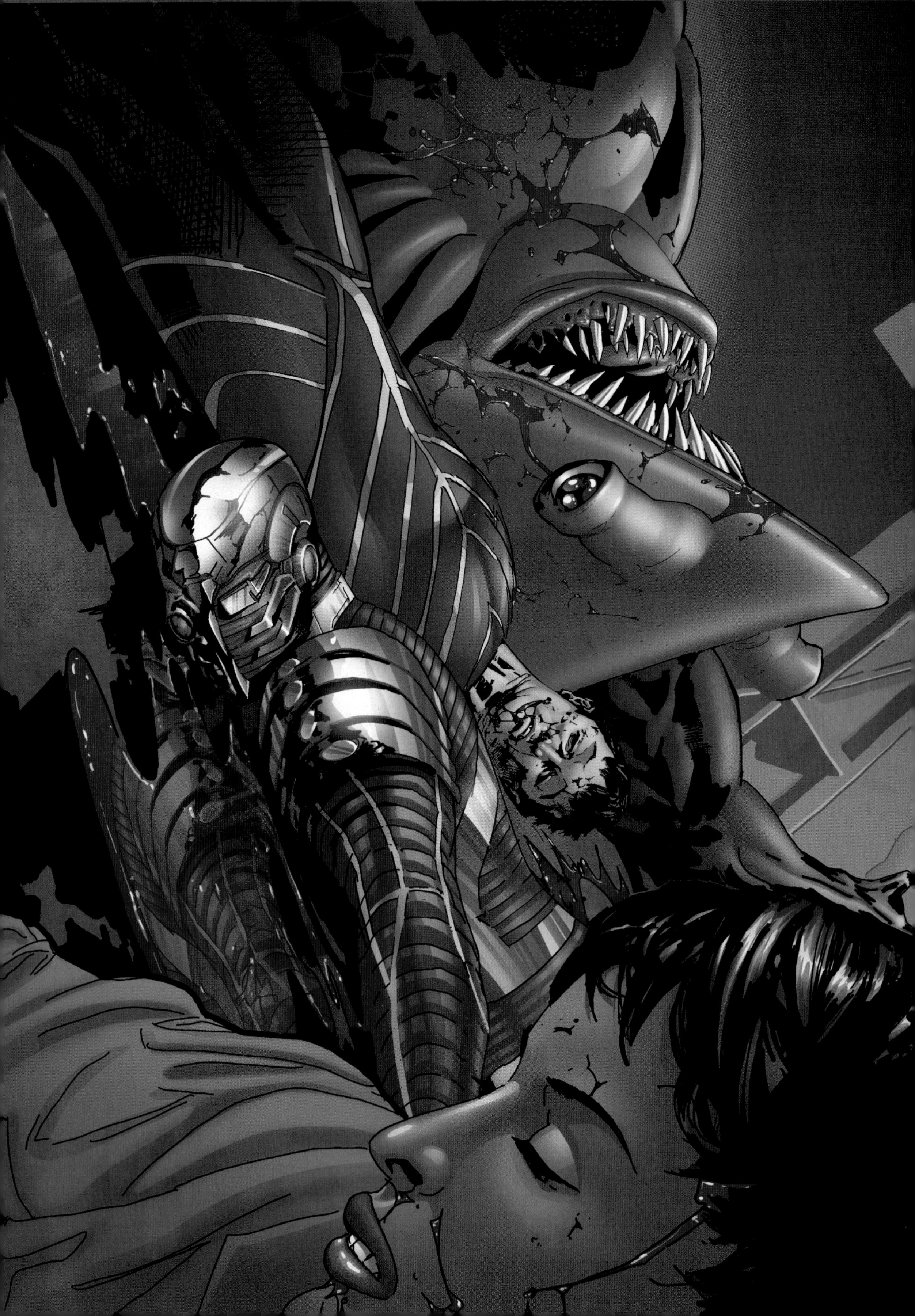

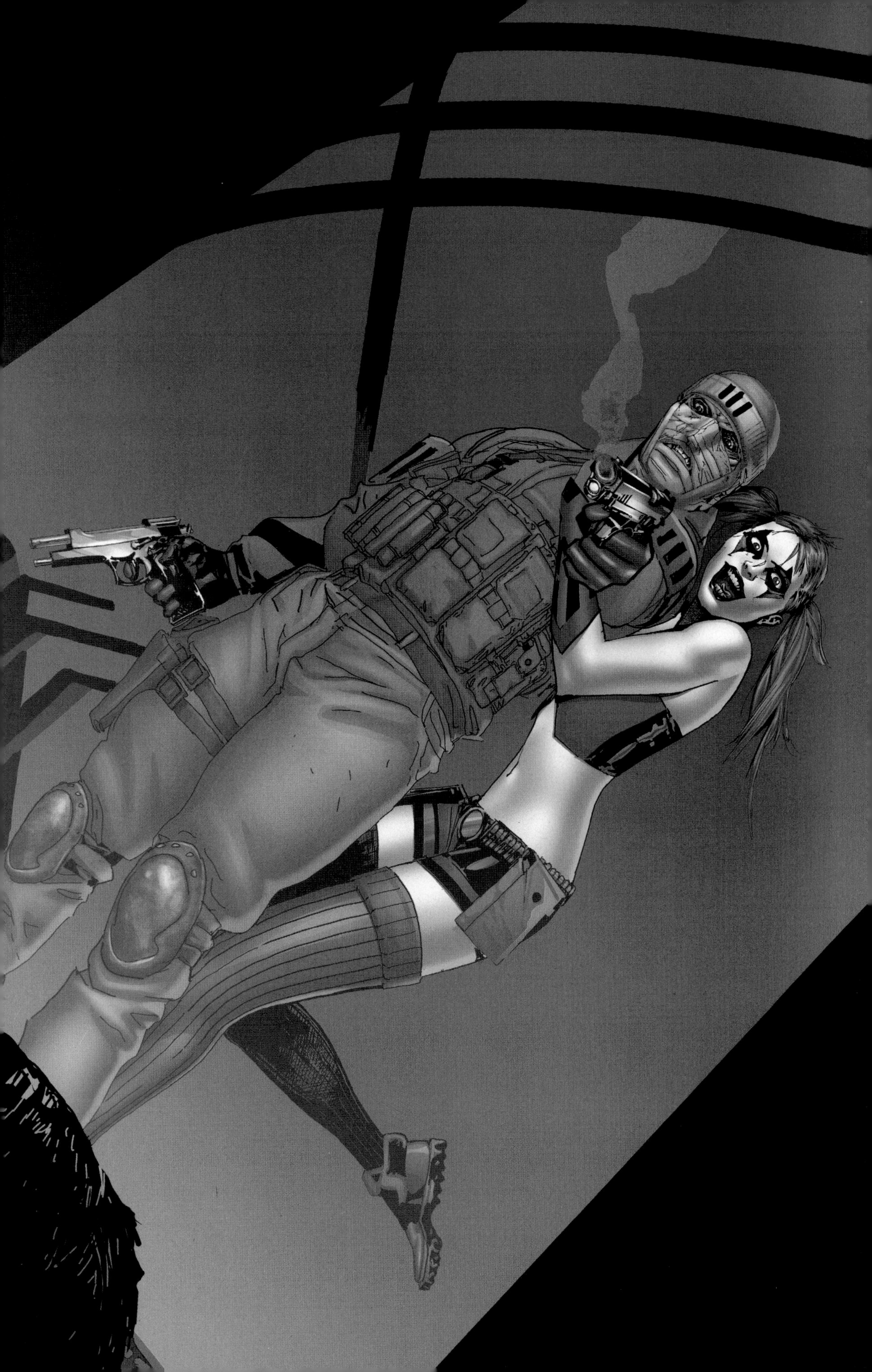

SUICIDE SQUAD

ISSUE #14 SKETCHES AND INKS BY FERNANDO DAGNINO

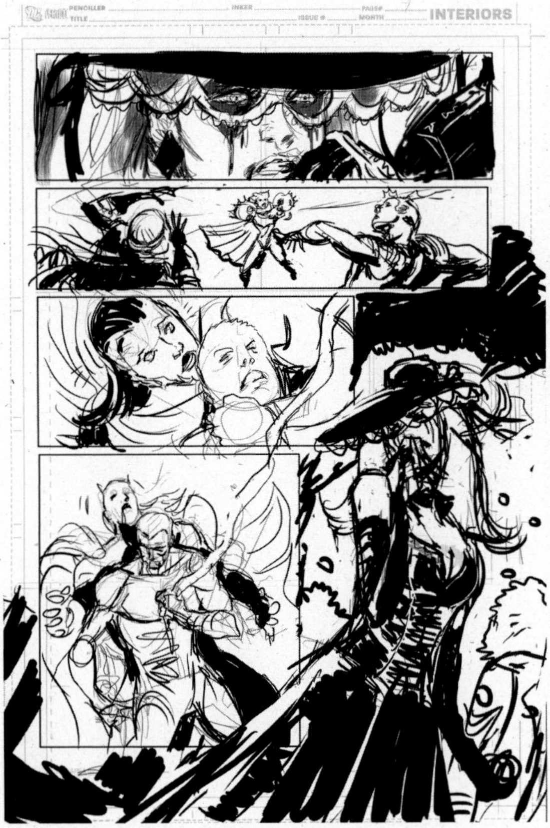
INTERIORS

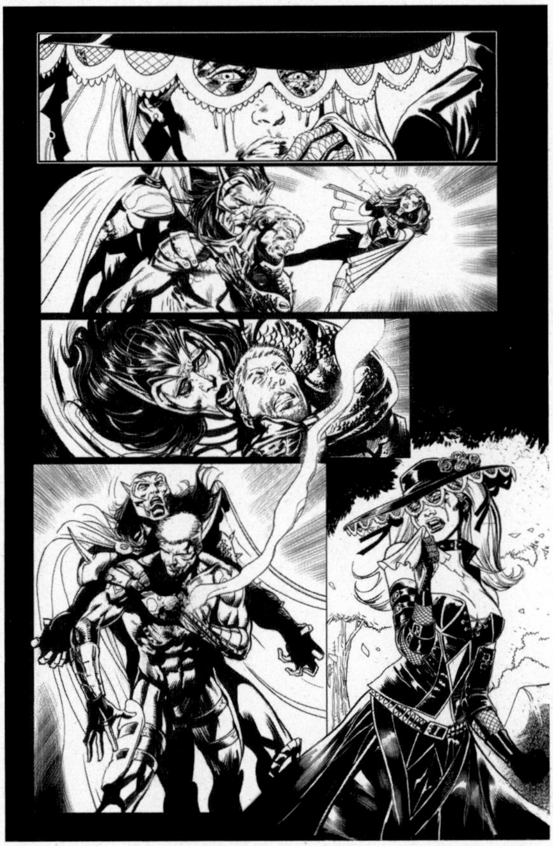

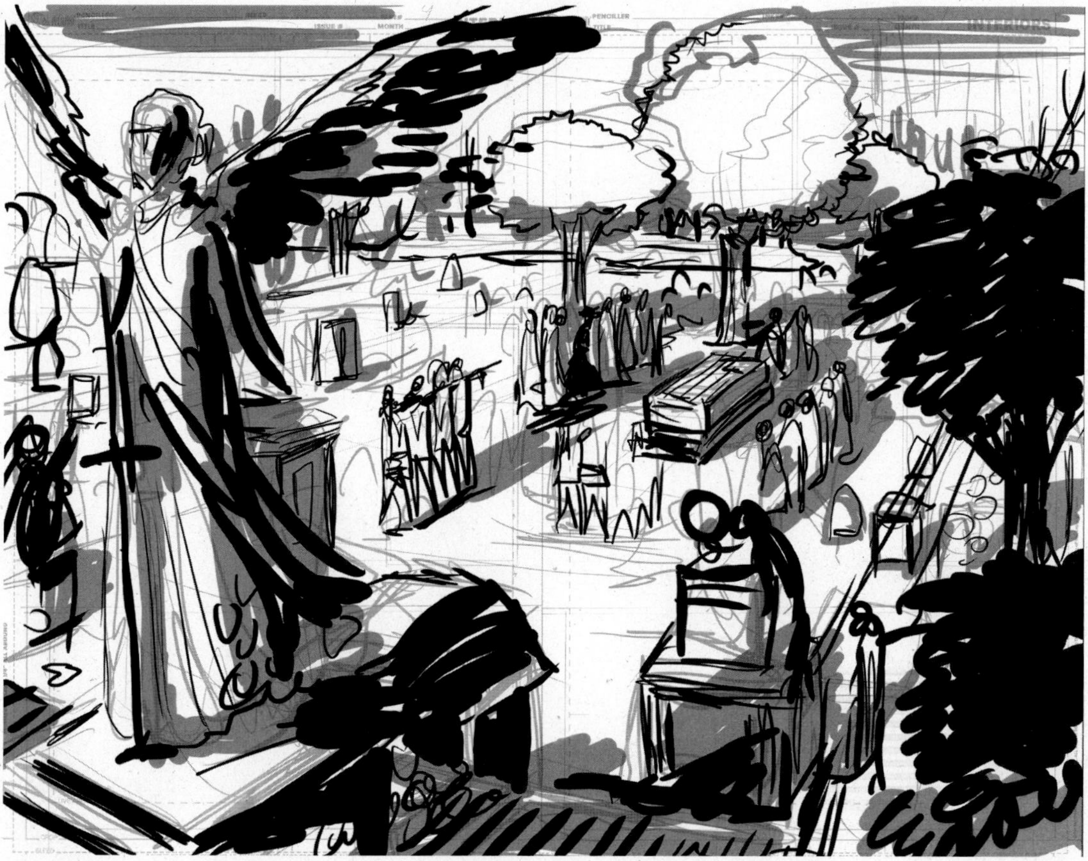

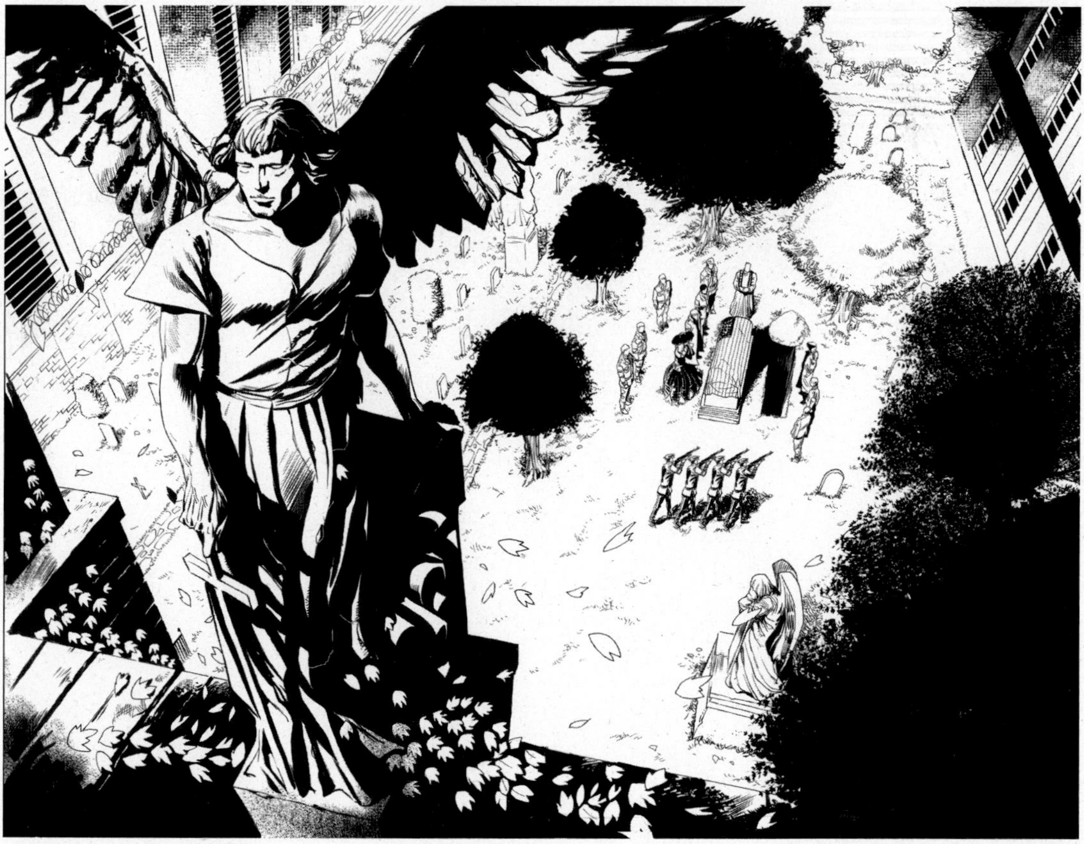

PENCILLER
INKER
PAGE# 4
TITLE
ISSUE #
MONTH
INTERIORS

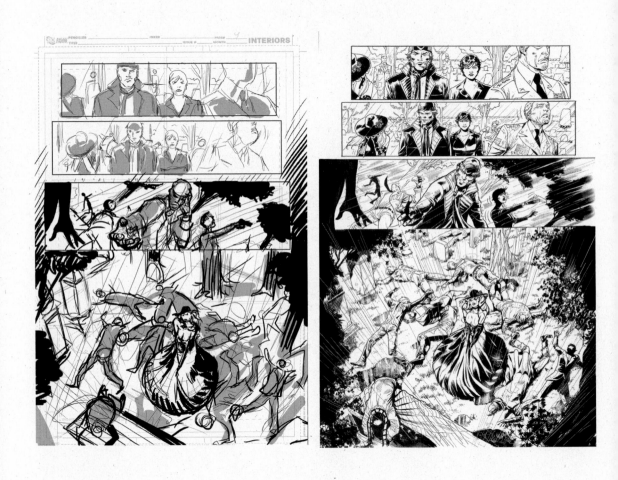

SUICIDE SQUAD
ISSUE #17 PENCILS BY HENRIK JONSSON

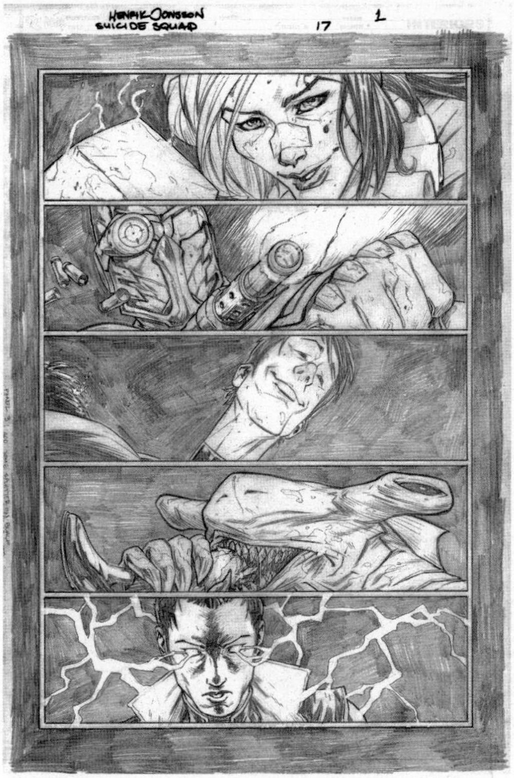
HENRIK JONSSON
SUICIDE SQUAD
17
1

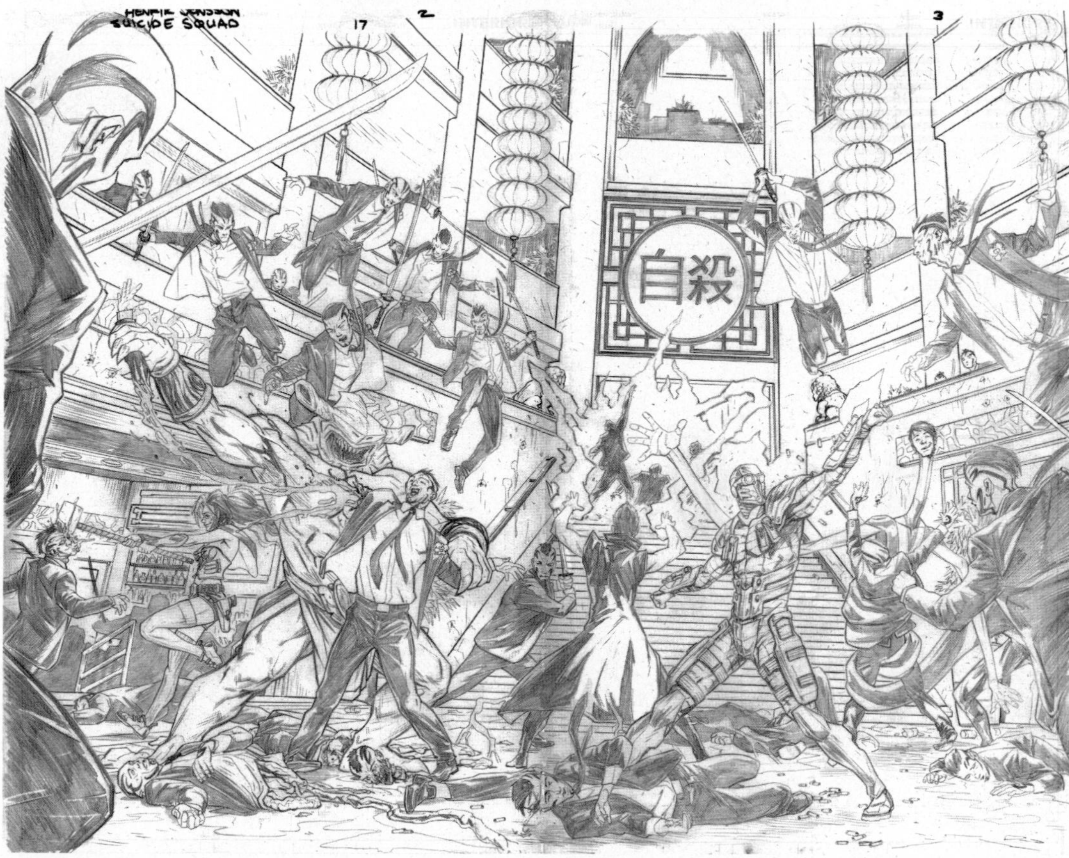
HENRIK JONSSON
SUICIDE SQUAD
17
2
3
自殺

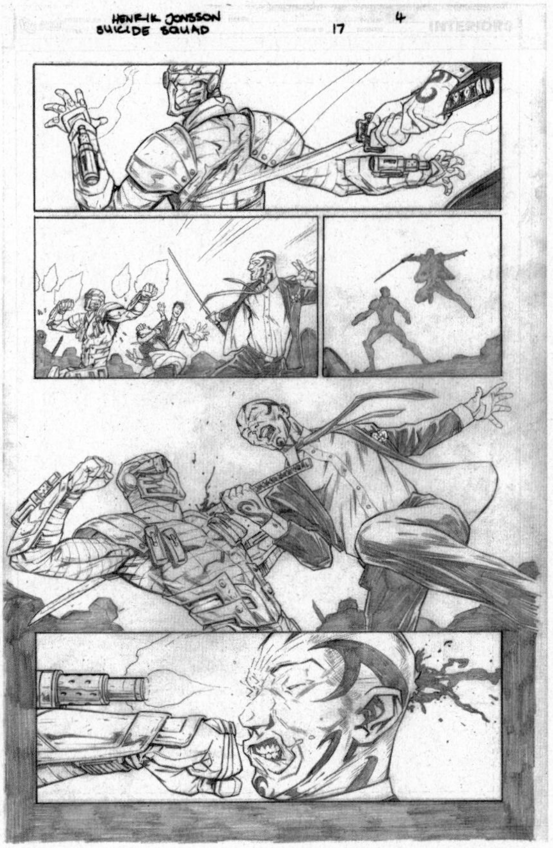
HENRIK JONSSON
SUICIDE SQUAD
17
4

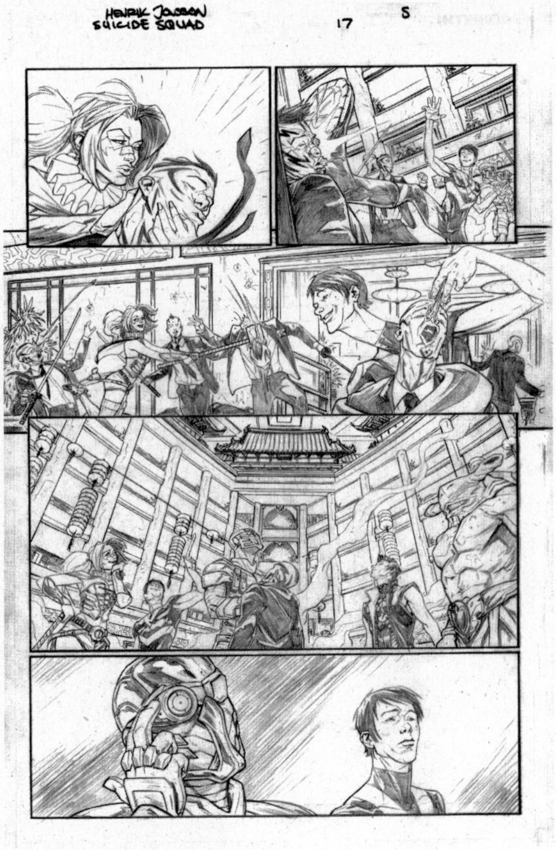
HENRIK JONSSON
SUICIDE SQUAD
17
5

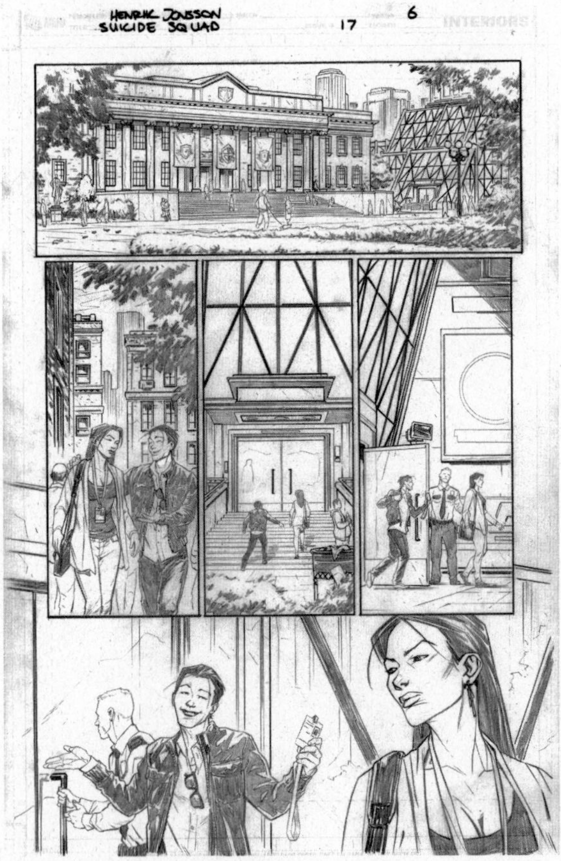
HENRIK JONSSON
SUICIDE SQUAD
17
6